Setting the Conflict COMPASS

Activities for Conflict Resolution and Prevention

Michelle Cummings
with Mike Anderson

Kendall Hunt
publishing company

Images used on the title page, design, and page 9 © Shutterstock, Inc.
Images used on pages 5, 10, 13, 34, 35, 53, 54, 55, 64, 105, 111, 122, 131, 176, 177, 181, 199, 200, 249, 266, 270, 277, 317, 338, 339, and 341 © JupiterImages Corporation.

Kendall Hunt
publishing company

www.kendallhunt.com
Send all inquiries to:
4050 Westmark Drive
Dubuque, IA 52004-1840

ISBN 978-0-7575-8457-2

Printed in the United States of America
10 9 8 7 6 5 4 3 2

Contents

PART 6 Conflict Activities in a Youth Environment 141

Foreword

A compass can be used in many ways, from telling which way is North, to finding hidden treasure, to following an unmarked path over wilderness terrain. In any conflict, you have to get your bearings on what happened. This helps you best determine how to resolve the issue. Conflict is inevitable, and despite how many of us feel about it, conflict is not always a bad thing. People have varying degrees of comfort with conflict as well. Some thrive in it, and some prefer avoiding it at all costs. Conflict is neither good nor bad; it is simply a predictable occurrence within any relationship or team. Dealing with conflict is critical to success in all areas of your life. Learning how to manage and resolve conflict is to your benefit. Another key component of conflict is to understand that no two conflict situations will be identical. This in itself makes dealing with conflict more difficult.

The activities in this book will help participants become aware of how they perceive and handle conflict. There will be suggestions and strategies for dealing with conflict as well. It will also remind individuals to think of the perspective of others. This will be achieved while gaining tools and techniques for increased collaboration, resolving disputes, and ultimately finding win/win resolutions to workplace and classroom conflicts.

A Note of Thanks

No doubt you will notice, as you read through the pages of this book, that we have been the fortunate recipients of great ideas shared by our friends and fellow facilitators. One of the most outstanding features of the experiential education world is the unique and generous sharing that goes on between members of this field. We are grateful to every person who has allowed us to share their unique insights and their wonderful ideas for exploring conflict resolution and prevention.

In every way we could imagine, we have attempted to thoroughly research the origins and creators of the activities in this book. To the best of our ability, we have tried to credit those who deserve recognition for their contributions.

If, after reading this book, you are aware of any activity for which we have not yet given an appropriate reference or credit, it would be our pleasure to correct this situation in the next printing of this book. Please direct any information you have related to appropriate crediting to Michelle Cummings at michelle@training-wheels.com. We also enjoy hearing from you about your usage of the activities in this book. Please tell us your stories, tales, and experiences with the audiences you serve, both within the United States and abroad. And, if you happen to create a new Conflict Resolution Activity that you would like to share with the world, send us a photo and activity description. If we use it in a future publication, we will send you a copy of that book.

Sincerely,
Michelle Cummings and Mike Anderson

Disclaimer

All activities contain some inherent risk of injury, whether it be physical or emotional. Michelle Cummings and Mike Anderson have devoted reasonable attention to the safety of the activities in this book. The reader assumes all risk and liability for any loss or damage that may result from the use of the materials contained in this book. It is your responsibility to obtain the expertise and experience necessary to avoid an injury during one of these activities. Liability for any claim, whether based upon errors or omissions in this guide, are the sole responsibility of the reader.

Michelle Cummings, Mike Anderson, and their affiliates are not responsible for the misuse of the information and activities in the book.

Safety

Your ability to create a mentally and physically safe environment is the foundation of this book. We have spent a few decades discussing and challenging each little detail of these activities and have done the best to eliminate as much risk for injury as possible. There can be no substitute for you, the facilitator, and your team members taking responsibility for safety. It is up to you to obtain the necessary skills to keep the events safe.

We have given you the basic outlines for the activities to act as the foundation for your learning. No amount of training can prepare you for the infinite number of situations that may arise during these events. You must be ready for anything, trust yourself and be clear with your participants about their choice to participate and their responsibility for safety. Be very clear that it is each person's CHOICE how they participate and all choices are supported.

How to Read the Activities

Each activity is broken down into components to make them as user-friendly as possible. Here is what you will find and what it means.

Type of Initiative: This tells you the intended timing and type of activity. Activities will range from Icebreakers, Discussion Tools, Problem-Solving, Communication and Debriefing Tools, to name a few.

Purpose: This is a brief overview of some outcomes you should expect from this activity.

Props Needed: What materials and props are needed for the activity.

Group Size: A recommended number of participants for the activity.

Directions: Provides the necessary set-up information. Provides the directions, rules and goals of the activity.

Variation: Variations of the activity.

Debriefing Topics: Questions and topics that may be explored with the group after or during the activity.

Where to Find It/ How to Make It: Many of these props are available commercially. There are many cost effective ways to make them on your own as well.

Facilitator Notes: We like to leave room at the end of each activity for you to write some helpful notes on facilitating each activity. Once you have led one of the activities from the book, please jot down some helpful hints to help you remember what went well and what you might do differently next time.

Be aware of the 'Activity Directions' trap. This is the mindset that an event can only be done the way it is written in the instructions. As you look through the descriptions keep in mind that none are set in stone. The setup, rules and questions to ask are open to modification and imagination. This book has been written to guide you through the process of facilitating the events. Use the event as is or be creative! Keep your mind open to the possibilities and potential of each activity.

PART 1

Compass Basics:

What Is Conflict?

If someone were to ask you your definition of conflict, what would you say? What is conflict? Is it a fight between two people? Is it ongoing? Can you see it? What does it look like? Is it measurable?

Dictionary.com describes Conflict as:

Con·flict [v. *kuh* n-flikt; n. kon-flikt]

-verb (used without object)

1. to come into collision or disagreement; be contradictory, at variance, or in opposition; clash: *The account of one eyewitness conflicted with that of the other. My class conflicts with my going to the concert.*

2. to fight or contend; do battle.

-noun

3. a fight, battle, or struggle, esp. a prolonged struggle; strife.

4. controversy; quarrel: *conflicts between parties.*

5. discord of action, feeling, or effect; antagonism or opposition, as of interests or principles: *a conflict of ideas.*

6. a striking together; collision.

7. incompatibility or interference, as of one idea, desire, event, or activity with another: *a conflict in the schedule.*

8. *Psychiatry.* a mental struggle arising from opposing demands or impulses.

So what is conflict? Well, it depends on whom you ask. We can give you many definitions, lots of examples, and lots of strategies stemming from years of research, but the answer might still elude you. Conflict, to us, is simply a difference of opinion. The stronger your opinion, the more intense the conflict. It does not seem to matter if we are talking about politics, religion, how many children we'll have, our taste in music, the food we like, what shows we watch on television, the movies we rent, the kind of automobile we drive, the sports teams we cheer for, standing in line, waiting for service, how we raise our kids, whom we associate with, etc. The list can go on and on, but one thing remains constant . . . OPINION.

So the question then becomes, "what forms our opinions?" Unfortunately that answer is as ambiguous as the answer is to the question "what is conflict?" Our opinions seem to be formed by our history, our family, our experiences, our friends, our upbringing, our culture, etc. To make things more complex, there does not seem to be any absolute rubric for determining our or anyone else's opinions. Every hour of every day our experiences change how we look at the world. We're not really talking about extreme situations or massive role reversal here. We're more interested in the day-to-day conflicts that occur in our schools, our homes, and our jobs.

Assuming we can all agree that it is NOT just where and how we grew up that determines how we feel about certain subjects, then the development of our opinions must also come from our learned preferences and our interests. As an example, Mike is the only person in his ENTIRE family that has any tattoos. He did not have older relatives who had tattoos, and he always looked at folks with tattoos as "weird." Then one day when he was 19 years old, he got one, and almost 20 years later he has A LOT of them. In fact, he's still getting them—much to the chagrin of his parents. He can't tell you what happened to his opinion of tattoos, and he cannot identify a specific experience that changed his preference toward tattoos. It just changed.

It is that statement "it just changed" that makes dealing with conflict so hard. Our opinions just change. One day a phone solicitation does little to raise our blood pressure, and the next it sends us into a tailspin. Often our opinions on a variety of matters are rooted in a fluid environment. Meaning, that from the moment we wake up in the morning, our life is in a state of constant flux. As a business owner, hardly a day goes by that everything goes exactly as planned. As a parent, hardly a day goes by that your children do everything as you hoped and expected them to do. The world as a whole will not cooperate in the fashion that you expect it to. So, what are we to do about it?

Our lives are controlled by our emotions, and when our emotions get out of whack things start to go horribly wrong for us. Our ability to control our emotions is a critical piece to consider when attempting to deal with a conflict. Some will say that to effectively diffuse a conflict leave your emotion at the door. Others will tell you that your emotion is what solves the conflict. Our opinion is that you need all your faculties to effectively resolve any conflict situation. Some conflicts will require to you be extremely analytical, while others are purely emotional. What we have tried to do in the pages of this text is provide you with some simple tools that prove helpful in creating environments where conflict can be dealt with in a healthy manner. Remember, conflict is unavoidable . . . how out of control the conflict gets *IS* avoidable.

Conflict might be easier to deal with if it were in only one area of our lives. Everywhere you turn, the potential for conflict exists. Conflict with ourselves (Should I eat that piece of pie? Should I get up and exercise, or sleep in? Should I cut my hair short?); conflict with others (I was next in line. That waitress was rude. That guy cut me off!); conflict at work (Why is the project over-budget and late? Who left this mess? That's not my job!); conflict at home (No, you cannot have dessert before dinner. No texting at the table. Why can't I go to the game tonight?) Conflicts also may occur in almost any social situation, and range in importance from trivial to profound.

When we accept and understand conflict, we allow ourselves to grow, change, and be empowered. Understanding different conflict styles will also assist us in dealing with conflict. There are a few general styles described here.

As a culture, we are taught to be uncomfortable with conflict and find it difficult to deal with. As stated earlier, conflict is natural and inevitable. Conflict is neither good nor bad; it is simply a predictable occurrence within any relationship or team. Conflict can be scary due to many factors; a fear of loss of control, loss of self-esteem or affection, criticism and hurtful remarks, or anger and confrontation. Many people view conflict as inevitably having a winner and a loser.

There are several styles of handling a conflict, including:

Collaboration—the most useful tactic. The aim here is to focus on working together to arrive at a solution where both sides have ownership of and commitment to the solution. This results from a high concern for your group's own interests, matched with a high concern for the interests of other partners. The outcome is "win/win." This strategy is generally used when concerns for others are important. This approach helps build commitment and reduce bad feelings. The drawbacks are that it takes time and energy. In addition, some participants may take advantage of the others' trust and openness. Generally regarded as the best approach for managing conflict, the objective of collaboration is to reach consensus.

Compromise—each party gives up something to settle on a halfway point or come to resolution. This strategy results from a high concern for your group's own interests along with a moderate concern for the interests of the other party. The outcome is "win some/lose some." This strategy is generally used to achieve temporary solutions, to avoid destructive power struggles, or when time pressures exist. One drawback is that participants can lose sight of important values and long-term objectives. This approach can also distract the parties involved from the merits of an issue and create a cynical climate.

Competition—fighting for your way at all costs (the "winner"). This strategy results from a high concern for your group's own interests with less concern for others. The outcome is "win/lose." This strategy includes most attempts at bargaining. It is generally used when basic rights are at stake or to set a precedent. However, it can cause the conflict to escalate, and losers may try to retaliate. Those who compete may get their way frequently but at a high cost to their relationships at work or at home.

Accommodation—giving in to another's desires for the sake of keeping peace (the "loser"). This results from a low concern for your group's own interests combined with a high concern for the interests of other partners. The outcome is "lose/win." This strategy is generally used when the issue is more important to others than to you. It is a "goodwill gesture." It is also appropriate when you recognize that you are wrong. The drawbacks are that your own ideas and concerns don't get attention. You may also lose credibility and future influence.

Avoidance—withdrawing from or side stepping the conflict entirely; refusal to engage in the situation. This results from a low concern for your group's own interests coupled with a low concern for the interests of others. The outcome is "lose/lose." This strategy is generally used when the issue is trivial or other issues are more pressing. It is also used when confrontation has a high potential for damage or more information is needed. The drawbacks are that important decisions may be made by default. Those who accommodate and those who avoid may smooth over disagreements, but their needs may not be met, and they may harbor resentments that eventually damage the relationship.

All of these styles may be appropriate to use at times, but when used exclusively may result in unresolved or escalating conflict.

No matter how you define conflict, the reality is that it is a part of life. It is important that you recognize and deal with it appropriately. You can either let conflict, or the potential for conflict, drag you down, or you can use it to lift you to new levels of performance. Understanding what conflict is and why it exists will help shape your response. We will go into this in more detail in the section: Strategies for Dealing with Conflict.

CHARACTERISTICS OF A COMPASS; CHARACTERISTICS OF CONFLICT

With the title of this book being, *Setting the Conflict Compass,* we are going to use the metaphors of a compass, direction, and other map-related jargon throughout the book. You might learn a little about how to work a compass in the process of dealing with conflict!

There are hundreds of compass styles. These range from simple compasses that tell you the direction you're facing to compasses that have an accuracy of a few tenths of a degree. There are marine compasses, aeronautic compasses, and many others. For basic back country use, most hikers use the mountaineers' compass. The diagram on page 6 shows two types of compasses and describes some of the parts.

Image © 2010 JupiterImages Corporation.

Although not shown 'b' has all the parts 'a' does, but some of these were removed for clarity. The type 'a' compass is a good compass for beginner use, as the number of gadgets is limited. Type 'b' compasses are excellent for outdoor use, as they take the most accurate measurements.

With any conflict situation, the more practice you have at resolving conflict the better you will be at it. Learning to resolve conflict starts when we are born and we begin to interact with others. As the diagram here indicates, a beginner compass has limited gadgets as we learn to resolve conflicts. As we grow, we develop the basic tools to be successful with resolving conflict. (No, no, you can't take away someone else's toy because you want it. Say you are sorry. It's not nice to hit. You need a time-out to think about what you have done.) As we encounter more conflicts and practice our responses to conflict, the more tools we develop. (What tone of voice did you use when you told your brother to leave you alone? What could you do differently in the future? Please be respectful when talking to your mother.)

As we mature, we are given more tools and gadgets that help us deal with conflict. The further our brains develop, the more capable we are of identifing positive ways to resolve conflict. After all, the reason car insurance rates go down after the age of 25 is because the human brain is more developed. Scientific evidence proves that brain function and cognitive abilities are more mature after the age of 25 than at 13. Therefore, is it safe to deduce that as we get older we should be capable of maturely handling conflict situations? Do you agree with that? Why does dealing with conflict seem to get harder as we get older?

We wish that dealing with conflict was as simple as laying out a diagram with pointy little arrows showing where the conflict began, who was involved, how it began to escalate, and what could have been done to prevent it. Although a timeline map might be a good activity,

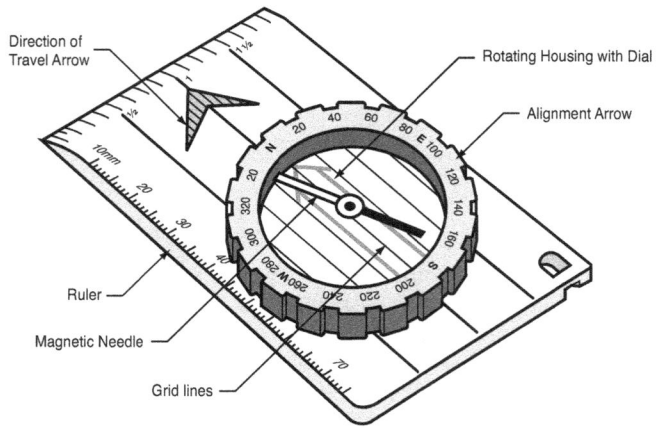

Direction of Travel Arrow — Rotating Housing with Dial — Alignment Arrow — Ruler — Magnetic Needle — Grid lines

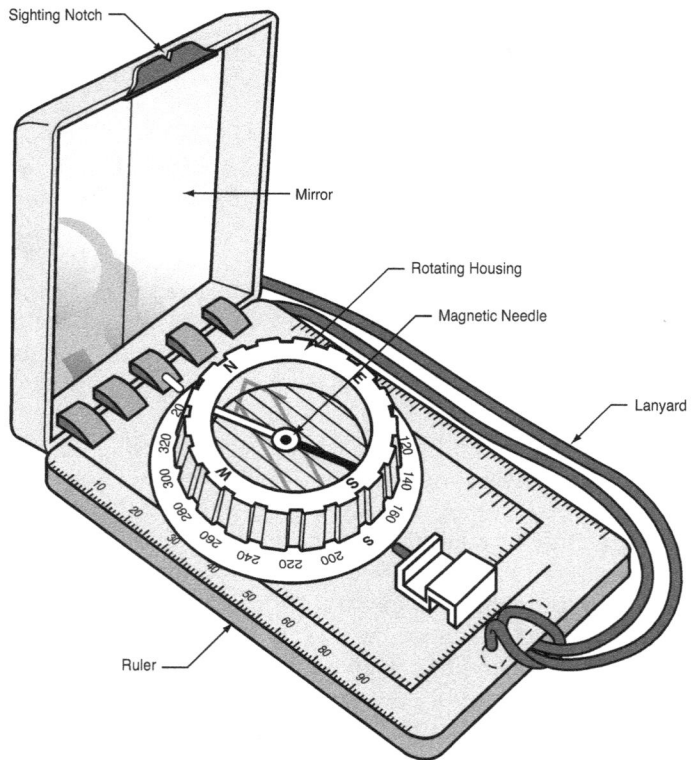

Sighting Notch — Mirror — Rotating Housing — Magnetic Needle — Lanyard — Ruler

it's usually not that simple. There are many obstacles that get in the way or prevent us from resolving the conflict situation. The following pages provide compass metaphors to aid in discussions for conflict resolution.

COMPASS PARTS AND HOW THEY RELATE TO CONFLICT

Compasses have several working parts and roles, much like the various roles in any conflict situation. Following are several descriptions of common compass parts and what they do. We then align the compass part to a metaphor for conflict.

Magnetic Needle—this is the heart of a compass. The needle is the part of the compass that determines direction. It is magnetically charged and freely floats in the dial. It will align itself with the earth's magnetic field. Generally speaking, the red end points North and the other end points South.

    Conflict Metaphor: Generally, when someone thinks about a compass they think about a device in which a needle will point you in a desired direction. Determining the direction a conflict interaction follows depends on the balance of incentives to compete or cooperate to resolve it.

    At the heart of conflict lie emotion, passion, and identity. Conflict is often emotionally charged, and we internally stew in our own 'stuff' until we align our thoughts with something that makes sense to us. Like the magnetic needle aligns itself with the earth's magnetic field, we too will align with what feels right to us. Conflict often reveals a common human pattern. When faced with conflict, we tend to focus passionately on what our opponent has done wrong or should do to make things right. Whether it is something trivial or completely profound, emotions generally point us in the direction to conflict will go.

Rotating Housing—An important part of the mountaineers' compass. This dial has magnetic bearings printed on it (in degrees) as well as the alignment arrow. This is used to enter or determine bearings.

    Conflict Metaphor: When a conflict situation arises you have to first determine what happened, or in other words, figure out your bearings. On a compass the Rotating Housing piece is a dial you actually spin around to get an accurate bearing. Metaphorically speaking in conflict, there are often times you feel like your head is spinning from the many angles or details that are involved. You may feel overwhelmed by the complexity of what has happened. On a positive spin, open discussions in conflict can allow you to sharpen your perceptions and get reliable bearings on different issues in the real world.

Alignment Arrow—this is printed on the rotating housing. It is used to align the magnetic arrow. When the magnetic arrow is within this arrow the compass will point along the desired bearing.

    Conflict Metaphor: The Alignment Arrow we liken to having a shared mental model of the end goal to the resolution of the conflict. When your mental model of the resolution is in alignment with the desired goal, as well as the mental model of the person(s) you are in conflict with, that is when positive movement forward will begin.

Another metaphor to think about with the Alignment Arrow is your perspective. What you see depends on where you stand. Your perspective is very different depending what side of the conflict you are on. There are several activities in this book that deal with perspective. Understanding someone else's perspective usually requires a great deal of questioning and thought. Sometimes conflict can be avoided if people just take the time to hear the other person out.

Mirror—some compasses have a sighting mirror. This allows the compass to be easily aligned while taking a bearing.

Conflict Metaphor: Mirrors are devices that allow people to see themselves the way others see them. Using the metaphor of a mirror in conflict is a technique designed to help people see how their approach to conflict looks to others. The metaphor of a mirror asks individuals to put aside their prejudices and stereotypes and, at least temporarily, look at the world from the perspective of others. This technique helps people understand why proposals that may seem perfectly reasonable to them are viewed as unacceptably selfish by others. It also helps people understand why strategies that some think are reasonable and moderate are viewed as provocative and inflammatory by others.

Ruler—can be used to measure distances on a map, the size of animal tracks, and the size of that mosquito . . .

Conflict Metaphor: There are many ways to measure Conflict. Whether it is the size of the argument or the amount of money it takes to dispute it, conflict is measurable. Conflict can be demonstrated by not returning phone calls, filing complaints, grievances, or lawsuits. At its extreme, conflict involves physical violence. In a quick Internet search, we found at least a dozen different profile tools that have been developed to measure conflict. One thing is for certain—conflict is everywhere and the costs are measurable. In the corporate world, several commonly tracked employee functions can provide Human Resource managers with a wealth of data to analyze and track the true costs of conflict. You can deduce that time spent, absenteeism, turnover, and grievance filing are indicators of workplace conflict. Measuring the costs of each of these factors can be used by Human Resource managers to prove the added value of human resources interventions such as training and performance management.

Direction of Travel Arrow—this arrow is printed on the base plate and points in the direction of the bearing.

Conflict Metaphor: This feature gives us the general direction in which to travel. To quote a Successories poster: "Success is in the Journey, not in the Destination." Sometimes we all know what the end product will look like, but the journey that gets us there can be difficult. In conflict situations, throughout this journey there will be many moments when people feel stuck and want to withdraw. We all know that we're supposed to be 'nice' to people, but sometimes it's not as easy as it sounds. In Robert Fulghum's book, *All I Really Needed to Know I Learned in Kindergarten,* he points out that the most important lessons of life are those that can be learned by a child. A few of them include:

1. Share everything.
2. Play fair.

3. Don't hit people.
4. Put things back where you found them.
5. Clean up your own mess.
6. Say you're sorry when you hurt somebody.
7. When you go out in the world, watch out for traffic, hold hands and stick together.

We smile when we realize Fulghum's ingenious simplicity. **Of course he is right.** These are lessons that a five-year-old can understand and that a sixty-five-year-old can be miserable at. But having a general direction in which to travel is important when dealing with conflict. Transforming conflict into something positive is a process aimed at humanizing people's relationships and improving them without resorting to violence.

Base Plate—the bottom of the compass.

Conflict Metaphor: We liken this metaphor to getting to the bottom of what the conflict is. By analyzing what leads to conflict or what could be the root of the conflict, we can identify personal and group responsibility. The key here is establishing a foundation for communication quickly and implementing a policy to resolve misunderstanding rather than carrying frustration and mistrust about on a daily basis. Identifying and resolving conflict is not a function of who wins and who loses, but the company being more effective and productive with confident employees that can communicate effectively in demanding situations. These employees, when needed, can quickly get to the bottom of conflict issues, resolve them efficiently, and in the end build a stronger organization.

FINDING A BEARING

Finding a bearing on a map requires you to know two things. First, you have to know where you are on the map, and secondly you have to be able to find your destination on the map. That's it! Once you have these two things, it is simple to find a bearing from the map. If you don't know these two things, you are in trouble.

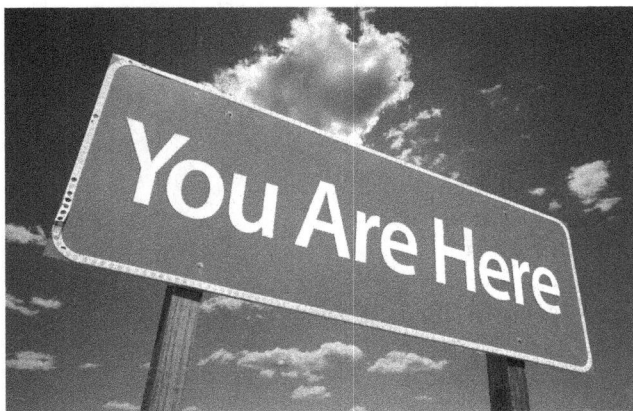

Great! Thanks for telling me! Image © 2010 by Feverpitch. Used under license from Shutterstock.

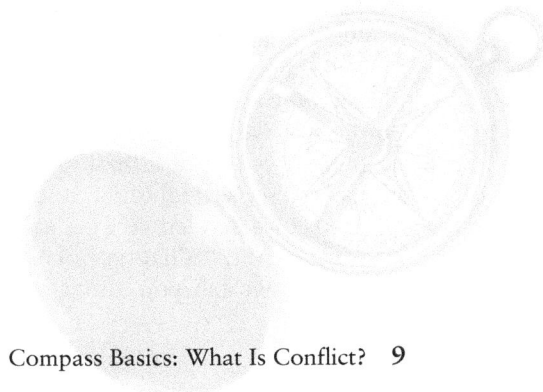

Finding your bearings in a conflict situation is essential to getting anything resolved. Sometimes the signs are obvious and other times they are harder to pinpoint. Wouldn't it be nice if there were signs everywhere that told you where you were? Like this one:

In conflict, knowing what destination creates a win/win situation for all involved will essentially help you chart your course. That course will often present us with different challenges or directions to go, but ultimately we need to have a goal in mind for our final destination.

We've all been to the mall before. These giant twenty-acre monstrosities are home to retail merchandizing gurus. There are some people that absolutely love the mall—the thrill of exploring each store to find a good bargain or unique find. The allure of the ambiance of the holiday decorations and special hours can

SUCCESS

Image © 2010 JupiterImages Corporation.

draw them in like flies to light. Then there are others who absolutely loath the mall scene. They don't enjoy wandering aimlessly from store to store in hopes of finding that one little gem to scratch off their list. Regardless of which type of mall shopper you are, The Map Kiosk can be your friend and guide to a pleasant mall shopping experience. You walk up and immediately look for the words printed on the big red dot, "YOU ARE HERE." You think to yourself, "Oh good, I've found myself!" Now to find your destination . . . You scroll through the categories ("children's shoes . . . no; women's apparel . . . no; books . . . yes that's it!") Then you find the name of the store you are looking for ("ABC's Children's Books . . . no; Read or Write Books . . . no; Books-n-More Books . . . yes!') You're getting closer. Location: F9. Now you need to chart your course between the YOU ARE HERE dots to F9. You check for landmarks: what is it near? is it beyond the food court? what other stores are nearby? . . . . You think to yourself, "OK, I know how to get there." You now have a mental map of how to get to F9. You begin your course at a brisk pace. You walk by several stores; you see several of the landmarks that were on the map. All of a sudden you get accosted by a cell phone kiosk attendant, "What type of cell phone service do you have? Can we tell you about some new features? We

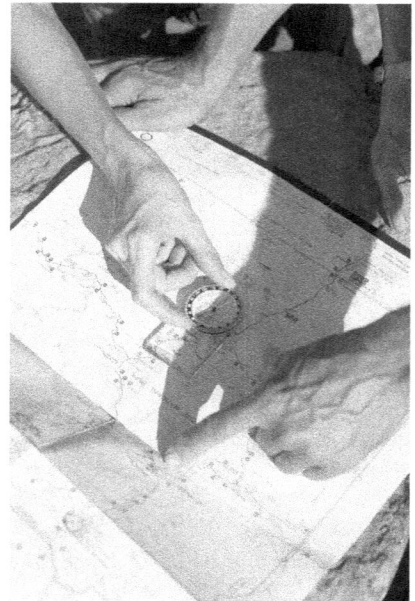

Image © 2010 JupiterImages Corporation.

have many new models. . . ." You think to yourself, "What? No! I was on track! I was headed in the right direction!" You get distracted for a moment, and you don't want to be rude. You stop briefly and then reply back, "No, thanks" and continue your journey. You start walking again, but all of a sudden you look up and you don't exactly remember which way you came from. Which direction were you headed? What corridor did I just come down? What direction was I supposed to go? Did I already pass that water fountain thing? Oh great, I'm lost. Where's another map kiosk? Why don't they put more of those out? What was the name of the store I'm going to? Ahhhhhhhh!!!!!

OK, so maybe it's not that dramatic, but you can see it is easy to get taken off course. Whether it be from a mall kiosk salesman or an argument between co-workers that needs some attention—going off course is an expected occurrence.

FOLLOWING A BEARING

Following a bearing isn't as easy as it sounds. Unfortunately, things tend to get in the way, and you have to be able to move around them without moving off your bearing. Does that sound like solving a conflict to you? What is interesting about map and compass skills is that you actually *have* to go off route to get to the end destination. If you tried to go in a straight line from point A to point B it would be extremely difficult, if not impossible. In the book *Flight Plan,* by Brian Tracy, he writes that any airplane headed for any destination will be off course 99 percent of the time because of air turbulence. But, by locking in on its destination, taking off, and making continual course corrections, the plane will arrive as scheduled. The same is true of people's journey through life and in conflict situations. We always need to adjust our course to deal with the 'stuff' that comes up. Most of the time conflict situations are unplanned and unpredictable, but knowing that they will come up and having a support system in place to help you deal with them will inevitably make your journey a little easier.

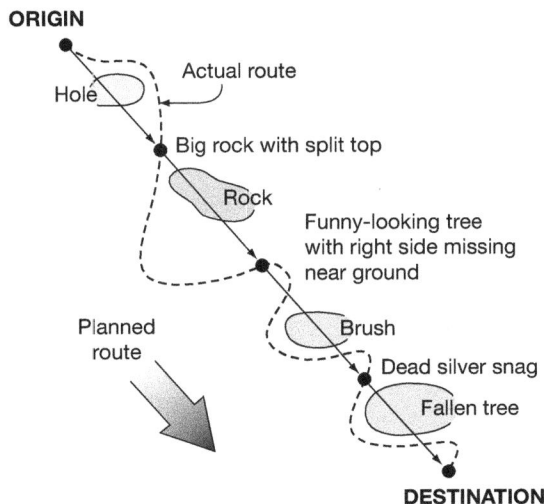

When following a bearing on a compass, there are several ways to accomplish this:

Following a Bearing Method 1: Find an obvious landmark along the bearing. This landmark should be easy to find and not too distant. Make your way to this object, and then find another object along the bearing and repeat. It is essential that the object be exactly along the bearing, as this type of navigation tends to amplify errors.

Here is a graph of what this might look like:

Conflict Metaphor: In a conflict situation the ORIGIN might be the event in which the conflict took place. The Destination would be the conflict diffused. The Planned Route would be the steps needed to take place in order to resolve the conflict. The Actual Route would be how effectively the two people in conflict communicated with one another.

Following a Bearing Method 2: This method is similar to Method 1. What you have to do in this case is locate two landmarks, in line with each other, *behind you*. These objects should be large, and it is acceptable if they are somewhat distant. Navigating like this is easy because you know you are on the right bearing as long as these two objects are in line with each other. This method of navigation is more accurate than Method 1, but it gets less accurate the farther you move away from your reference points.

Conflict Metaphor: Looking behind you is another way of saying *reflection*. We've all heard the saying, "You can't see the trees because of the forest." Oftentimes when we examine and identify clues as to how a conflict started, it's quite easy to pinpoint. We just didn't see the potential triggers at the time. Identifying a few larger events that started the conflict can be helpful in preventing them from happening again. As we reflect and discuss these events, they can also help us stay focused on the resolution of the conflict.

Following a Bearing Method 3: This method requires two people. One person moves ahead, working his/her way around obstacles. When they get around the obstacle they move back onto the bearing. The person who stayed in place moves their partner back onto the bearing using voice commands. This person then moves to their partner's location, where this process is repeated. Although slow, this process is extremely accurate. This method also has the advantage that it can be used in low visibility conditions or in places where landmarks are lacking (i.e., heavy forest, plains, etc.).

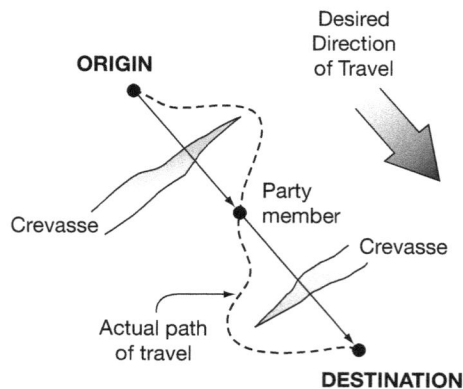

Conflict Metaphor: Having a mediator to resolve a conflict can be a welcome and rewarding experience. For this scenario, the mediator would be the person who moves ahead and sets a goal for the next bearing. The two people in conflict would set about the course working together and overcoming the obstacles in the way to make it to the next bearing location. Once there, the mediator would do a check in and see what the next steps for resolving the conflict would be. The mediator would move ahead and the two in conflict would do the work necessary to make it to the next check point.

Like any journey, these methods can be mixed to get to your destination. It would be nice if we could use a fancy GPS unit (global positioning system) and just select our destination to end a conflict.

Origin: Rude tone of voice and sarcastic comment

Select Destination: Peaceful ending

Suggested Route: Arrange a face-to-face meeting with involved parties

Quickest Route: Apologize and take responsibility for your actions

Warnings: On GPS units if you take a wrong turn the screen will flash big red arrows and announce that you have gone off track. It would be nice if this could happen in the real world! "Warning! You have just insulted your boss! Apologize for using inappropriate humor and verbalize an action plan for what you will do differently in the future."

Image © 2010 JupiterImages Corporation.

Having strategies for dealing with conflict are essential to healthy relationships. We will explore these strategies further and present a framework for conflict management in the pages of this book. This framework can be described as an experiential learning approach for helping individuals understand the influence of contextual factors and perspective in conflict resolution and management.

PART 2

Strategies for
Dealing with Conflict

Communication—talking about the conflict—is the first step toward resolving it.

Conflict generally results from poor communication, disruptions in routines, unclear goals or expectations, the quest for power, ego massage, differences in value systems, or hidden agendas. It is often expressed in rude, discourteous, and sometimes hostile behavior; selfishness; strident and defensive language; lack of respect; and increased stress.

If you are called to assist in resolving a conflict, you must get both parties to a place where they will at least listen to and respect the other party involved. If this is not achieved, it will be very difficult to resolve the conflict. At the point where either party hears themselves criticized, diagnosed, or intellectually interpreted, their energy will turn toward self-defense and counter-accusations rather than toward resolutions that meet everyone's needs.

People have varying degrees of comfort with conflict. Some prefer avoiding it at all costs. Unfortunately, those costs tend to increase the longer issues are left unaddressed. Therefore, learning how to manage and resolve conflict is to your benefit.

The following are some guidelines and suggestions that will help you deal with conflict.

- **Treat it as normal and expected.** Conflict is inevitable, and despite how many of us feel about it, conflict is not always a bad thing. Conflict need not be catastrophic or personal. Conflict is simply part of being human.

- **Deal with issues as they arise.** Avoiding conflict makes situations worse. Time does not resolve matters. Instead, it decreases the chance of a positive outcome.

- **Brainstorm.** There might be a variety of solutions if everyone is focused on a positive outcome and engaged in the process. Challenge yourself and others to be creative about the possibilities available to you. Conflict yields better ideas, as free markets create better products.

- **Attempt to understand the other person's point of view.** Dismissing the other's views, assigning blame, and exclusive focus on your own perspective are all counterproductive. Encourage each party to state what they agree with or like about the other's position.

- **Keep a positive outlook.** If you expect good things to happen, they will. Conversely, if you expect bad things to happen, you had better believe you won't be disappointed. Your attitude will govern your response.

- **Concentrate on what you can control.** What should you take ownership of and fix? What falls under your sphere of influence? What impact will you have on the desired outcome? Learn to focus your attention and activities where you can make a difference. Don't get caught up in areas beyond your control. You've got to learn to let go of those.

- **Don't judge emotions.** No one's feelings are more or less "right" than the other's. Emotions reflect a *valid* perspective of an individual. Even if you don't understand it, acknowledge the other person's reaction as important.

- **Focus on the behavior, situation, or problem area without attacking the person involved.** Ask open ended questions to show that you wish to understand and are willing to listen.

- **Dig out hidden agendas.** For example, one manager may be resisting a new idea simply because he or she developed the old one or because the other party is seen as an enemy. Try to determine if there is old 'stuff' being used to fuel the fire. Help them understand how the new idea builds on, rather than devalues, the old.

- **Think win-win.** In conflict, one party does not have to win and the other lose. Sometimes disagreement will lead to a more effective solution. An excessive drive to win will lead to lose-lose outcomes. Sometimes a good decision is reached when everyone has to give a little. To change is not to lose your own identity. As a matter of fact, by changing you find yourself and you find others. The only way to find a solution that benefits all sides is to learn more about each other. That beats a power struggle any day. Successful conflict resolution requires emotional intelligence on both sides to create win-win solutions.

- **Do not assume your values or beliefs are "right" and find common ground.** Your values and beliefs reflect a view of the world from your unique perspective. Respecting another's viewpoint as equally valuable as your own opens an opportunity for learning and growth. What common ground can you find? Are there common goals, values, beliefs? Finding areas of agreement can help to make other parties realize that you are not rejecting everything they are saying.

- **Get to the root of the problem.** Try to find the cause of the disease instead of just treating the symptoms. Start by trying to get to the bottom of the conflict. What is causing the conflict, and why are you reacting the way you are? Everyone involved in the conflict needs to agree on a definition of the problem before the problem can be tackled. This could mean describing the problem in terms of each person's needs. There's an old saying that a problem well defined is already half solved.

- **Ground yourself.** When lightning strikes, lightning rods take the electrical current and run it harmlessly to the ground. So, too, can you take the jolts and divert them harmlessly away if you have a well-constructed foundation of core values that you adhere to. Having designed a personal mission statement that clearly articulates who you are and where you are going will help provide guidance and direction before the conflict even occurs. The old country song says it best, if you don't stand for something, then you'll fall for anything.

- **Avoid using authority to stifle conflict.** This will breed resentment, which will surface elsewhere. This only prolongs the conflict.

- **Eliminate emotions.** Separate your feelings from the problem. When your emotions get mixed up in the conflict, the outcome is in doubt. Emotions color your perceptions and your logic and cloud the rational thinking that is essential to arriving at a solution.

- **Look for warning signs.** Be in touch with who you are. Part of handling conflict is to be aware of your own personal strengths and weaknesses, your beliefs and perceptions, and how they shape your response. For instance, if you perpetually run behind and you've got an important date, leave a little earlier than normal so that if you encounter traffic, you won't lose your cool and overreact. Build "fluff" into schedules. Likewise, set realistic deadlines for yourself and others.

- **Maintain a sense of humor.** Learn to laugh—harder and more frequently. Remember how hysterically upset some people can get and how comical it is. Don't let your boorish behavior provide comic relief for someone else. Laugh it off.

- **Stay in control.** Recognize that when you're dealing with people, not everyone will live up to your expectations all of the time. Reframe the stressful situation to keep your composure. Instead of overreacting when someone cuts you off on your morning commute, look for opportunities to be "nice" and let someone cut in front of you. Don't sink to their level. When you lie down with dogs you get fleas.

- **Establish ground rules.** When conflict happens, set goals for how to resolve it. What would happen if we don't fix this? What would a successful resolution look like? Look for common ground. Keep focused on a positive, solution-based outcome. Perhaps the only thing you can agree on is to agree to disagree, but do it in an agreeable manner.

- **Sleep on it, especially if you are angry.** Having control over emotional responses is difficult, so before you react in anger ask for time to think about it. Statements like, "Thank you for bringing this to my attention; I will get back to you tomorrow on this" is an appropriate response and allows you time to think before you react. Ask yourself the appropriate questions, think first, and then consider which technique will be the most helpful to you and to the other party.

- **Take action.** Once you've arrived at a win-win solution, accept it and implement it. Don't second-guess. Make sure each person takes responsibility for agreeing with the decision. Helping parties in conflict maintain self-esteem and save face is critical and should be a part of the action plan. And remember, no action is still an action. Don't avoid the resolution of the conflict.

Dealing with conflict does not need to be dreaded or feared. Interpersonal conflict is a natural component of human interaction. In fact, if the problem is the object of focus rather than the people involved, disagreements can generate new ideas and growth. Dealing with issues as they occur, acknowledging the other party's feelings and perspective, and avoiding judgment or blame further increase the chance of productive conflict resolution.

When we accept and understand conflict, we allow ourselves to grow, change, and to be empowered.

PART 3

The Importance
of Processing and Debriefing

THE VALUE OF REFLECTION

An important concept to consider when facilitating experiential activities is to provide opportunities to process, or reflect, on the experiences. The educational philosopher John Dewey (1933), who is known as one of the forefathers of experiential education, believed that in order to truly learn from experience there must be time for reflection.

Processing helps learners make connections between their educational experiences and real-life situations. It helps them recognize their skills and strengths by naming them. By recognizing and naming the skills and strengths used in an experience, individuals become more cognizant of the inner resources that can be used in future life situations. The practice of reflection itself is one of the most useful human skills in that it develops insight, which is one of the hardest important tools to teach and learn. Experiential activities followed by processing help people develop insight skills.

PARTICIPANT-DIRECTED PROCESSING

There is no one set way to process; using a variety of techniques and activities that give learners the power to take the lead in reflection is an engaging and effective way of viewing processing. Participant-directed methods of processing are a term coined by Steve Simpson of The Institute for Experiential Education (1997). In this orientation towards processing, participants decide what meaning to attach to the activity. Rather than being involved in more didactic discussion, there may be some guidance from the facilitator/teacher initially, but for the most part these activities allow for the spontaneity of individual interpretation of the experience. Many participant-directed methods involve the use of props or symbolic representations of the experience that provide a tangible object upon which participants can attach their thoughts.

METAPHORIC OBJECTS AND IMAGES

Using objects as symbolic representations of an experience or personal attribute can be a very effective approach to processing. These activities engage participants in creating or choosing symbols representing a group success or individual strength or accomplishment. The strength of these types of activities is that they are not threatening to participants and facilitators and leave the opportunities for creative and meaningful interpretation of an experience wide open. Participants can attach their thoughts to a tangible object that they can touch and show to a group during group discussion or take away with them to represent their experience. This helps thoughts and ideas reach depth and character in a way that doesn't happen with dialogue alone. Because the participants can talk about the object or image rather than about themselves directly, they sometimes express thoughts that otherwise would be left unsaid (Cain, Cummings, and Stanchfield 2004). Objects and images can be used to liven up the traditional sharing circle by providing interactive, kinesthetic ways to engage participants in group dialogue. For more ideas about effective ways to process and debrief with groups, please reference the book, *A Teachable Moment, A Facilitators Guide to Activities for Processing, Debriefing, Reviewing and Reflection*, by Jim Cain, Michelle Cummings, and Jennifer Stanchfield.

TRUST THE PROCESS

Fundamentally, all of the activities in this book serve as catalysts to dialogue. We have included some starter questions and debriefing topics with each activity. These questions are designed to begin the dialogue. It will be important for you, the facilitator, to ask two to three follow-up questions based on the responses of the participants. Ask questions about issues raised by the group, not what you want to hear. It's not the activity you should be concerned with, but rather what is talked about as a result of the event. **Trust this process.**

PART 4

Quotes on Conflict

Here are some useful quotes on conflict. These pages may be photocopied for discussion aids. Simply cut the quotes apart on the photocopied pages and hand one to each participant. Ask individuals to share the quote with a partner or small group and discuss what the quote means to them or how it applies to them.

Difficulties are meant to rouse, not discourage. The human spirit is to grow strong by conflict. —*William Ellery Channing (1780–1842)*

The greatest conflicts are not between two people but between one person and himself. —*Garth Brooks, country music*

Nonviolence is the answer to the crucial political and moral questions of our time; the need for mankind to overcome oppression and violence without resorting to oppression and violence. Mankind must evolve for all human conflict a method which rejects revenge, aggression and retaliation. The foundation of such a method is love. —*Martin Luther King Jr. (1929–1968)*

Our first and most pressing problem is how to do away with warfare as a method of solving conflicts between national groups within a society who have different views about how the society is to run. —*Margaret Mead (1901–1978)*

Conflict is going to happen whether you want it or not. People will butt heads. Sometimes when you least expect it.
—*Jimmy Bise Jr., Us and Them: A Blog Conversation Survival Guide, SXSW 2006*

As the networks evolve, so do my opinions toward them, and my divergent feelings bring out conflicting points of view. In advance, I apologize to those who expect a consistent position from me. —*Clifford Stoll, Silicon Snake Oil, 1995*

In dwelling, live close to the ground.
In thinking, keep to the simple.
In conflict, be fair and generous.
In governing, don't try to control.
In work, do what you enjoy.
In family life, be completely present.
—*Tao Te Ching*

Fortunately (psychoanalysis) is not the only way to resolve inner conflicts. Life itself still remains a very effective therapist. —*Karen Horney*

The harder the conflict, the more glorious the triumph. What we obtain too cheap, we esteem too lightly; it is dearness only that gives everything its value. I love the man that can smile in trouble, that can gather strength from distress and grow brave by reflection. 'Tis the business of little minds to shrink; but he whose heart is firm, and whose conscience approves his conduct, will pursue his principles unto death. —*Thomas Paine (1737–1809)*

Washing one's hands of the conflict between the powerful and the powerless means to side with the powerful, not to be neutral. —*Paulo Freire*

One hour of thoughtful solitude may nerve the heart for days of conflict—girding up its armor to meet the most insidious foe. —*Percival.*

Conflict builds character. Crisis defines it. —*Steven V Thulon*

In life we make progress by conflict and in mental life by argument and disputation . . . . There must be confrontation and opposition, in order that sparks must be kindled. —*Christopher Hitchens*

The fact is that a person does not wish to purge himself of the world, as it first appeared, but of his own difference from society. If he is thoroughly absorbed into society with no conflicts, then (he himself admits) everything is in order; if not, then he must attend to the matter as speedily as possible; and if necessary he will clean himself away. So dependent is he on the outside world for his own definition, and does not realize it. —*Christian Enzensberger,* Smut: An Anatomy of Dirt

Whatever you do, you need courage. Whatever course you decide upon, there are always difficulties arising that tempt you to believe your critics are right. To map out a course of action and follow it to an end requires some of the same courage that a soldier needs. Peace has its victories, but it takes brave men and women to win them.   —*Ralph Waldo Emerson (1803–1882)*

Creativity comes from a conflict of ideas.   —*Donatella Versace*

I am a woman in process. I'm just trying like everybody else. I try to take every conflict, every experience, and learn from it. Life is never dull.   —*Oprah Winfrey*

Peace is not just the absence of conflict. It's the presence of justice.   —*from the movie,* Air Force One *with Harrison Ford*

Beautiful light is born of darkness, so the faith that springs from conflict is often the strongest and the best.   —*R. Turnbull*

The most dramatic conflicts are perhaps, those that take place not between men but between a man and himself—where the arena of conflict is a solitary mind.   —*Clark Moustakas, humanistic psychologist*

It is the eternal struggle between these two principles—right and wrong. They are the two principles that have stood face to face from the beginning of time and will ever continue to struggle. It is the same spirit that says, "You work and toil and earn bread, and I'll eat it."
                        —*Abraham Lincoln (1809–1865), sixteenth president of the USA*

Change means movement. Movement means friction. Only in the frictionless vacuum of a nonexistent abstract world can movement or change occur without that abrasive friction of conflict.   —*Saul Alinsky*

Reason and emotion are not antagonists. What seems like a struggle between two opposing ideas or values, one of which, automatic and unconscious, manifests itself in the form of a feeling.   —*Nathaniel Branden, American expert on self-esteem*

Whenever you're in conflict with someone, there is one factor that can make the difference between damaging your relationship and deepening it. That factor is attitude. —*Timothy Bentley, Canadian family therapist*

If we cannot end our differences at least we can make the world safe for diversity. —*John F. Kennedy (1917–1963), thirty-fifth president of the USA*

The split in you is clear. There is a part of you that knows what it should do, and a part that does what it feels like doing. —*John Cantwell Kiley*

During the last century, and part of the one before, it was widely held that there was an unreconcilable conflict between knowledge and belief. —*Albert Einstein (1879–1955), German-born American physicist*

I'm not a combative person. My long experience has taught me to resolve conflict by raising the issues before I or others burn their boats. —*Alistair Grant, business executive, chairman of Argyll Group*

When one ceases from conflict, whether because he has won, because he has lost, or because he cares no more for the game, the virtue passes out of him. —*Charles Horton Cooley*

A good manager doesn't try to eliminate conflict; he tries to keep it from wasting the energies of his people. If you're the boss and your people fight you openly when they think that you are wrong—that's healthy. —*Robert Townsend*

Peace is not the absence of conflict but the presence of creative alternatives for responding to conflict—alternatives to passive or aggressive responses, alternatives to violence. —*Dorothy Thompson*

As such people achieve influence within the organization, whenever there is a conflict between their own interest and the interest of the organization, their interests will win out. —*Robert Shea*

There is an immutable conflict at work in life and in business, a constant battle between peace and chaos. Neither can be mastered, but both can be influenced. How you go about that is the key to success. —*Philip Knight*

Peace is not absence of conflict; it is the ability to handle conflict by peaceful means. —*Ronald Reagan*

To observe people in conflict is a necessary part of a child's education. It helps him to understand and accept his own occasional hostilities and to realize that differing opinions need not imply an absence of love. —*Milton R. Sapirstein*

Conflict is the beginning of consciousness. —*M. Esther Harding*

PART 5

Conflict in Corporate Environments

Arrows

TYPE OF INITIATIVE

Opening activity

SOURCE

Bill Michaelis, from *The Game and Play Leader's Handbook*. The version presented here was shared with us by Chris Cavert. This writing explains the directions for an activity containing an incredibly valuable lesson.

PURPOSE

We like to use Arrows at the beginning of a program to introduce how easy it can be to make mistakes. The more complex the situation, the easier it is to make mistakes.

PROPS NEEDED

—A piece of paper with a well-defined arrow on it.

GROUP SIZE

4–100

DIRECTIONS

The facilitator stands facing the group—be sure that everyone in the group can see the facilitator and that each person has an arm's length of room to either side of them. In this activity the facilitator will be moving the arrow to point in one of four directions—Up, Down, Left, or Right. The group will have a different task in each round.

This is written as if spoken by the facilitator:

Round 1: "I will be showing you an arrow. It will be pointing in one of four directions—Up, Down, Left, or Right. In this round the challenge will be to thrust your arms in the same direction the arrow is pointing and, at the same time, say out loud the direction it is pointing. Are there any questions? Let's give this a try." Give a few seconds for each direction. Show about six or seven different directions in the first round. Don't forget to celebrate the effort.

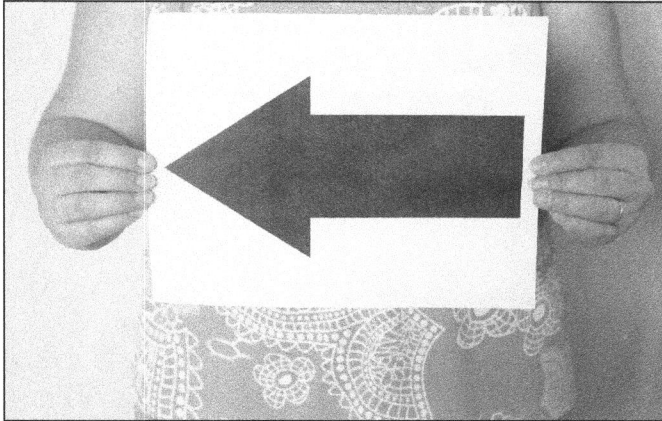

Round 2: "Okay, in this second round the challenge will be to thrust your arms in the direction the arrow is pointing and say out loud the *opposite* direction it is pointing. So, if the arrow is pointing left, you thrust your arms left and, at the same time, *say* 'right.' Are there any questions? Let's try." Again, show six or seven directions. Celebrate.

Round 3: "This time the challenge is to thrust your arms in the *opposite* direction and say the *correct* direction of the arrow. Any questions? Let's try it."

You will need to decide how fast you change the direction of the arrow—the faster you get the more challenging it becomes. Also, please remind the group that this activity is about the effort and not the succes—trying is key. Celebrate.

DEBRIEFING TOPICS

Remind everyone that we all make mistakes and that some mistakes are easier to make than others. Usually, mistakes are unintentional. One point to reinforce when addressing conflict with a group is to suggest that not all conflict starts with an intentional wrongdoing. Stepping back and looking at solutions to the conflict may seem simple in nature. Following through with the solutions is much harder. We can still make mistakes in the process.

- How did it feel to do the activity correctly? How did it feel to do it wrong? Why do we put so much emphasis on the errors we make and not the successes we have as an individual, team, or group?
- How is this activity like a conflict situation?
- Describe a time where simple mistakes created a conflict with a colleague or friend.
- What are some other insights you formed from this activity?

WHERE TO FIND IT/HOW TO MAKE IT

Print an arrow from a clip art program onto an 8.5 × 11-inch piece of paper or card stock. Laminate it for longevity. Or simply draw a large arrow on a piece of paper.

FACILITATOR NOTES

As If

TYPE OF INITIATIVE

Icebreaker

SOURCE

Relayed to us by Chris Cavert who learned it from "Steve the Aussie" at the 2006 National Challenge Course Practitioner Symposium.

PROPS NEEDED

None

GROUP SIZE

2–100

DIRECTIONS

Divide your group into pairs. Begin this activity by letting participants know that you will give them a relationship role to play for the upcoming interaction. Have the pairs stand about 15 feet apart from one another. Have them determine which partner will be the "greeter" and which partner will play out the "role." Each interaction is approximately 20–30 seconds in duration. Then announce the first interaction.

Ask your group to greet another person in the room **AS IF** you are:

* long-lost friends

Let this interaction go on for 20–30 seconds. Afterwards, briefly process what happened in this interaction, what some of the feelings were, and the general mood of the interaction. Then proceed with another role. Here are some examples of other roles you could use:

- college roommates
- someone you have had a conflict with at work
- your boss
- the author of your favorite business book
- The President of the United States
- a colleague you are intimidated by
- a famous musician
- someone who does not speak English (or the dominant language of the group)
- someone interviewing for a job
- a favorite actor or actress

You can come up with as many different AS IF scenarios as you wish. This is a great follow-up activity to the Handshakes activity.

When introducing this exercise tell the group that there may be periods of uncomfortable interaction, or there may be periods of joy, anger, or frustration. You will find that the way people greet one another is open to an incredible amount of interpretation. For example, just about everyone greets their high school friend with a hug or a handshake, and it typically involves some shouting and lots of asking "how are you." However, a greeting between college roommates can vary greatly. Some people have no interest in seeing their college roommates again, but some folks are as close today as they were while living in the dorm 25 years ago. By the time we see folks introducing themselves to the President, we observe many different approaches . . . some are thrilled, others are rude, and some pretend to be violent. My response is "really?" That is REALLY how you would greet the President? My comments following this activity are always the same, and they typically go something like this: "Would you agree that everyone we greeted today is human? Is it safe to say that all humans deserve the same respect in terms of being polite to one another? We don't have to agree with what the President does or even like our college roommate, but these are just two examples of how our attitude and belief systems affect our ability to be respectful of one another. Does that make sense?"

DEBRIEFING TOPICS

- What did you notice?
- Who was uncomfortable with some of the early "as if" situations?
- What about the later introductions?
- What did you notice about non-verbal body language with the different roles?
- How did your attitude change during the exercise?
- Would you agree that everyone we "greeted" today is human? Is it safe to say that all humans deserve the same respect in terms of being polite to one another?

FACILITATOR NOTES

The Body Part Debrief™

Embodying Conflict

TYPE OF INITIATIVE

Debriefing tool

PURPOSE

The Body Part Debrief™ was one of the first activities Michelle Cummings created at Training Wheels. It is by far one of the most popular debriefing tools available and her personal favorite. She uses it with 90% of the groups she facilitates with great success. For more information about the general use of this tool, please consult the Training Wheels website at www.training-wheels.com. The Body Part Debrief™—Embodying Conflict is an adaptation of the metaphors of the body and how conflict affects us as leaders and team members.

PROPS NEEDED

—Objects or pictures of different body parts.

DIRECTIONS

Conflict exists at all levels in an organization. Conflict is not reserved for specific titles and roles. Organizational excellence or organizational disaster can often be measured by a team's ability to resolve conflict.

This can be achieved by embodying the characteristics and practicing the skills necessary to resolve conflict, sustain performance, and encourage each other to keep a healthy work environment.

Present the following body part metaphors to use for conflict to the group. Allow the group time to discuss what the parts mean to them and how these tools can help resolve a conflict they may be experiencing.

THE ELEMENTS OF EMBODYING CONFLICT

The Heart

Speak from the heart and be honest with your feelings. Build trust and respect among those we work with by taking to heart constructive feedback.

The Mind/Brain

Individuals must think strategically when resolving a conflict, translate that strategy into tactical actions, and make sound decisions that are fair to all parties involved.

The Core of Conflict/Spine

Being courageous enough to stand up for what is right. Get to the core of the issue to prevent it from happening again.

The Ears

Actively listening to others and hearing what is important to them. Be a good listener when someone has a conflict with you. Remember, there are always two sides to the story.

Walk Your Talk/Foot

Be accountable for your actions. Do what you say you are going to do. Don't stick your foot in your mouth by doing the opposite of what you said you would do.

The Eyes

Have a sound vision for the future. Be open to new possibilities—even ones you did not come up with.

Your Voice

When trying to resolve a conflict, speak in a tone in which the other party will hear you. If your tone is disrespectful, your words will mean nothing.

Know when to speak up for the good of the organization.

Full Body or Shoulder

Take responsibility for your actions. Do not blame others for your behavior.

WHERE TO FIND IT/HOW TO MAKE IT

The Body Part Debrief™ activity is trademarked through Training Wheels, www.training-wheels.com. You may purchase this activity through their website. You can also provide the group pictures of the different body parts.

FACILITATOR NOTES

Bright | Blurry | Blind

TYPE OF INITIATIVE

Discussion tool

SOURCE

Michael Cardus, www.create-learning.com

PURPOSE

Creating a sense of community; intra- and inter-departmental communication; develop transparency and trust within organizations; allows participants to openly speak about issues of conflict within the team and organization.

PROPS NEEDED

—Flip chart paper—enough for two sheets per group
—A variety of markers and writing utensils
—Metaphor cards—cards with images on them with no definitive meaning. These cards are a way for participants to discuss and determine the team's BRIGHT | BLURRY | BLIND areas.

GROUP SIZE

5–500; participants are asked to work in their existing teams (i.e., Accounting is together in one team, Human Resources is together in another team, Sales, etc.)
The important point is that the teams are made up of people that work together sharing similar tasks, supervisors, roles, responsibilities, and culture.   .

GOALS

Giving the teams and participants an opportunity to think and speak about concerns and give accolades to each other so a powerful bond is created. Additionally, by illuminating topics within departments and the organization teams can brainstorm and strengthen the team. Facilitating a "one team" atmosphere and then empowering the participants to share information and techniques that are successful. Often, this information has not been shared in an open forum.

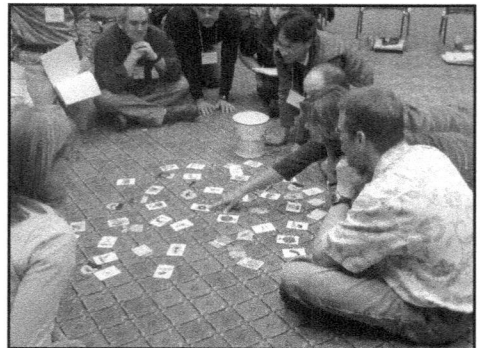

DIRECTIONS

Ask the groups to split into their work teams (mentioned above). Ask for a representative to come and receive two pieces of flip chart paper, some markers, and a stack of metaphor cards. With large teams it helps to have clearly marked areas where the team should be located. Have the materials already in place in a brown paper bag. Ask participants to inventory the contents according to the inventory sheet inside.

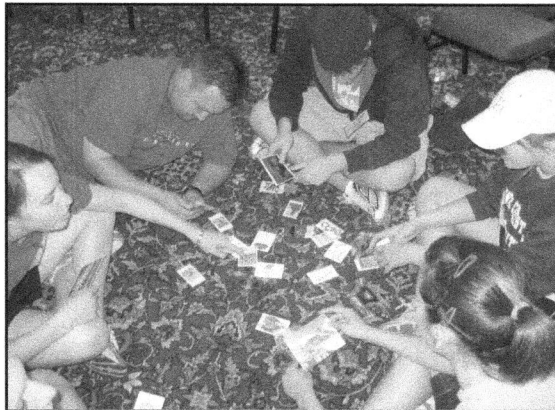

Once the teams settle, give the following direction:

"Within our small teams and within the organization there are several ideas and issues that seem obvious to us and not to anyone else. As a team it is important to create a culture of transparent and open communication of needs and requirements for our teams and individuals to be their most effective.

In a moment I am going to ask each small team to choose three metaphor cards with different meanings attached to them. The team must be in agreement of which three cards to use and what each card will symbolize for each small team.

—One card is going to represent BRIGHT—**Bright** is an issue or topic that is out in the open, clearly evident to the team about the organization. Bright is common knowledge everyone knows that this is an area of concern for the team and the organization.
—The second card represents BLURRY—**Blurry** is known and not spoken about enough; a subject that should become Brighter. Blurry is the undercurrent water cooler talk—the area that the team feels insecure about in reference to the organization and its status within the organization. Blurry is a topic or issue that, if it was made brighter, much of the "gossip" would cease to exist and questions would be answered.
—The third card represents what the team feels is BLIND—**Blind** is **not** known, lacking from the shared understanding and knowledge of the organization. Blind issues and topics are ones that the team feels only they struggle with and no other teams are aware of. If the Blind issues and topics became Brighter the organization would become transparent and create a paradigm shift towards excellence."

The teams are asked to choose the three metaphor cards (one for BRIGHT, one for BLURRY, and one for BLIND) and write these on flip chart paper. Each group should present the BRIGHT | BLURRY | BLIND findings to the entire organization and teams that are present for the activity.

DEBRIEFING TOPICS AND NOTES

BRIGHT | BLURRY | BLIND is an initiative that can stir up some powerful emotions and discussions. Be prepared to be open to the team criticizing and touching on topics that create conflict. The way this initiative ends can create some real growth and increase trust within the organization.

After each team has had the chance to present their BRIGHT | BLURRY | BLIND charts, ask them to hang them on the walls. Give participants approximately 15–30 minutes (more time if necessary) to walk around and view the other teams' flip charts; allow for some unstructured speaking and question-and-answer sessions.

Following the unstructured viewing time, call the participants back into their functional teams and ask them to gather by their flip chart papers. Some possible processing questions:

- How were the metaphor cards chosen for the BRIGHT and BLURRY and the BLIND?
- How effective was the group's communication process?
- In what ways were disagreements settled?
- What was the easy part? What made it easy?
- What was the challenging part? What challenges were faced?
- Are there any common themes that we noticed among all the departments?
- What BLURRY topics can we discuss right now to make BRIGHT?
- Any surprises that were found among teams with the BLIND areas?
- Are the areas that were BRIGHT to one team BRIGHT to all or other teams?
- What are the causes of BRIGHT | BLURRY | BLIND topics within organizations?
- How can we as a team minimize the BLIND areas?
- What are we going to do with this information?

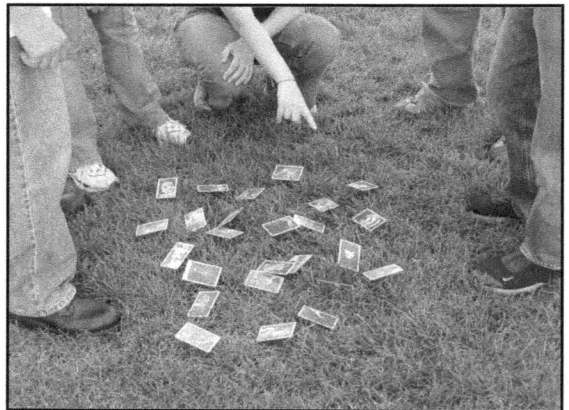

* Possibly end the day by creating a team of individuals who are responsible for addressing and developing a system to enhance transparency and communication within the organization. The team can use the information gathered for a starting point.

*** **DO NOT LET THIS INFORMATION GO UNUSED!** If you lead this team-building activity and do **nothing,** you will create an environment that can be more hostile and subversive than before you began.

WHERE TO FIND IT/HOW TO MAKE IT

You can make your own cards using index cards and cutting out and pasting various images on the index cards or they can be purchased. Metaphor cards and Chiji Cards are available through Training Wheels, www.training-wheels.com.

FACILITATOR NOTES

Buzz Ring
Talking in Circles

SOURCE

Introduced by Pat Rastall; further developed by Michelle Cummings, *A Teachable Moment*, pp. 67–68.

PURPOSE

This physics phenomenon will have your participants talking about the 'Buzz Words' of conflict in a unique way.

TYPE OF INITIATIVE

Problem Solving, Processing

PROPS NEEDED

—One Buzz Ring

GROUP SIZE

Maximum of 15 people per ring.

DIRECTIONS

- To begin this activity, identify the "buzz" words that your group may encounter during a conflict. For example, your group may come up with the words: communication, respect, positive language, trust, and conflict.
- Explain to the group that it takes a lot of effort to keep communication, respect, positive language, trust, and conflict working together simultaneously. Like most group work, it takes time and practice to master a new skill. Explain to the group that you are going to start the buzz ring and give them a task that is quite difficult to accomplish. Explain that you are not certain if they will be able to successfully complete the activity but would like to see how they do. Then start up your buzz ring.

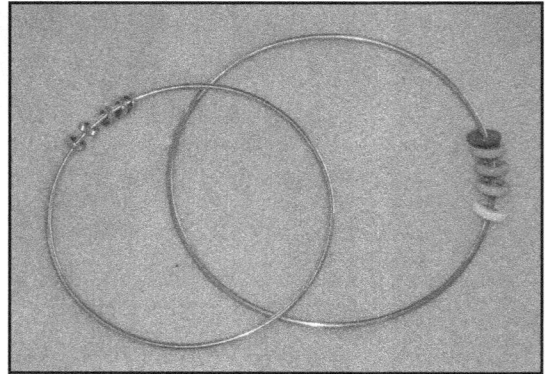

- The object is to pass the buzz ring around the circle without stopping any of the rings from buzzing. As previously stated, this is a difficult task, and the majority of groups will not be successful their first attempt.
- While the group is passing the ring around, you can talk about the buzz words and what they will encounter in a typical work day.
- If someone in the group makes the rings stop, process it immediately. This person is feeling some embarrassment, disappointment, stress, and may feel that they have let the group down. First, encourage them to get the rings going again. If they are unsuccessful, ask the group the following questions: "Has anyone ever done this before? Is it acceptable to the group that we do not have to be perfect the first time we attempt new tasks? How many people hoped that someone else would be the first to stop the rings before it was their turn?"
- At this point you can have the group set goals based on the number of mistakes they want to allow in one pass of the ring. Then help the group get the rings going again.
- Verbal encouragement from the facilitator helps in the group success. Encouraging statements include: "It's a simple hand-over-hand motion. Communicate with the person next to you when you are ready to release the buzz ring into their possession."
- Encourage the group to celebrate after the ring makes it all the way around the group.

DEBRIEFING TOPICS

There are several things to bring up as you process this activity. Here are a few examples:

- Was anyone nervous to be the one receiving the ring? Why? Examples they may give include not wanting to fail in front of the group or not wanting to let the group down by making a mistake. This opens up a great opportunity to talk about how those issues might come up throughout the program as the group works together. It is also good to point out that most people have not handled a buzz ring before, so being willing to try new things in front of the group is important. It encourages risk taking and emphasizes how small failures enable us to have success in the end.

- Starting the program with this activity creates a safe environment for participants to talk about any fears they may have about the day. Ending the program with this activity lets the group see how much they have learned together as a group.
- Sometimes if the rings stop in the process, a participant will make a good effort to get the rings going again but only get three of the five rings buzzing and then continue passing it around. This gives you a good avenue to talk about how difficult it can be to keep all five of the buzz words they came up with (communication, respect, positive language, trust, and conflict) going at one time. Can we have trust if we do not have respect at the same time? Some great dialogue around conflict can develop from this.
- Another way to use the buzz ring is to ask who in the group is good at multitasking. After those people admit (or do not admit!) to the skill, pass the buzzing ring around the circle and ask each participant to tell the group three things about themselves while keeping the rings buzzing. This is difficult for even great multitaskers!

SPECIFIC DEBRIEFING QUESTIONS

- Were you nervous to receive the ring? Why?
- What did your body do as the ring got closer to you?
- Did you hope that someone else made a mistake before the ring got to you?
- Has anyone ever tried this before? Is it acceptable to make mistakes the first time you try new tasks?
- In what ways can we as a group create an atmosphere of support and respect so people feel comfortable trying new things?
- How difficult is it to be successful at (the buzz words they chose) trust, teamwork, communication, bullying . . . at the same time?
- Was it risky to try something new in front of this group?
- How likely would you be to try something new in front of someone who had bullied you in the past?

SEQUENCING

The Buzz Ring can be implemented in many different ways. Here are a few suggestions:

1. Start and end the training with the Buzz Ring.

   Sequencing the Buzz Ring at the beginning of a program can set the tone for what you want to accomplish with the group. Giving them a task that is difficult to achieve, allows them to think metaphorically, creates some performance anxiety, and has the potential to push them outside their comfort zone is a wonderful first step when talking about the hard topic of conflict. Dealing with conflict is critical to successful teams and people and often takes a step-by-step approach to resolve. Being successful at the Buzz Ring activity is also a step-by-step sequence. Oftentimes we are not 100% successful at our attempts. The sequence of starting the program with the Buzz Ring allows the group to have the initial experience with the ring itself.

Ending the program with the Buzz Ring allows the group to have other experiences during the day of working together, effective communication, and more conversation about how to deal with conflict and each other. The more practice we have at resolving conflict and working together, the better we will be at it. Experience has shown that groups that end the program with the Buzz Ring have a higher success rate at completing the task with little to no errors. You will be amazed at how well groups do with this.

2. Use the Buzz Ring as a stand-alone activity.

   The Buzz Ring activity works well as a stand-alone activity for many reasons. Because the buzz ring is such a unique tool participants often buy-in quickly due to the 'coolness factor' of what it physically does. Multiple learning styles are utilized—auditory, visual, and kinesthetic—so right away you have engaged a large percentage of your audience.

3. Debrief the Day: Pass the Buzz

   Using the Buzz Ring as a wrap-up at the end of a training or workshop can be an effective way to encourage participants to 'Pass the Buzz' about what they learned.

   At the end of the training, invite participants to form a circle.

   Present the buzz ring and start it buzzing. Then ask: "How do we keep the buzz going from this workshop?"

   While keeping the buzz ring in motion, model a response by saying: "I learned more about the conflict styles of my co-workers. I'm going to use this knowledge to approach individuals differently if I have conflict with them (or whatever else may be appropriate from the workshop content)." Then pass the buzz ring to the next person in the circle.

When the next person gets the ring, he/she states what he/she will take from the workshop and passes the buzz ring to the next person. This pattern continues around the circle until the ring gets back to the facilitator.

If the ring stops buzzing as it goes around the circle, the person has to restart the buzz and mentions what might be an obstacle that could stop the buzz. After sharing this they proceed with the initial question.

The fascination with the buzz ring combined with the reflection helps participants leave with a smile and an action plan.

GETTING THE BUZZ RING STARTED

Getting the rings to start can be tricky, and practicing ahead of time is a must. There are multiple ways to start the rings so finding your 'style' just takes some practice to figure out which system works best for you. Some place their palm down on the still rings and give them a good spin. By turning the large ring at the same time, the rings start buzzing. Others will slap straight down at the rings and turn the large ring at the same time to get them buzzing. Practice to see which method works best for you.

HERE ARE SOME BASIC INSTRUCTIONS

1. Hold the large metal ring in either hand.

2. Use the other hand to spin-out the washers.

3. After the washers begin "spinning," quickly use both hands to smoothly rotate the large metal ring toward you.

The washers should continue to spin as long as you rotate the large ring.

WHAT ARE THE PHYSICS BEHIND THE BUZZ RING?/HOW DOES THE BUZZ RING WORK?

The buzz ring is really just five little tops of unusual design strung on a metal ring. Do you remember how tops appear to start "wobbling" as they slow down? This rotation of the spin axis is called precession and causes the ring to press on one side of the hole in the spinning top. The contact point between the ring and the top can be thought of as a gear that changes the motion of the upward-moving ring into the top's spinning motion.

FACILITATOR NOTES

Change Debrief

TYPE OF INITIATIVE

Processing tool

SOURCE

Michelle Cummings. This activity was created out of an Internet story that circulated. Origin unknown. Michelle added parts to the activity to add more metaphor to the group application.

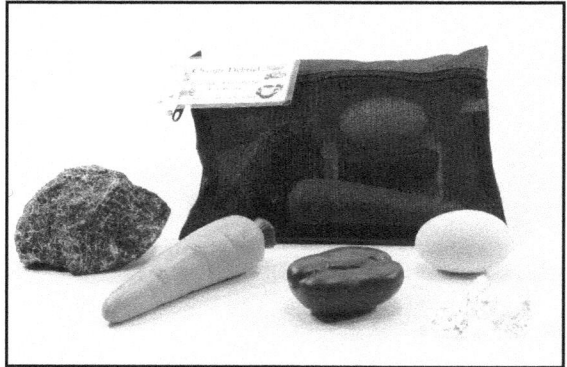

PROPS NEEDED

Objects shaped as an egg, a carrot, a coffee bean, a rock, and an ice cube. Props could be pictures of each item, the item itself, or stress relievers in the shape of each item.

GROUP SIZE

1–20

DIRECTIONS

Here is a truly unique tool to help organizations and individuals deal with change.

Set these props out in front of your group and ask them to describe their actions when put in a "hot water" situation. Frontloading the metaphors that accompany each part is important to the level of depth participants will share.

Egg

- In "hot water" situations, are you like an egg?
- Do you look the same on the outside but turn hard on the inside?
- How easy is it for you to put your "game face" on when talking to teammates about a decision that, on the inside, you are quite unhappy about?
- If an egg is left in boiling water too long, it will crack or explode.

Carrot

- What happens to a carrot when placed in boiling water?
- A carrot will turn soft and change itself dramatically as an effect of the hot water. Do you turn to mush and do whatever the "hot water" wants you to do when faced with a change?

Coffee Bean

- Are you like the coffee bean; do you change the "hot water" situation?
- Do you get energized about new changes or try to influence how the changes get implemented?

Rock

- When a rock is placed in a pot of boiling water, it will sink to the bottom and not change. What do you do with the "rocks" in your team—those that refuse to change while the change is happening around them?
- How does this change style encourage conflict within a team?

Ice Cube

- How are you like the ice cube?
- Do you try to diffuse the hot water situation?
- Are you a small ice cube that attempts to cool things down and then become overwhelmed with the situation and melt back into it?
- Or are you a large ice cube that really affects the hot water situation and sticks with it to diffuse it?

Oftentimes, individuals will go through each stage in a changing environment. Use the props as a timeline to describe a person's journey through the change.

DEBRIEFING QUESTIONS

- What do you think is your typical change stage when first faced with a new change?
- Does this stage encourage or prevent a conflict with others?
- How do you approach others who have different perspectives and opinions about the change?
- Describe the positive aspects of knowing what change stage each individual is in.

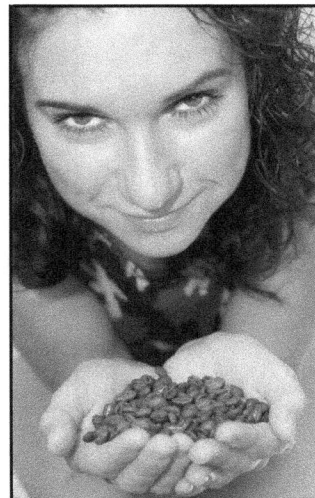

VARIATION

Here is a story that could be a good topic of discussion to use with The Change Debrief.

IN THE TEST KITCHEN OF LIFE

A young woman was complaining to her father about how difficult her life had become. He said nothing but took her to the kitchen and set three pans of water to boiling. To the first pan, he added carrots; to the second, eggs; and to the third, ground coffee. After all three had cooked, he put their contents into separate bowls and asked his daughter to cut into the eggs and carrots and smell the coffee. "What does this all mean?" she asked impatiently.

"Each food," he said, "teaches us something about facing adversity, as represented by the boiling water. The carrot went in hard but came out soft and weak. The eggs went in fragile but came out hardened. The coffee, however, changed the water to something better."

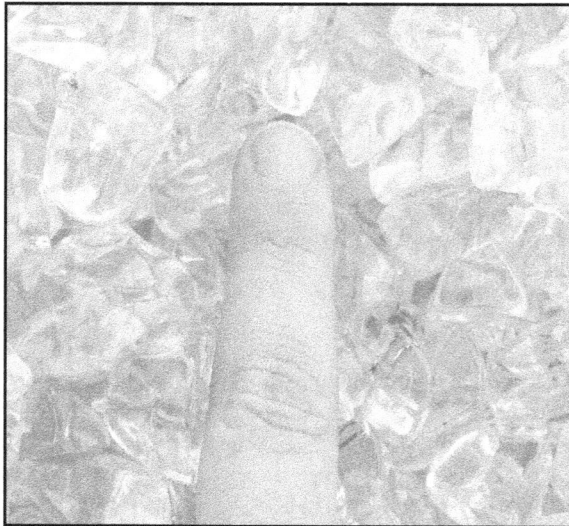

"Which will you be like as you face life?" he asked. "Will you give up, become hard, or transform adversity into triumph? As the 'chef' of your own life, what will you bring to the table?"

WHERE TO FIND IT/HOW TO MAKE IT

Training Wheels sells a set of stress reliever parts for this activity. There are five parts packaged in a tidy 7 × 9-inch mesh envelope. The stress relievers are all made of polyurethane. Latex free. Visit www.training-wheels.com for more information.

You can also source all of these items from your kitchen and back yard. We recommend hard boiling the eggs before you bring them to your group!

SUGGESTION

If you are trying to encourage everyone to be like the coffee bean and be energized about the new changes, you could send everyone home with a bag of coffee beans encouraging them to be energetic change agents.

FACILITATOR NOTES

Conflict Resolution
Thumball™

TYPE OF INITIATIVE

Icebreaker, Problem Solving, Processing tool

PURPOSE

Here is a truly unique tool to help organizations and individuals resolve a conflict.

PROPS NEEDED

Conflict Resolution Thumball™

GROUP SIZE

1–100; small groups of 10 people per ball is recommended

DIRECTIONS

Here is a truly unique tool to help organizations and individuals resolve a conflict. There are 32 different conflict resolution or peer mediation questions pre-printed on the panels of the ball. The ball is made of soft material.

- Invite your group to sit or stand in a circle.
- Ask participants to toss the Thumball™ to a teammate. This teammate should catch it, look under their thumb, and respond to the question found there.

Participant responses can vary each time you play. Here are a few suggestions:

- Respond to the panel under your thumb by answering for yourself.
- Respond by asking another player to answer.
- Predict the answer another player would give.

Once a group has played together several times, you can add the challenge of recalling an answer provided by another player on a previous day. You may also ask them to recall an answer given by another participant that may be helpful in solving a new conflict.

Sample questions found on the Conflict Resolution Thumball™:

1. What is one thing you could have done differently?

2. How would you like to see the conflict resolved?

3. How did you approach the other party?

4. Describe your initial reaction to the conflict.

5. Is there old stuff you are using to fuel this fire?

6. In the grand scheme of things, how important is this conflict?

7. Are you trying to cast blame?

8. What are you doing that is blocking the resolution of this problem?

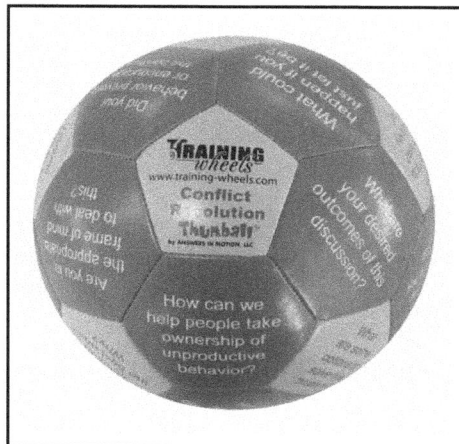

VARIATION

Read the group a conflict scenario and then ask them to toss the ball around and respond to the questions based on how they would try and resolve the conflict.

VARIATION

This is a wonderful processing tool for one person. If you are going through a conflict of some kind, toss the ball in the air and look under your thumb to reflect on the question silently. The 32 questions are well thought out and may give you insight on how to solve your own inner conflict.

WHERE TO FIND IT/HOW TO MAKE IT

The Conflict Resolution Thumball™ is a custom design of Michelle Cummings. You can purchase the Conflict Resolution Thumball™ from the Training Wheels website at www.training-wheels.com. You could make a similar ball by writing conflict resolution questions using a permanent marker on a beach ball or other soft, tossable sphere.

FACILITATOR NOTES

Cross the Line

TYPE OF INITIATIVE

Diversity, Behavior Awareness, Empathy

SOURCE

Idea provided by the staff at Making the Peace; further developed by Michelle Cummings

PROPS/MATERIALS NEEDED

Two ropes or masking tape, large room (big enough for entire group)

GROUP SIZE

4–100

PURPOSE

This activity is one of the more powerful activities in this book. In everyday speech when someone has "crossed the line," it usually means that they have gone too far or stepped over a boundary. These scenarios are breeding grounds for conflict. This activity will allow participants to reflect on times when they have demonstrated a behavior (or one demonstrated toward them) that crossed the line.

TIME NEEDED

20 minutes for activity; 30–45 minutes to debrief

DIRECTIONS

Step by Step Procedure

1. Put two ropes (or tape lines) parallel to one another in the center of the room on the ground. Place them 8–10 feet apart and span the length of the room.

2. Ask your participants to line up on one side of the rope you placed on the ground. Everyone should be on the same side of the room, facing the line.

3. Introduce the activity: Explain to the group that this activity involves people's feelings. It requires four things: respect, sensitivity, silence, and not judging others.

Specifically describe these four things with the participants:

- **Respect:** Being respectful means that you will refrain from intruding upon or interfering with someone's experience.

- **Sensitivity:** This means you will be aware of and responsive to the feelings of others. Let them know that they might experience strong feelings during this activity—sadness, anger, guilt, etc.

- **Silence:** The activity should be done in silence to create a safe environment for individuals to cross the line. If laughing or side comments were allowed, it may inhibit a participant's willingness to share.

- **Not Judging Others:** You have the choice to cross the line or not cross the line—even if the prompt pertains to you. It is important not to judge others because of this rule. An individual may choose to not cross the line, even if the prompt is truthful for them. It may be tempting to form an opinion about someone else in the room from circumstances presented in the activity.

4. Verbalize to the group that this activity is about individual choices, not their friends or the people standing next to them.

5. Once you have covered the "rules" to the activity, you may ask the group if they feel they are ready to begin. Once they are able to be quiet, respectful, and sensitive, they may cross the line.

6. Explain to the group that you will read a statement out loud. If that statement is true for them or if they identify with that group, they may cross the line. Explain that they should walk across to the other rope, step across the line, turn around, face the other participants on the other side of the line and pause there. Give an example: "if you are a male, please cross the line." After the participants have crossed the line you say out loud: "Notice how it feels to cross the line; look who is with you, look who is not with you and cross back over."

7. Allow for a few seconds of reflection time before you begin your next prompt.

The goal of this activity is to help break down the barriers between people that perpetuate acts of unkindness. Participants become aware that others face many of the same insecurities, fears, and challenges that they do. They learn that showing your feelings does not make you a weak person, rather it takes courage. They learn that other individuals can be appreciative and supportive when they reveal those feelings. Be careful not to be judgmental or shaming in this activity. Be supportive and accepting. All participants will most likely have a reason to cross the line. Some participants will need your support in realizing that they may be modeling behaviors that they have seen or passing along treatment they have received.

CROSS THE LINE PROMPTS FOR TEACHERS

- Cross the line if people routinely mispronanouce your name.
- Cross the line if you've ever been judged or teased because of the color of your skin.
- Cross the line if you have ever been the only person of your race/ethnicity in a classroom.
- Cross the line if you've ever been put down for the way you teach your students.
- Cross the line if you have ever thought your subject matter is more important than others.
- Cross the line if you've ever wanted to connect with others at (insert school name here) but don't have the time.
- Cross the line if you feel you connect with high-performing kids better than lower-performing kids at (insert school name here).
- Cross the line if you feel you connect with low-performing kids better than higher-performing kids at (insert school name here).
- Cross the line if you have ever made assumptions about a student's academic performance based on the way they dress.
- Cross the line if you have ever intentionally hurt someone's feelings.
- Cross the line if you feel you change your teaching methods based on your students' abilities.
- Cross the line if you have ever been teased because of the part of the world or country you or your family comes from.
- Cross the line if you've ever felt pressure from your friends or a colleague to do something you didn't want to do and felt sorry for it afterward.
- Cross the line if you have ever judged another educator's teaching style because it was "different" than yours.
- Cross the line if you've ever stood by and watched while someone was hurt and said or did nothing because you were too afraid.
- Cross the line if you feel that you have a unique strategy for connecting with kids that you would be willing to share with others.

DEBRIEFING TOPICS

- What are some feelings that came up for you during this activity?
- Why was it so important to be quiet, respectful, and sensitive?
- Why was it important not to judge others?
- What was the hardest part for you?
- What did you learn about yourself? About others?
- What do you want to remember about what we've just experienced?
- Why is it important to be allies to each other?
- How can we avoid treating others poorly in our school?

These prompts are examples. You may customize a list of prompts that fit the needs or issues within your group.

CROSS THE LINE PROMPTS FOR CORPORATE POPULATIONS

- Cross the line if you've ever been teased or called a bad name or made fun of in the office.
- Cross the line if someone else has taken credit for your work.
- Cross the line if you've ever been reprimanded without getting a chance to explain yourself.
- Cross the line if you've ever been judged or teased because of the color of your skin.
- Cross the line if someone continually brings up a mistake you made a long time ago.
- Cross the line if you have ever gossiped about another co-worker.
- Cross the line if you have been bullied by someone at work.
- Cross the line if you've ever borrowed something from a co-worker and not returned the item.
- Cross the line if you have intentionally hurt someone's feelings.
- Cross the line if you've ever felt pressure from a colleague to do something you didn't want to do and felt sorry for it afterward.
- Cross the line if you've ever stood by and watched while someone was hurt or put down and you said or did nothing because you were too afraid.
- Cross the line if you have ever started a rumor about someone at work that was untrue.
- Cross the line if people routinely mispronounce your name.
- Cross the line if you routinely miss important deadlines.

DEBRIEFING TOPICS

- What are some feelings that came up for you during this activity?
- Why was it so important to be quiet, respectful, and sensitive?
- Why was it important not to judge others?
- What was the hardest part for you?
- What did you learn about yourself? About others?
- What did you want to remember about what we've just experienced?
- How can having a healthy level of empathy for some of these things reduce the amount of conflict in our office?

These prompts are examples. You may customize a list of prompts that fit the needs or issues within your group.

FACILITATOR NOTES

Grizzli Grapefruit

Teaching Guide

SOURCE

Noam Ebner and Yael Efron, Tachlit Mediation Center, Jerusalem

TYPE OF INITIATIVE

Conflict Simulation

PURPOSE

Grizzli Grapefruit is a negotiation and mediation simulation game. Its storyline is generally similar to the well-known "Ugli Orange" game that has inspired negotiation teachers and students for so many years—with a few important distinctions described (see "Simulation Note").

SCENARIO

Two scientists have come across pharmaceutical solutions for crises about to wreak turmoil in two different locations. Unfortunately, they each need the same resource in order to manufacture their product: The peel of the Grizzli Grapefruit. There is simply not enough of this fruit in existence to go around. The scientists must negotiate with one another in order to secure the resource for their project. Wary of each other, they have decided to hold a mediated negotiation session.

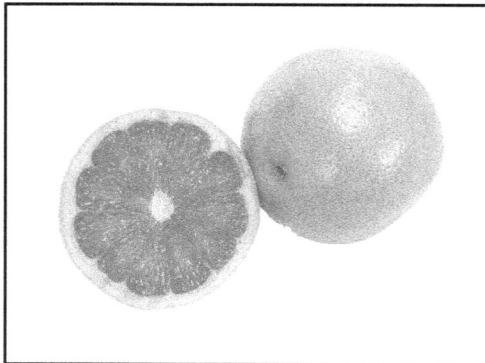

SIMULATION NOTE

This simulation game, while based on the Ugli Orange role-play, is different in several important ways:

1. It has been written as a mediation simulation, not as an unassisted-negotiation scenario.

2. The 'magic key' solution, wherein participants come to the realization that one party needs the fruit and the other needs the peel, has been written out. Both parties need the peel and will need to find other ways to reach agreement.

3. Ugli Orange has both sides equal in resource power and information. In Grizzli Grapefruit, one party has more money to spend than the other does. The other party, though, has more information, knowing there are an additional 1,000 grapefruits still out there on the market.

Our experience in using this simulation game indicates that besides its advantages for use in a mediation course, the more complex scenario makes for more demanding interactions; participants are never excused from the tough job they are facing by stumbling across a text-based 'magic key' solution. In addition, in many of the courses in which we have used this simulation, at least one participant had participated previously in Ugli Orange or in one of the many variations being used for training. Their assumptions regarding how the simulation should be "solved" set them up for a rude awakening—and for an important discussion about assumptions and perceptions in negotiation and mediation.

GROUP SIZE

2–4 participants (see Variations).

TIME REQUIREMENTS

1.5–2.5 hours
Participant Preparation Time: 15–20 minutes.
Running Time: 45–75 minutes.
Debrief Time: 30–45 minutes.
Note: If used in a framework with a class meeting weekly, this simulation game can be run over two (or more) weeks, with separate debriefing sessions.

PROPS NEEDED

1. Forms A,B,C, and D—Participant Instruction Forms (provided at the end of this activity)

2. Debriefing Guide

DIRECTIONS

1. Break participants down into groups of two negotiators and two mediators each. Hand out roles, allowing sufficient time to read instructions carefully (one printed page each). The roles can also be handed out (or sent to participants by e-mail) a day or so before the "meeting."

2. Instruct negotiators to read their role material carefully, to consider their information, and to try and flesh out their instructions with their own knowledge, emotions, and experience. Explain that through their "owning" the role in this manner, the simulation will not only become more lifelike, it will also enable them to understand what parties to a conflict managed by a third party truly experience, enabling resulting insights to be highly transferable to real-life situations. Remind them of their role as negotiators: they must decide on their goal and choose a negotiating strategy.

3. Instruct mediators to set up the mediation area and to decide on their game plan. They should consider the type of process they wish to manage, its ground rules, the stages it will go through, and the atmosphere they wish to create. Remind them that they are not being tested. Rather, they are being given a chance to test their skills and improve them. If mediators are working together in pairs (co-mediation), suggest they use the time to coordinate their efforts.

4. Tell participants they may begin as soon all the members of their group are ready.

5. Participants are usually quite comfortable in their roles and capable of managing this simulation with very little external tweaking. It is recommended that you let participants play it out in whatever way they see fit. Trainers might choose to intervene with process tips or reminders (e.g., reminding the mediators that they might call for a break or initiate private sessions with each party).

6. The simulation ends when parties reach either an agreement or an insurmountable impasse. If time constraints demand it, the simulation can be cut off at any arbitrary moment. This sometimes helps to focus the debrief on the mediation process itself, rather than on any outcomes achieved.

For more suggestions on running the simulation/game, see Variations.

VARIATIONS

As opposed to the original Ugli Orange simulation/game, this simulation includes roles for two mediators and incorporates the rationale for mediation in the storyline. Depending on teaching goals and on the number of students, this simulation can be used as a negotiation exercise (by teachers telling participants to ignore the mediation information or informing them that the mediators got caught in a traffic jam and could not make it), as an exercise in solo mediation (by simply not assigning one of the mediator roles), or in co-mediation.

The simulation/game can be structured in such a way that parties initially meet and discuss the issues, unassisted, for a limited period of time (recommended: up to one hour). If negotiations are unsuccessful, they can agree on a future meeting. During the waiting period, a mediator can be appointed (someone who either observed the first meeting or was absent) who can offer their services to the parties. This allows participants to observe and compare unmediated and mediated negotiation.

If there are unassigned participants, they can be assigned as observers in each simulation group. Alternatively, they can be assigned other roles such as that of a negotiation consultant to one of the parties who has been hired for the purpose of this all-important negotiation. These consultants are not given role information and know only what the party employing them chooses to share with him. These consultants might play a fly-on-the-wall role during the meetings and advise through notes or during team caucuses—or advocate for their employer throughout the mediation session. This will introduce participants to a new way of utilizing their negotiation skills, as well as make for interesting intra-team dynamics.

If a mediation session seems to be progressing but time has run out, you might allow parties (or mediators) to send draft agreements to one another by e-mail until an agreed text is reached. This can be used to show the importance of small details and the complexities added to a situation by involving different forms of communication.

FACILITATOR NOTES

Grizzli Grapefruit

Debriefing Guide

Begin the debrief by asking which of the groups reached agreement and then asking a couple of them for the main points of their agreements. Next, ask a group who did *not* reach agreement whether there had been a last refused offer on the table or what their impasse looked like (this is done mainly to allow participants still engrossed in the game to join the group, others to vent a bit, and, in general, to stress the joint-but-separate experience of the groups, transforming them back into one large learning group). Next, focus the discussion on specific themes, according to training goals, and the dynamics that unfolded in each group's process.

Following are some themes and related questions for managing the debrief session, but these are not intended to limit the scope of questions or discussion themes:

Negotiation Strategy

- How would the scientists define their overall strategy? (You might assist participants in framing a short strategic definition, such as "working together" or "trying to win out over the other guy.")
- Why did they choose this strategy? Did it prove to be effective? Did they stick to it?

Communication Skills

- What communication tools did the parties and the mediators use throughout the discussions?
- What communication techniques did the mediators employ for the purposes of trust-building and information gathering?
- Did any notable communication problem arise over the course of the negotiation? What was its source? How did the parties or the mediator address it?

Information Sharing

- Was an atmosphere of trust built between the parties?
- Did the parties share information openly, or were they more restrained?
- What did the mediators do in order to allow or promote information sharing?

Exploring Options

- Did the search for options focus on elements that were very much on the table, or were attempts made to expand the pie?
- Did the mediators take an active role in generating or evaluating options for agreement? What effect did this have on the process? What might have been done differently?
- Was any attempt made by the mediators to *impose* a solution upon the parties? If so, what effect did this have on the process?

Mediation Process Management

- Did the mediators set/discuss process management rules? What were these? In retrospect, were they suitable to the context and to the situation?
- What effect did these rules have on the process? Was there any need to remind parties of these rules, or to enforce them, during the process?
- How did the mediators manage the process? Do the mediators feel they managed the process "by the book"—that is, moving from one stage of the model they learned to the next in a conscious and controlled manner? Do they feel that the structured process they tried to manage got away from them every so often?
- What effect did the process have on the parties' relationship? Do the parties feel that their relationship shifted somehow at different stages of the mediation? What was the mediator's role in bringing this about (if any)?
- Do parties feel that the process was a suitable one for working out their differences?
- Do mediators feel that the process was a suitable one for assisting the parties? Did they feel constrained, or overwhelmed, in their roles?

FACILITATOR NOTES

FORM A

Grizzli Grapefruit

Background for Dr. Shane

You are Dr. H. Shane. You work as a research biologist for a U.S. pharmaceutical firm. The firm is under contract with the U.S. government to develop methods to combat enemy uses of chemical warfare.

Recently, several World War II experimental nerve gas bombs were moved from the United States to a small island, just off the U.S. coast, in the Pacific Ocean. In the process of transporting them, two of the bombs developed a leak. The leak is presently being controlled by holding the bombs in specially sealed chambers, but government scientists believe that the gas will escape within two weeks. They know of no method of preventing the gas from escaping into the air and spreading to other islands; depending on wind conditions, it could easily spread to the U.S. West Coast as well. If this occurs, it is likely that thousands of people would incur serious brain damage or die and large areas of land would remain uninhabitable for up to three years.

You've developed a "countergas"—a vapor that will neutralize the nerve gas if it is injected into the bomb chamber before the gas leaks out. The countergas is made with a chemical extracted from the peel of the Grizzli grapefruit, a very rare fruit. Unfortunately, your sources inform you that only about 4,000 of these grapefruits were produced this season. You've been informed that a Mr. A. McKenna, a fruit exporter in the Australian Outback, is in possession of 3,000 Grizzli grapefruits. The chemicals from this number of grapefruits would be sufficient to neutralize the gas if the serum is developed and injected efficiently.

You have also been informed that Dr. M. Delaney is also urgently seeking purchase of Grizzli grapefruits and that he is aware of Mr. McKenna's supply. Dr. Delaney works for a firm with which your firm is highly competitive. There is a great deal of industrial espionage in the pharmaceutical industry. Over the years, your firm and Dr. Delaney's firm have sued each other for violations of industrial espionage laws and infringement of patent rights several times on all sorts of issues; two of the cases are still in court. The U.S. government has asked your firm for assistance. You've been authorized by your firm to approach Mr. McKenna to purchase the 3,000 Grizzli grapefruits. You have been told he will sell them to the highest bidder. Your firm has authorized you to bid as high as $10,000,000 to obtain the oranges.

Before approaching Mr. McKenna, you have decided to talk to Dr. Delaney to influence him so that he will not prevent you from purchasing the grapefruits. You invited him to a meeting, and he suggested you have someone present to facilitate the discussion. You agreed to meet at the office of Dr. H.K. Lander, a well-known commercial mediator, to discuss issues of mutual interest.

FACILITATOR NOTES

FORM B

Grizzli Grapefruit

Background for Dr. Delaney

You are Dr. M. Delaney, a biological research scientist employed by an Irish pharmaceutical firm. You have recently developed a synthetic chemical useful for curing and preventing Peditis-3.

Peditis-3 is a disease contracted by pregnant women. If not treated in the first four weeks of pregnancy, the disease causes serious brain, eye, and ear damage to the unborn child. Recently, there has been an outbreak of Peditis-3 in Montenegro and several thousand women have contracted the disease. You have found, testing on volunteer victims, that your recently developed synthetic serum cures Peditis-3 in its early stages as well as inoculates women against contracting the disease. You've demonstrated that your synthetic serum is in no way harmful to pregnant women and has no side effects. The U.S. Food and Drug Administration has approved the production and distribution of the serum as a cure for Peditis-3. Unfortunately, the present outbreak was unexpected, and your firm had not planned on having the compound serum available for six months. Your firm holds the patent on the synthetic serum, and it is expected to be a highly profitable product when it is generally available to the public.

Unfortunately, the serum is made from the peel of the Grizzli grapefruit, which is a very rare fruit. Only a small quantity of these grapefruits was produced last season, and they have been hard to track down. As they are seasonal fruit, there will not be another crop of Grizzli grapefruits until next season, which will be too late to cure the present Peditis-3 victims.

You have recently been informed that Mr. A. H. McKenna, a fruit exporter in the Australian Outback, is in possession of 3,000 Grizzli grapefruits in good condition. If you could obtain all 3,000 you would be able to both cure the present victims and provide sufficient inoculation for the remaining pregnant women in Montenegro.

You have recently been informed that Dr. H. Shane is also urgently seeking Grizzli grapefruits and is also aware of Mr. McKenna's supply. Dr. Shane, employed by a competitor pharmaceutical firm contracting to the U.S. government, works on chemical warfare. There is a great deal of industrial espionage in the pharmaceutical industry. Over the past several years, Dr. Shane's firm and your firm have sued each other for infringement of patent rights and espionage law violations several times over different issues.

You've been authorized by your firm to approach Mr. McKenna to purchase all the Grizzli grapefruits. You have been told he will sell them to the highest bidder. Your firm has authorized you to bid as high as $12,000,000 to obtain the 3,000 available grapefruits.

Before approaching Mr. McKenna, you decided to talk with Dr. Shane to influence him so that he will not prevent you from purchasing the grapefruits. Strangely enough, just before you picked up the phone to call him he called you himself, suggesting you meet to discuss issues of mutual interest. Due to the strained relations between your firms, you suggested you have someone present to facilitate the discussion; after receiving Dr. Shane's agreement, you scheduled a meeting with Dr. H.K. Lander, a well-known commercial mediator.

FACILITATOR NOTES

FORM C

Grizzli Grapefruit

Background for Dr. Lander, Mediator

You are Dr. H.K. Lander, a well-known international commerce mediator specializing in disputes between companies in the pharmaceutical and bio-tech industries.

You recently received a call from a Dr. M. Delaney, who asked you to facilitate a meeting between him and Dr. H. Shane. Both are researchers with large corporations; you have worked with both firms in the past, and they were pleased with your services. You recall that Dr. Shane's firm, based in the United States, does research in the field of chemical weapons and defense; Dr. Delaney's Ireland-based firm specializes in pharmaceuticals.

Dr. Delaney did not specify what the issue to be discussed was, although he did sound somewhat pressured on the phone. He told you your fee would be split between the two firms and asked that a meeting be set quickly due to time pressure. You agreed on a time, and they are due to arrive soon. You asked your associate, Dr. L.M. Sanders, to be your co-mediator. You have no idea the nature of the topic, but should sketch out a game plan to manage the discussion, no matter what type of a session it turns out to be.

FACILITATOR NOTES

Grizzli Grapefruit

Background for Dr. Sanders, Mediator

You are Dr. L.M. Sanders, a well-known international commerce mediator specializing in disputes between companies in the pharmaceutical and bio-tech industries. You work with an associate, Dr. H.K. Lander; together you have co-mediated many issues successfully.

Dr. Lander recently received a call from a Dr. M. Delaney, who asked him to facilitate a meeting between him and Dr. H. Shane. Both are researchers with large corporations; he has worked with both firms in the past and they were pleased with his services. He recalls that Dr. Shane's firm, based in the United States, does research in the field of chemical weapons; Dr. Delaney's Ireland-based firm specializes in pharmaceuticals.

Dr. Lander told you that Dr. Delaney did not specify what the issue to be discussed was, although he did sound somewhat pressured on the phone. He told him that the mediation's cost would be split between the two firms and asked that a meeting be set quickly due to time pressure. They set up a time, and they are due to arrive soon. Dr. Lander asked you to serve as his co-mediator. You have no idea the nature of the topic but should sketch out a game plan to manage the discussion, no matter what type of a session it turns out to be.

FACILITATOR NOTES

Helium Pole

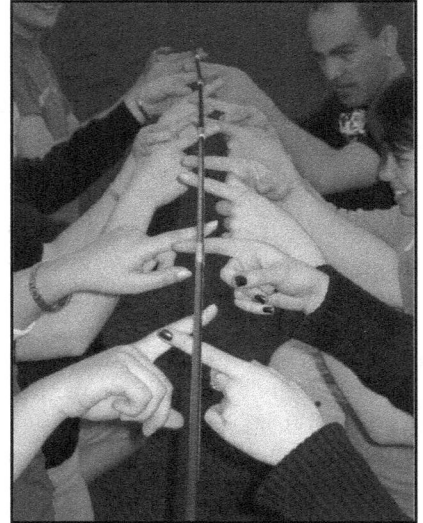

TYPE OF INITIATIVE

Problem Solving

SOURCE

Karl Rohnke (we think)

PROPS NEEDED

A tent pole or hula hoop, ideally something very light weight

GROUP SIZE

8–20

DIRECTIONS

- Ask the group to divide into two subgroups and stand in two lines facing one another. Ask each participant to stick out their right index finger as if they are pointing at the team across from them. Depending on the overall length of the tent pole, you may be able to accommodate up to 10 people per side. The difficulty level of this activity increases with adding people to each side.
- Explain to the group that you are going to lay the tent pole on their extended index fingers. The only thing that can touch the tent pole is the top of the index finger. They must remain in contact with the pole AT ALL TIMES! The tent pole must continually rest across the top of the right index finger. Encourage the group to keep their fingers straight and pointing at the person across from them. You may want to demonstrate proper form for the pole laying on the TOP of the index finger; otherwise some folks may not do this properly.
- Instruct the group that the object of the activity is to lower the pole to the ground. This sounds easy, but it will challenge them beyond belief. It is a difficult task because it sounds so simple and groups will begin with that assumption.
- It's called Helium Pole because usually the pole will rise above the participants' heads before it will be lowered to the ground. The pole is light enough that any amount of pressure will raise the pole, which is the opposite direction of where they want to go. Groups really have to focus and work together to get the pole to do what they want it to do.
- Facilitate this one carefully, as some groups will get so frustrated that they may want to give up.

- Oftentimes you will see people blaming others for the pole going up and not down, and while they are blaming their fingers are not touching the pole. This is a great example of being worried about what others are doing and not taking care of your own responsibilities.

DEBRIEFING TOPICS

- Why does the pole seem to float higher when the object is for the team to lower it to the floor?
- Why is lowering it so difficult to do while keeping contact with each person's finger?
- After instructions were given, did this seem like an easy task? How did your assumption play into how difficult the task was?
- How important was focus during this activity? Describe behaviors that made it hard to focus. Describe behaviors that made it easier to focus.
- How was the beginning of this activity different from the completion?
- Describe how the group communicated during this activity.
- Did anyone become frustrated with another member of the team? How did you deal with that frustration?
- When you have a conflict with someone, what is your typical response?

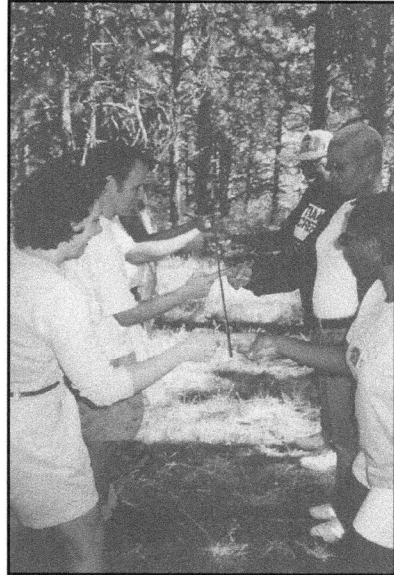

FACILITATOR NOTES

Knot Exchange

SOURCE

Sam Sikes, DoingWorks, www.doingworks.com

TYPE OF INITIATIVE

Problem Solving

PURPOSE

Create a large tangle of rope in the middle of a team and then see how quickly another team can undo it. Allows for great discussions of how one team makes a mess and another team has to clean it up.

PROPS NEEDED

One 5-foot rope or cord for each pair of people in the room

GROUP SIZE

12 or more

DIRECTIONS

Figure out the group size that you want beforehand. Ideally, every team will have six or eight people in it. If there are an odd number of people, one person can grab two ends of the rope instead of one.

Lay three or four ropes on the ground in an asterisk formation for each group. Divide participants into groups of six, and have each group form a circle around an asterisk of rope.

Instruct the group that you would like everyone to grab one end of a rope, lift it off the ground, and hold on to it. Have them imagine that the rope is now superglued to their hand. In other words, they may not let go of the rope or break contact with the rope.

Tell the group that when you say, "Go" you want them to take two minutes to make the biggest tangle of rope in the middle of their team. The more you weave it, the bigger and more tangled it will be.

After two minutes are up, ask the group to carefully lay their rope ends back on the ground and let go of the ropes. Now everyone should move to a new area and pick up the ends of the ropes of another team. Wait until you give them the signal before they begin untangling their mess. You can have this be a competition to see who can untangle the mess the fastest. The rules about the superglued hands are still in effect.

VARIATION

Ask people to close their eyes. It is possible; it just takes longer to untangle.

VARIATION

Use much longer cord. Everything starts looking like a May Pole event without the pole. People also may tie real knots in the cords since the cords are longer.

DEBRIEFING TOPICS

- Tell me about the teamwork you used to untangle this mess.
- What was your reaction when we switched to a new tangle of rope?
- What was it like making a mess compared to undoing someone else's mess?
- How is this activity like solving a conflict between two co-workers?
- Have you ever witnessed a conflict begin because you were constantly cleaning up someone else's mess?

WHERE TO FIND IT/HOW TO MAKE IT

You can make this out of any type of rope. We recommend clothesline or other small rope that comes in multiple colors.

FACILITATOR NOTES

Lines of Communication

PURPOSE

This incredibly challenging communication activity will evoke conflict between the three groups. Success in the activity will require creative problem solving and communication.

PROPS/MATERIALS NEEDED

Large, open area for this one. Rope or tape. Soft tossables and bag or box. Blindfolds are optional.

SET UP

Divide your group into three smaller groups. If there are uneven numbers, Group 3 should be the largest.

The goal of the activity is to put all of the objects back into the bag provided, but the information has to pass through a few people before it gets to Group 3 (the workers). This is a powerful communication activity that needs to be debriefed well.

DIRECTIONS

Set up two ropes (or lines of tape) on the floor about 15 feet apart from one another. Divide your group into three subgroups. Separate them so they cannot hear or, ideally, see each other. Sometimes this is not an option, but it is ideal.

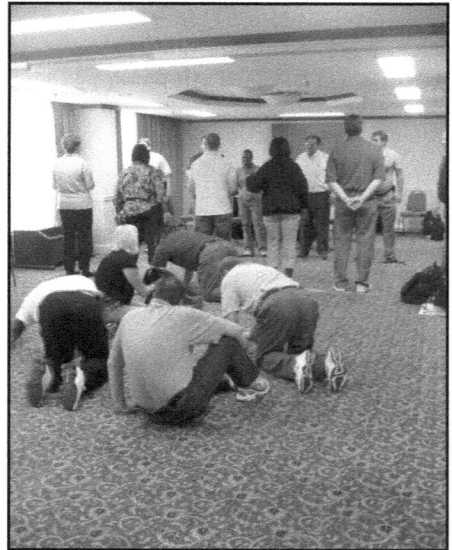

THE FOLLOWING DIRECTIONS SHOULD BE NOT BE HEARD BY THE OTHER GROUPS:

Group 1

They are given the most information about what is to happen in the activity. Instruct this group that, from this moment on, they do not have the resource of their voice. They cannot ask questions or talk to one another to strategize. Tell them that they have to communicate to the rest of their team to pick up all of the tossables on the ground and put them in a bag. They must stay behind the first line at all times.

Group 2

This group has all of their faculties but must make a commitment to never look behind them for the duration of the activity. Instruct them that all of the information they need to be successful in the activity will be given to them by the rest of their team. Position them in front of the second rope and remind them that, from that moment on, they cannot look behind them.

Group 3

This group is asked to make a commitment to be blindfolded (or keep their eyes closed) for the duration of the activity. (Note: If any participant is not comfortable with that, invite them to be an observer of the activity. It's fascinating to watch.) The group is then told that all of the information they need to be successful in the activity will be given to them by the rest of their team. Lead the sightless group to their position behind the second rope.

After each group is in position set out all of the tossables as quietly as possible in the area where the blindfolded people are. After you are finished laying out the items, signal Group 1 that they may begin.

GROUP 1

Stands behind first rope facing Groups 2 and 3. Can see but cannot use their voices. Are given the instructions to have all of the non-seeing people pick up the objects on the floor and put them in the bag provided. Are told to begin after the facilitator gives them the thumbs up.

    1   1   1   1   1   1

GROUP 2

Stands in front of second rope facing Group 1. Can use their voices and can see in front of them but cannot look behind them. Are told that the rest of their team will give them the instructions.

```
      2         2         2         2         2         2
          o             o                   o    o
      3             3             3
  o       o   o         o         o         o            o
      o
          o   3   o         3   o         o   3    o
```

GROUP 3

Are told they will be given everything they need to be successful in the activity by the rest of their team. After Groups 1 and 2 are in place, Group 3 is led with eyes closed (or blindfolded) by the facilitator to stand in an area behind the second rope.

TYPICAL GROUP REACTIONS

Usually Group 1 starts to 'mime' directions to Group 2. Group 2 usually takes a few minutes to figure out that they are responsible for relaying the information to Group 3. Sometimes Group 3 members will get distracted with conversation between one another and are not very good listeners when it comes time for Group 2 to relay information to them.

Some teams will create a trio of information passers; one member from Group 1 will mime specific instructions to one member of Group 2, which gets relayed to one specific member of Group 3. Teams that figure out this information trio are generally the most successful.

DEBRIEF SEQUENCE

1. After the group successfully places all of the tossables into the bag, tell Group 3 they may open their eyes. There will be a few minutes of loud laughter and conversation. Allow them to applaud and briefly discuss their experience. Then ask the group to sit in a circle so you can debrief the experience.

2. Usually I start the discussion with an explanation of the structure of the activity. This is done primarily for the members of Group 3 who are generally pretty clueless as to what has just happened.

3. After you discuss the structure of the activity, I ask the members of Group 3 to explain to the rest of the team what their experience was like. I start with this group because they are given the least amount of information, have the least amount of resources, and generally do not know what just happened.

   Allow this group to talk for several minutes and prompt individuals who struggled to discuss what it was like to be in their position.

4. Next, move on to Group 2 and allow them to discuss their experience. Ask them what was most frustrating for them and how they were able to communicate the message to Group 3.

5. Lastly, ask Group 1 to discuss their experience. Have them discuss how they communicated the directions to Group 2. Also have them discuss how they changed the way they communicated when the style they originally chose was not successful.

6. After each group has had the opportunity to discuss what the experience was like, ask them to start making connections between what happened in the activity to what happens back in the real world. Here are some examples:

DEBRIEFING TOPICS

Think about how the group communicated in this activity. Do you see any connections to communication trends on your team?

What are some of the challenges this team has in communicating to one another?

What do the tossables represent to this group in the real world?

How important is the element of empathy in this activity? How does that translate to management and the different roles in our company?

How did the challenge of communication barriers increase the level of conflict in the group? How is this similar to a conflict scenario that has happened in the real world?

FACILITATOR NOTES

Pocket Processor

TYPE OF INITIATIVE

Processing Tool

SOURCE

Institute for Experiential Education, Buzz Bocher, Steve Simpson, and Dan Miller, *A Teachable Moment,* pp. 176–177.

PROPS NEEDED

Pocket Processor Cards

PURPOSE

The Pocket Processor is a processing tool based on the theory of the yin and the yang. This theory describes two ends of a continuum, with each end having the seed of the other. A healthy being does not stay at one point on the continuum but flows continuously between the two extremes. The Pocket Processor helps participants examine the flow along the continuum.

DIRECTIONS

There are several ways to use the Pocket Processor.

BASIC USE

The most basic use of the Pocket Processor is to debrief an activity by spreading all cards out and asking each participant to choose the card that best represents some kind of progress made (either individual or group progress). Then allow each person to explain his or her choice (e.g., "I chose the competing/cooperating card because I am naturally very competitive, but I successfully fought off my desire to complete the initiative faster than the other group").

VARIATION 1

Rather than allowing each person to pick a card, the facilitator may ask the group to come to consensus on the one card (or two or three cards) that best exemplifies progress made by the group. The narrowing down of the cards then may become the topic of discussion and the participants will start processing all of the issues to narrow it down to the top one. Give each group 8–10 cards to work with. Ask the group specific questions about conflict.

Come to consensus on the biggest challenge the group is experiencing right now.

Come to consensus on the card that represents a conflict the group needs to work on.

Discuss the cards shown and put the cards in order from the least significant to the most significant card in relation to the healthy/unhealthy environment the team is working in.

FRONTLOADING

The Pocket Processor is an excellent frontloading tool. If a group has multiple goals or a poor idea of what its goals are, spread out the cards prior to the day's activities. Then have the group pick out one or two themes that they want to work on that day. After the day's activities are complete, pull out the cards chosen and ask them to assess their progress on the goals that they set for themselves at the beginning of the day. Goals can be individual or as a group. Rather than setting group goals, a facilitator may frontload by allowing each member of the group to choose his or her own card.

HUMAN CONTINUUM

It is important to remind the participants that the two phrases on each card are extremes of a continuum, not dichotomies. One way to convey this information is through a human continuum.

- Have two sides of a room (or an open space) be two extremes of a continuum. You can place a piece of webbing or rope to mark the center.
- Instruct the participants to stand on the line. Explain that the line has a value of 0 and the walls on either side of the line have a value of 5. The space in between the line and the walls represent from 1,2,3,4, and the walls are 5 on both sides.
- Then read the two sides of the card and allow every participant to physically place him or herself anywhere on that continuum. For example, a facilitator can say, "this side of the room is avoiding conflict. The other side of the room is confronting conflict. I want each of you to find the place on the continuum where you most fit today."
- The human continuum then lends itself to discussion—for example, "If most of you usually avoid conflict, what impact does that have on our group? If a conflict arises in our group today, how will it get handled? What are the pros and cons of this arrangement?"

WHERE TO FIND IT/HOW TO MAKE IT

To make this activity you could use index cards and write down categories on each card and use it the same way as described. To purchase a deck of the Pocket Processor Cards, contact the Institute for Experiential Education, www.chiji.com; Training Wheels; High 5 Adventures; or Project Adventure.

FACILITATOR NOTES

Rejection

TYPE OF INITIATIVE

Diversity, Get to Know You, Cultural Differences

GROUP SIZE

20 or more

SOURCE

Idea from Rick Bosch

PLAYING THE GAME

This activity should be played as an initial mixer with a twist. Give each participant a card. Ask them to find a partner with a card that has something in common with their card. (This could be the suit, the number, or the color.) Depending on the outcomes you have planned for your program, you could have them discuss one of the following things or come up with your own. Here are a few suggestions:

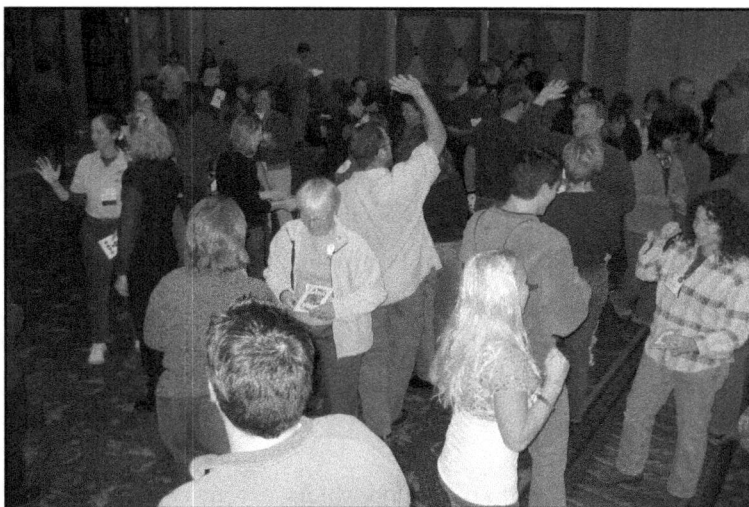

GET TO KNOW YOU TOPICS

- Find three things you have in common with your partner
- Share a goal you have for the day
- Share why you came to the program/workshop
- Discuss your favorite office tool
- Describe the first car you ever owned

Encourage the group to keep mingling and try to connect with at least 5–6 people. The twist in this activity is in the directions. As you hand out the cards, the participants that receive a red card are given normal instructions for the activity. Participants that are given a black card are given the same instructions with the additional rule they are not allowed to talk to anyone with a red card.

With large groups, there are many options for everyone to mill around and find a partner to discuss the chosen topic. At first those with red cards may be unaware that there are participants in the group that are not allowed to talk to them. After 5 minutes, nonchalantly start exchanging red cards with black cards and give the new instructions to these participants. As the milling about continues, there will be visible moments of participants with black cards avoiding the participants with red cards. Stop the activity after this is seen a few times, and ask the group to get into a circle to debrief what happened. Always inform the group of the two sets of rules that were being played so the participants with red cards understand that they were being avoided on purpose.

VARIATION

Mike Pollack, Leadership Development International, Tianjian, China, shared this wonderful cross cultural variation of this activity. Set the rejection exercise up as indicated previously and add these instructions:

Pairs have to find three things in common and have to share a goal for the training day and a goal for a work project they are working on.

* Black suits could not talk to red suits was the original 'rule' given only to the black suit cards

However for added cross-cultural fodder add (taped to the back of the cards):

* Face cards cannot smile
* Odd numbers do not ask or answer direct questions
* Red cards with even numbers are embarrassed to talk about themselves and will excuse themselves rather than answer

Each person has their own rules and are told not to discuss the rules. Each person has to find at least six partners in 10 minutes.

From Mike Pollack: "The results of this variation are great! It definitely stirs up the issues of cross-cultural work with students and staff. It brought up the necessity to defer judgment and to practice patience when we don't know the 'rules' others are playing by, as well as insights about rejection."

DEBRIEFING TOPICS
* How did this activity make you feel?
* How did it feel to have a black card? What were some of your strategies for encountering a participant with a red card?
* If you had a red card, describe an interaction you attempted to have with a black card.
* How is this activity like society?
* Describe how interactions in a conflict situation might mimic the same interactions that were demonstrated or observed here.
* Did anyone experience any anxiety or inner conflict with the rules of the activity?

After a large-group discussion has been completed, invite group members to find a partner and share for a few minutes their experience with the activity. This allows for everyone to verbalize any feelings or thoughts on the experience.

FACILITATOR NOTES

Rope Puzzles

Each of these activities presents a visual puzzle for a team to solve. However, the solution is only part of the puzzle. Working toward consensus within the team is the ultimate goal and the teachable moment for these unique puzzles.

TYPE OF INITIATIVE

Problem Solving, Perspective

SOURCE

Teambuilding Puzzles

PROPS NEEDED

2B or Knot 2B requires five different colors of rope or webbing. Each rope segment should be about 10 feet (3 meters) in length. The Missing Link requires two different colors of rope or webbing. Each rope should be about 10–16 feet (3–5 meters) in length. Not Knots requires just a single piece of soft, flexible rope or webbing. This rope should be about 6 feet (2 meters) in length.

DIRECTIONS

Figure A, **2B or Knot 2B,** shows an arrangement of four colorful pieces of rope or webbing that have been joined together by a fifth piece. This puzzle is presented in such a manner that it is not immediately obvious which rope is the one holding the other four together. The challenge for the group is to discover which rope is holding the other ropes together and to achieve consensus on this selection before touching any of the ropes.

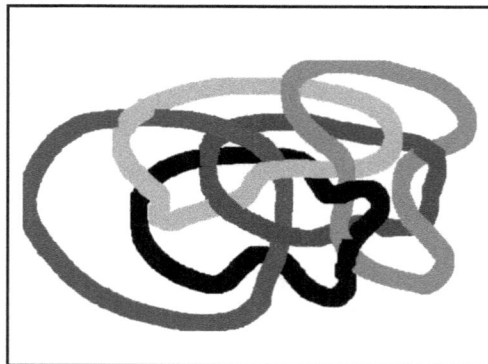

Figure A   2B or Knot to 2B

The goal of **The Missing Link,** shown in Figure B, is for a group to decide if the two segments of rope are linked together (like links of a chain) or unlinked, by visually checking them and without touching them.

While the actual solution may be simple or complex, the real value of this activity comes from a team working together to achieve a group consensus, listening to each other, and learning the skills that it takes to get everyone on the same page. We like to begin this activity by a process called 'pairing and sharing,' which involves everyone working with a partner in an attempt to convince one other person before trying to convince the entire group.

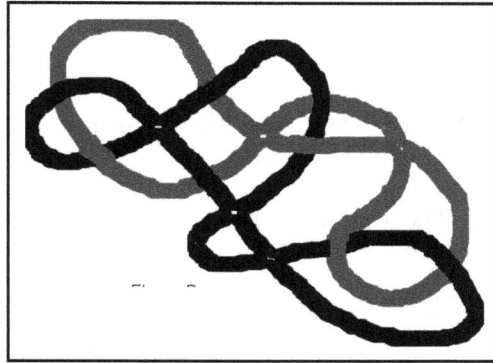

Figure B   The Missing Link

A natural consensus-building activity to follow 2B or Knot 2B or The Missing Link is **Not Knots,** shown in Figure C. In this activity, which can be accomplished with only a single piece of rope or webbing, a "doodle" is constructed and the group is given the choice of whether this doodle will create a KNOT or NOT A KNOT (i.e., a straight line) when the ends of the rope are pulled away from each other.

The object here is to provide the group with some tools to use when they cannot easily form a consensus. Typically, upon analysis, about half of the group thinks the doodle will form a knot, and the other half a straight line. If this is the case, ask participants to partner with another person that has a different viewpoint (i.e., one partner from the KNOT side, and one partner from the NOT A KNOT side). By learning how to listen to a person with a different viewpoint, group members learn how to cooperate. After this discussion, ask participants to choose sides, with the KNOT decision folks on one side of the knot doodle, and the NOT A KNOT folks on the other side. At this point, it is likely that there will still not be a complete consensus within the group. Prior to slowly pulling the ends of the knot doodle, let the members of the group know that you will pull the knot doodle slowly, and they can change sides at any time during the unraveling of the knot doodle (this illustrates the ability to make an initial decision but still be flexible as more information becomes available).

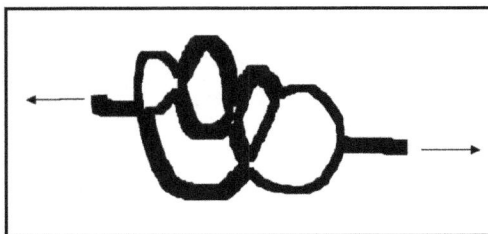

Figure C   Photo of Not Knots
Configuration

HINTS AND CLUES

For 2B or Knot 2B, consider not only which rope appears to be the correct rope, but also which ropes can be eliminated from the choice because they are obviously not the correct rope. Also, look for the 'hint rope.' Any rope that is only attached to one other rope indicates which rope is the correct one.

For The Missing Link, counting the number of times each rope passes over or under another rope may provide some insight.

DEBRIEFING TOPICS

- How did this activity allow you to see the perspective of another group member?
- Were you persuaded to change your mind after you had more information?
- What are the similarities to this activity and solving a conflict between two individuals?
- Why is it important to hear another point of view or perspective?
- How does personal accountability factor into the answer in these activities? Was there a consequence for being wrong?
- How can we use this information in our group?

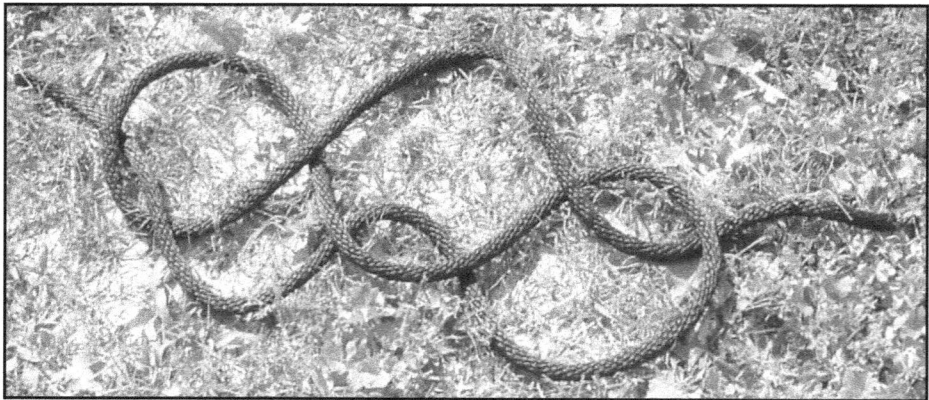

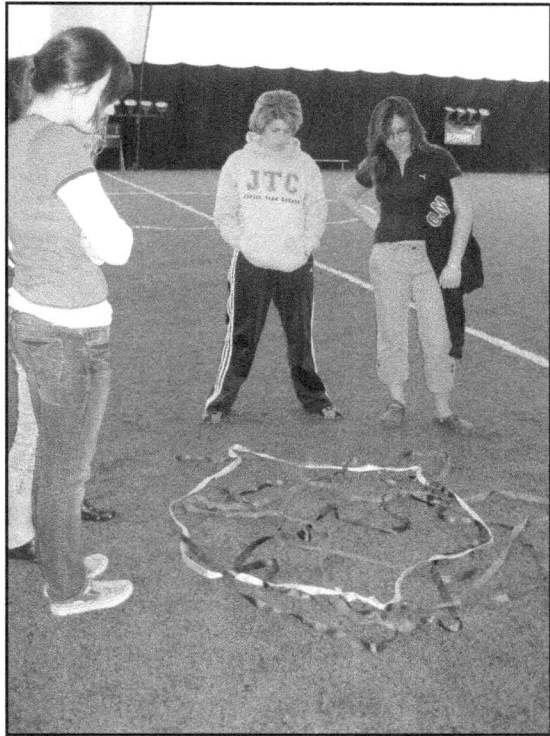

The Other Side

A Creative Look at Perspective

TYPE OF INITIATIVE

Problem Solving, Perspective Awareness

PURPOSE

This activity is designed to stimulate conversation about how there are always two sides to every story.

PROPS NEEDED

One copy of the book *The Other Side* by Isvan Banyai

GROUP SIZE

1–40

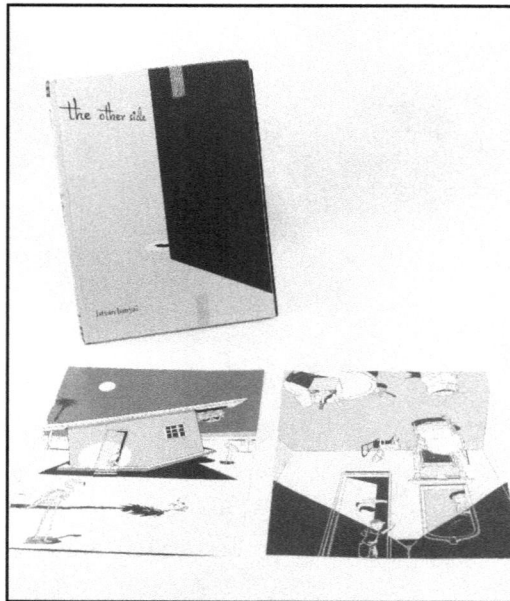

DIRECTIONS

The Other Side by Istvan Banyai is a visually dynamic and exciting book. There are few words in this book, but colorful graphic designs on each page offer intimate perspectives on the same scene. Each illustration in the book has another side. As you turn each page over, you will be surprised by the unique perspective on "the other side." The illustrations are amusing, thought-provoking, and surprising. The book is like a kaleidoscope—each page a reflection of the whole, yet showing a different angle and aspect.

The Other Side will have participants wanting to look, and think, twice. For example, one page of the book has a picture of several paper airplanes flying out of an apartment window and the other side of the page shows a boy inside an apartment releasing a flurry of origami planes out of the window. The very next page shows a jet flying over a city, and 'the other side' shows its seated, bored passengers.

To make this book into a conflict resolution activity:

- Carefully cut the pages out of the book and laminate them or use sheet protectors. We highly recommend protecting the pages or it will be a one-time use activity. The activity takes anywhere from 10–15 minutes to complete. By the time someone handles a piece of paper that long, it will be wrinkled, folded, rolled, or torn if it is unprotected.

PROCESS

- Invite your participants to find a partner.
- Slide one page of the book in between each pair. Try to distribute the pages to each pair so that each person in the pair only sees one side of the page.
- Have players closely examine their side of the picture for all of the details. Let them know that they are NOT to show their picture to their partner.
- Instruct players to discuss what is happening on their side of the page and then to listen to their partner's perspective from their page.
- Have each pair try to determine what event or story is taking place.
- After several minutes of discussion, allow participants to reveal their pictures to their partner and discuss the differences in the perspective of 'the other side.'

DEBRIEFING TOPICS

It is helpful for participants to debrief with their partner before debriefing with the large group. Ask the pairs to discuss the following questions:

- How was your perspective different from your partner's?
- Were you open to hearing the perspective of your partner's page?
- If you were in a conflict with your partner, how difficult would it be to hear his/her perspective?
- How did you communicate your page to your partner?
- What type of communication did you use to describe your perspective?
- What would happen if you openly listened in a conflict as you did in this activity?
- Why is it important to consider 'the other side' and another perspective?

After participants have debriefed in small groups, invite them to sit or stand in a large circle with their partner and their page of the book. Allow them to briefly describe their page and the different perspective on 'the other side' as well as any learning discovered in their small-group discussion.

WHERE TO FIND IT/HOW TO MAKE IT

This book can be purchased through the Training Wheels website, www.training-wheels.com, or through Amazon.com. It is published by Chronicle Books, www.chroniclebooks.com, **ISBN-10:** 0811846083 **ISBN-13:** 978-0811846080

ABOUT THE AUTHOR OF *THE OTHER SIDE*

Istvan Banyai, the acclaimed Hungarian-born creator of Zoom and Re-Zoom and illustrator of several other books for children, is also well known for his editorial illustrations, which have been published in *The New Yorker* and *Rolling Stone,* among other journals. His perspective, always unexpected (sometimes even to him), has made him one of the most original and iconoclastic illustrators today. He lives in New York and Connecticut.

FACILITATOR NOTES

Traffic Debrief

TYPE OF INITIATIVE

Processing tool

PROPS NEEDED

Items shaped like or resembling a stoplight, hard hat, traffic cone, police car, tire, or fire extinguisher.

GROUP SIZE

1–15

DIRECTIONS

One of our favorite processing tools to debrief conflict is the Traffic Debrief. Set these parts out in front of your group to set the stage for targeted metaphoric processing. Each part can be used independently or as a complete set. Following are examples of processing questions and information that relate to each traffic metaphor.

STOPLIGHT

This is one of our favorite metaphors to use to debrief a conflict.

A traffic light is used to help direct motorists while driving to keep them from crashing. The lights signify things a driver should do to keep things flowing smoothly. The three colors on the stoplight can be used as metaphors for behaviors: What are you doing well? (green light) What do you need to be careful of? (yellow light) What do you need to stop doing? (red light)

When a group has started to show negative behavior patterns or if a conflict arises, use the metaphor of the stoplight to debrief the situation. Frontload your discussion with examples for each color. You could also have the group give suggestions for each color.

- RED: What are things happening in the group that need to STOP in order for us to be more successful?
- YELLOW: What are things we need to be CAREFUL of as we continue? Suggestions have been to keep everyone safe, listen to all ideas, be aware of personal choices and boundaries, etc.
- GREEN: What are things we want to GO for? This could be group goals, as well as project suggestions. Ideas include being respectful, encouraging more, setting time limits, etc.

HARD HAT

A hard hat is a type of helmet predominantly used in workplace environments, such as construction sites, to protect the head from injury by falling objects, debris, bad weather, and electric shock. Inside the helmet is a suspension that spreads the helmet's weight over the top of the head. It also provides a space of approximately 1 1/2 inch between the helmet's shell and the wearer's head so that if an object strikes the shell, the impact is less likely to be transmitted directly to the skull.

Here are some specific debriefing questions for the hard hat:

- What areas are you being hard headed in?
- What do you need to protect yourself from?
- Often, hard hats are worn in construction/dangerous areas. When do you put on your construction hat each day?
- Describe an area of your life where you metaphorically put on a hard hat before you enter. What types of feelings do you experience as you go there?
- How would a hard hat be helpful/hurtful when dealing with conflict?

TRAFFIC CONE

Traffic cones are usually cone-shaped markers that are placed on roads or footpaths to temporarily redirect traffic in a safe manner. They are often used to create merge lanes during road construction projects or automobile accidents, though heavier, more permanent markers or signs are used if the diversion is to stay in place for a long period of time.

Here are some specific debriefing questions for the traffic cone:

- What problems do we need to avoid?
- What do we need to be careful of?
- What behaviors should you avoid when confronting a colleague?
- When you know there is a conflict between two colleagues, how can you help direct the conversation in a safe manner? If you feel this is not your place, what are other ways you can help resolve the conflict?

POLICE CAR

A police car is the description for a vehicle used by police to assist with their duties in patrolling and responding to incidents. Typical uses of a police car include transportation for officers to reach the scene of an incident quickly, transportation of criminal suspects, or patrolling an area while providing a high visibility deterrent to crime. For some people, the symbol of a police car is something positive. For others, it has a negative connotation and would be the last place they would go for help.

Here are some specific debriefing questions for the police car:

- Who do we go to if we need help?
- Who protects us?

- Do we follow the rules all of the time or just when the "rule enforcer" is nearby?
- What emotions do you feel when you see a police car?

TIRE

Tires are ring-shaped parts that fit around wheels to protect them and enhance their function. They are used on many types of vehicles, such as bicycles, motorcycles, cars, trucks, and aircraft. Tires enable better vehicle performance by providing traction, braking, steering, and load support. They form a flexible cushion between the vehicle and the road, which smoothes out shock and makes for a comfortable ride. We all know what happens when we get a flat tire and the obstacles this event presents us.

Here are some specific debriefing questions for the tire:

- What do we need to keep the wheels turning?
- How do we continue forward motion?
- How does our group respond if a conflict happens and we have to stop and "fix the flat"— that is, resolve the conflict?
- "Your Turn at the Wheel"—The tire could be used as a conversation tool if group members are talking over one another. Whoever has the tire has the floor.

FIRE EXTINGUISHER

A fire extinguisher is an active fire protection device used to extinguish or control small fires, often in emergency situations. It is not intended for use on an out-of-control fire, such as one that has reached the ceiling, endangers the user (i.e., no escape route, smoke, explosion hazard, etc.), or otherwise requires the expertise of a fire department. Typically, a fire extinguisher consists of a hand-held cylindrical pressure vessel containing an agent that can be discharged to extinguish a fire.

Here are some specific debriefing questions for the fire extinguisher:

- Where's the fire? What started it?
- What do we need to do to put out the fire?
- How do we prevent the fire from getting bigger?
- Is the fire/conflict one we can handle on our own, or do we need to call in the fire department/ human resources/manager?

WHERE TO FIND IT/HOW TO MAKE IT

Training Wheels sells a set of these—7 parts packaged in a 5 × 8-inch, snazzy stuff sack. The stress relievers are all made of polyurethane. Latex free. You could also use Matchbox cars, pictures of these items, or the actual items themselves.

FACILITATOR NOTES

Trash Can Conflict

TYPE OF INITIATIVE

Opening activity

SOURCE

Rey Carr from Peer Resources

PURPOSE

Rey Carr created this activity as a way to begin a workshop on conflict resolution and prevention. He often works with workshop participants who have been "sent" by a superior to participate in a conflict resolution session. This sometimes presents various degrees of attitude and/or resistance to participating. Rey often found that participants had their minds consumed by other things—something going on back at the office or a conflict or situation that is bothering them at work or at home. In other words, at the beginning of any training session, participants may have a focus on things other than what the session will be about. The activity Trash Can Conflict can help address some of the attitudes that may walk into your workshops.

PROPS NEEDED

Sheets of white paper, writing utensils

GROUP SIZE

1–50

DIRECTIONS

Ask participants to take a sheet of paper and take three minutes to write down a brief description of a thought, concern, worry, interfering behavior, or other event that may keep them from fully participating in the workshop. Inform the group that no one else will read what they write. What they write is confidential.

When they've finished writing, ask them to fold the paper in as many folds as possible and then make a unique mark on the outside of both sides so that they can identify their particular piece of paper.

Then place a garbage can (or bin or cardboard box) in the center of the circle and ask the participants to act like basketball players and shoot their piece of paper into the receptacle. If they miss, they can try again.

Once all the pieces of paper are in the can, make a big deal of lifting the can up while saying, "I'm now going to place your worry, concern, or interfering behavior just outside the door of the training room. This should help you release this issue while you are here in the training. Anytime you find yourself thinking about it, please feel free to go out the door, search through the pieces to find your mark, open it and read it. Then return to the group prepared to participate 100% again."

This usually gets a laugh but apparently provides a great deal of relief and reduction of conflict between being in the room and what was going on before they came into the room. Participants often seem more ready to learn and engage in the day's activities. During the day, it's not unusual for some of the topics that went into the can to come up as examples that participants want to work on or deal with more effectively within conflict resolution.

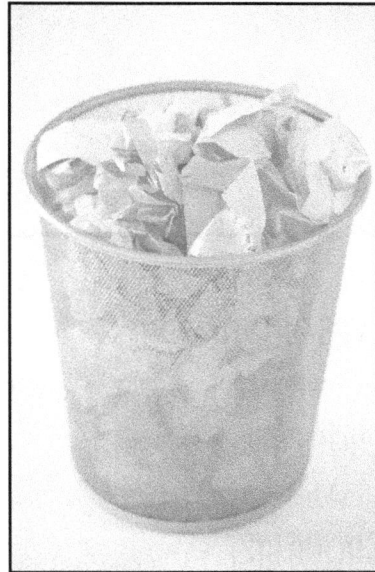

DEBRIEFING TOPICS

This activity is typically not debriefed right as it is completed, but here are some questions you could ask near the end of the workshop:

- Was it helpful to write down an inner conflict/worry/concern you were having? Why?
- Was it comforting knowing you had permission to revisit the concern throughout the session? Why?
- How could you use this type of activity back in the workplace?
- Is acknowledging the inner conflict we bring into the room helpful?
- What behaviors would be counterproductive today?
- Be sure to reiterate that everyone has permission to utilize their 'conflict' at any time.

FACILITATOR NOTES

UFO Ball

The Value of Connection

TYPE OF INITIATIVE
Debriefing tool, Attention Getter

PROPS NEEDED
UFO ball

GROUP SIZE
1–225

PURPOSE
This UFO ball may look like a simple ping-pong ball with two pieces of metal, but when both pieces of metal are touched simultaneously, the ball lights up and makes noise.

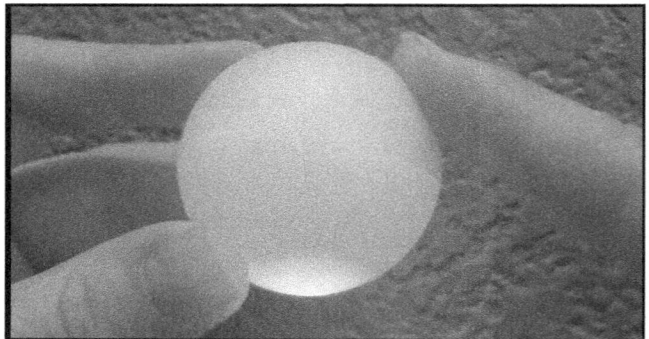

DIRECTIONS
- Invite your group to stand or sit in a circle.
- Conduct a brief discussion on the value of connection. Why is it important? What are the benefits of being connected to a group or an individual?
- As the facilitator, hold the UFO ball in your left hand and touch one of the metal plates with your left index finger. Ask 'Bob', the person on your left, if he will demonstrate the activity with you. Invite him to touch the other metal plate on the UFO ball with his right index finger without physically touching you (meaning, no skin-to-skin contact between the two of you).
- Now describe to the group that you may not know very much about 'Bob,' your partner, but you both work at the same organization (which is represented by the UFO ball). Explain that when you make a connection with 'Bob' exciting things can happen. At this moment reach up with your right hand and touch Bob's left hand. The moment you make physical contact with Bob's left hand the UFO ball will light up and make noise.

- Notice the "Ooooh's" and "Ahhhh's" that erupt from the group.
- This is a wonderful tool used to teach the value of connection in your team.
- Next, disconnect hands with Bob and invite the entire group to hold hands with the person standing next to them in the circle.
- Once everyone is connected hand to hand, reconnect hands with Bob. The ball will immediately light up and start making noise again. If one person disconnects from the team the ball will stop making noise. This is a powerful metaphor to debrief the effects on a team when someone is not giving 100%.
- The largest group we have experimented with was 225 people. It took about 45 seconds for the current to travel through the participants before the ball lit up.

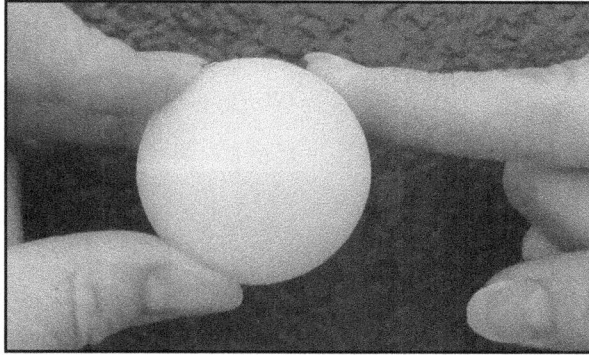

VARIATION

For school teachers and educational programs, it can be used to teach the science of closed circuits with amusement. If you use several UFO balls in one circle, you can teach polarities. Invite a group of participants to try and figure out how they can make all of the connections light up with four UFO balls in the circle. This initiative of determining the polarity sequence within the circle can take up to 15–20 minutes to complete.

VARIATION

Use the UFO ball in a one-on-one debriefing session. You can have a connection with yourself. If you are connected to yourself, your treatment plan, your exercise goals, your relationships, your (insert topic here); then we can have more meaningful relationships with others. After all, how can we expect to connect with others when we do not have a connection to ourselves? Plus, the attitudes and energy we bring to our external connections have an effect on those around us. If someone is committed to being connected to their treatment plan, they can have a more positive impact on their family or their team. The UFO ball can help make this point.

DEBRIEFING TOPICS

- In what ways are we connected to each other?
- How can we cultivate the connections on our team?
- When someone disconnects from the team, how does it affect the others?
- Describe a time when you felt disconnected.
- How can we keep a healthy level of energy in our team?

WHERE TO FIND IT/HOW TO MAKE IT

Training Wheels carries the UFO ball. www.training-wheels.com. It is often carried in science stores and other novelty shops.

FACILITATOR NOTES

Wagon Wheels

Logistics

TYPE OF INITIATIVE

Conflict Scenario and Role Play

SOURCE

Noam Ebner and Yael Efron, Tachlit Mediation Center, Jerusalem

NUMBER OF ROLES

3–4 (2 parties, 1–2 mediators)

SET-UP AND PREPARATION TIME

20 mins.

RUNNING TIME

45–60 mins.

DEBRIEF TIME

45 mins

LEVEL

Basic to Intermediate

LAW OR LEGAL ANALYSIS

Not required. Depending on the setting, participants may choose to apply their general knowledge in contract law or small-claims court outcomes; however, the simulation/game does not require such background knowledge.

ROLE ASSIGNMENT

Divide the group into groups of three (or four, if using co-mediation). If you are left with an odd student out, assign him/her as an observer. Assign one student to serve in each role, and hand out the following material:

Owners of Pizzarino's: General Information, Instructions for the Owners of Pizzarino's

Customer: General Information, Instructions for the Customer

Mediator: General Information, Instructions for the Mediator

GENDER ISSUES IN ROLE ASSIGNMENT– VARIATIONS

The simulation/game's story depicts a female customer and a male proprietor. Here are three possibilities for role assignment:

1. Assign roles randomly, as you might in any other simulation/game. Make sure every participant knows who his opposite is, and have them rewrite their role into their own gender, if necessary. For example, a male playing the role of the customer should change the story to revolve around a party he threw for his wife, a long-time regular at Pizzaroni's.

2. Assign male and female participants to the male- and female-written roles, accordingly (especially suitable if you intend to discuss the topic of gender in negotiation and mediation).

3. Assign male and female participants into roles designed for the opposite gender, and have them stick to the roles; in other words—a male participant will be playing a female customer (another way to address the same issue).

ROOM SET-UP

As you will have several groups working at once, try and space them out in different corners of the room, or use an adjacent room if available.

STUDENT INSTRUCTIONS

Instruct participants to read their information carefully, and try and flesh out their instructions with their own knowledge, emotions, and experience. Explain that through their "owning" of the role in this manner, the simulation will not only become more lifelike, it will also enable them to understand what parties to conflict truly experience. The resulting insights will, therefore, be highly transferable to real-life situations. Instruct participants to begin as soon as they feel prepared.

FACILITATOR NOTES

Wagon Wheels

General Information

The proprietor of Pizzarino's, a popular neighborhood pizza parlor, received a call from the wife of a long-time customer, ordering 20 Wagon Wheel Pizza Pies for the birthday party she was planning for her husband.

On the evening of the party, the pizza delivery didn't meet the customer's expectations, and an encounter she had with the owners of Pizzaroni's the next day left both parties angry.

The two have agreed to attempt to settle their differences with the assistance of a representative of a local community mediation center.

FACILITATOR NOTES

Pizzarino's

Instructions for the Customer

Your husband just turned 35! This year's celebration had to be special, and you decided to throw a surprise party for him in your home. Your husband had once commented that he'd never had a surprise party, and you wanted this one to be perfect. When the guest list passed 60 people, you decided to have the affair partially catered—and you knew just where to order the food . . .

Your husband loves pizza from Pizzarino's, the neighborhood pizza parlor. He eats there two or three times a week, always ordering pizza with extra cheese, onion topping, and a spoonful of Pizzarino's special garlic sauce. He has often tried, unsuccessfully, to obtain the sauce's recipe from the owner of Pizzarino's, who always turned him down with a smile, explaining that his grandmother had sworn him to secrecy. Although you aren't crazy about pizza, you have often accompanied your husband to Pizzarino's and were always impressed by the friendly atmosphere and by how they treated your husband as a special customer. Nothing would make him happier than a surprise pizza party.

It seems to you as if you didn't do anything that week but work on the party. Timing was crucial. You double-checked that every guest knew exactly when to arrive. On the day of the party, you cleaned the house and set it up for the party. You enlisted John, your husband's best friend, to keep him out of the house all evening, and to make sure they returned home between 21:45 and 22:00. Guests would be invited for 21:30, and you planned to order the pizza to arrive at 22:30. That afternoon, you called the owner of Pizzarino's, told him about your husband's party, and asked if he could supply the food you needed. He said he would be happy to, and you ordered 20 of his huge specialty Wagon Wheel Pizza Pies, with extra cheese and onion topping as well as a jar of his special garlic sauce. You agreed on a price of $500. The owner of Pizzarino's suggested the delivery arrive at 22:15, as the restaurant closes every day at 22:30, and you agreed.

That night, the house filled up quickly, and at 21:50 you received a text message from John saying they would arrive in a few minutes. At 22:00 exactly, there was a knock on the door. Someone turned the lights out, and when the door opened, everybody shouted "Surprise"—certainly surprising the two young men standing outside trying to juggle 20 pizza boxes. You began to protest that it was too early, and that they shouldn't be here when you heard your husband's voice from down the stairs, saying "Can you smell that pizza? I bet my wife ordered us dinner!" Your guests were so busy trying to unload the deliverymen and get everything into the kitchen that nobody noticed your husband standing in the doorway, looking around at the confusion. A couple of minutes passed before someone remembered to tentatively say "Surprise . . ."

This turned out to be only the first of the evening's disappointments. The pizzas delivered were barely warm, and most had olive topping on them, which your husband can't stand. When you asked the deliverymen about the garlic sauce, they shrugged and said it wasn't on their delivery form, so they hadn't brought any; they offered you little bags of oregano instead. You angrily called Pizzaroni's. The owner told you there was nothing he could do about the pizzas—the ovens were shut down for the night, and it would take an hour for them to heat up again. He promised to stop by after closing to bring you the garlic sauce, and indeed arrived twenty minutes later with two jars. You were busy trying to keep the party alive, and the two of you agreed to talk it over the next day. All evening you couldn't shake your angry feelings, and it seemed that the refreshments were a main topic of conversation at the party—for the wrong reasons.

Entering Pizzaroni's the next day, you complained that the faulty delivery ruined the party. The owner gave some offhanded apology, something like "Sorry, you know how these things are." You told him that wasn't enough, but he just continued serving pizza to customers in the restaurant, and you got the feeling he was trying to downplay the whole matter. When he handed you the bill for $500, you stared at him in shock. You told him you had no intention of paying for the bad service and product you received. To quiet you down, he offered to give you a $20 discount; you told him you wanted compensation for the ruined party. At some point you couldn't take it any longer, and left the restaurant.

You considered actually suing Pizzarino's in small-claims court for the damage he caused, but you followed a friend's suggestion to contact the local community mediation center first. They offered to contact the restaurant's owner and set up a meeting between the two of you. You're not sure you can control your anger in the presence of the owner of Pizzarino's, but you agree to the meeting. Consider your interests in this situation, and what it is you want to achieve; you are about to walk into the mediation room.

FACILITATOR NOTES

Pizzarino's

Instructions for the Owners of Pizzarino's

You own and operate Pizzarino's, a successful neighborhood pizza parlor. You attribute your success to two main factors: establishing a sense of community through warm personal connections with your customers, and your grandmother's secret recipes for pomadoro sauce and crushed garlic in olive oil and spices.

Last week you had a particularly busy evening at the store. Every couple of minutes the phone rang with a new order, and your deliverymen were taking three or four different orders with them every time they left the store. You received a call from a customer, requesting 20 of your gigantic specialty Wagon Wheel Pizza Pies for her husband's birthday party later in the evening. You knew this would be a hard order to cope with on a night as crazy as this one, but you pride yourself on never turning a customer down if you can help it. In particular, you don't want to turn down *this* customer—her husband is one of your regulars, coming in a couple of nights a week. She asked that the pizzas be delivered at 22:30 exactly. As this is your closing time, you suggested delivery take place a little earlier, in case there were any problems. She also requested some of your garlic sauce, and you promised to include it. Sometimes you think her husband comes for the garlic sauce and orders pizza just as an excuse or a platform for it. That's fine by you, as you enjoy his company in the shop. You agreed on a price of $500, slicing 10% off the usual price without even mentioning it and not charging for the delivery.

At about 22:00 your deliverymen were absolutely exhausted and preparing for their last round of deliveries—the large order and two smaller ones. After loading the pizzas into a small van you use for large deliveries, they left. About 15 minutes later, after you had shut down the ovens and were wiping down the counters and tables, you received an angry phone call from the customer, complaining that the delivery was too early. You thought it had been timed just as you had agreed, but she had already moved on to complain the pizzas were cold and that there was no garlic sauce. The ovens take an hour to heat up, so there was nothing to be done about the pizzas, but you promised to come by after you closed up with garlic sauce. You closed a few minutes early and hurried over with a couple of large jars—a special gesture for a special customer. Entering the house, you found your customer rushing about with trays in her hand. You handed her the sauce with an apology, but she seemed to be under a lot of pressure and suggested you talk about everything tomorrow. You asked her to say happy birthday to the birthday boy and went home.

The next day, just as the restaurant was filling up with your early-afternoon lunch crowd, the customer walked in. You were busy with the customers and hoped she wouldn't make a fuss, but she was very accusatory and blamed you loudly for ruining her party. People were turning to stare, so you tried to quiet her down by leading her over to the counter, away from the customers, and taking out the bill for the order. You told her you were sorry and offered to take $20 off the price to make up for whatever went wrong, but then she went ballistic, shouting that she wouldn't pay you anything and that she wanted compensation for her ruined party. You tried to reply, but at this point she turned and walked out of the restaurant, slamming the door behind her. Conversation seemed muted in the restaurant for the next few minutes, and you thought a few people finished their food rather quickly and left.

You asked your deliverymen for their side of the story. They said they didn't know exactly what time they had shown up at the party, but that even if they had come early, wasn't that better than being late (which, as all pizza deliverymen know, is what people always complain about)? They didn't know they had to show up at a precise moment, so they had just worked it into their rounds. You never keep your old order slips, so you can't check if anything might have gotten mixed up; however, you've been in this business for years now, and rarely, if ever, send out a faulty order.

A couple of days later, you received a call from someone representing the neighborhood community mediation center. You hadn't known this existed, or exactly what mediation is, but you do understand that there will be a chance for you to try and talk it out with your customer and to collect the money you are owed; you agreed to participate in a session with the customer.

Consider your interests in this situation, and what you want to achieve; you are about to walk into the mediation room.

FACILITATOR NOTES

Wagon Wheels

Instructions for the Mediator

You are a volunteer mediator at a community mediation center. The mediation center has been operating for about ten years and has successfully handled many disputes. The center prides itself on accessibility, both geographically and financially; parties are requested to voluntarily contribute $25 apiece to the center for handling their dispute, regardless of its financial value, or how much time and effort reaching agreement takes. You haven't been with the center for long and have only mediated a few cases so far.

You have been assigned a case scheduled to begin today. At first, the names meant nothing to you, but after rereading the scant information you were given, you realized that one of the parties is the owners of Pizzaroni's, and the claim has to do with faulty service or delivery.

While you have no recollection of Pizzarino's owners, you certainly remember the place; although not a regular, you must have stopped there after work a half-dozen times over the past couple of years. Good pizza, great garlic sauce, always good music on.

You're awaiting the parties in the mediation room. When you hear them in the waiting room, go out and greet them. Use the time you have until the parties arrive to prepare yourself and the room and to map out a game plan. Good luck!

FACILITATOR NOTES

Wagon Wheels

Teaching Notes

EDUCATIONAL OVERVIEW AND POSSIBLE USES

The Wagon Wheels simulation/game is an educational tool for mediation training. Designed for use at the beginner to intermediate level, the background information places participants in a setting whose elements are familiar from everyday life: a favorite restaurant and a party turned sour. The facts are relatively simple, with a few ambiguities planted in the participants' information in order to allow them to construct separate and conflicting factual "truths." Emotional issues such as mutual insult and shattered expectations add both to the situation's complexity as well as to the range of different levels on which the conflict can be managed. Finally, a powerful mutual interest in a positive future relationship allows mediators to practice helping parties to shift from focusing on the past to orientating on the future.

The relatively simple factual base has the additional advantage of allowing mediation to focus on the process and not on remembering details, thus laying the groundwork for a successful and confidence-building experience in process management.

Due to the possibility to address the conflict on the relational, contractual, financial, or other levels, this simulation/game is suitable for mediation training oriented towards either a problem-solving or a transformative approach.

Additionally, the simulation/game is suitable for triggering discussion on gender differences in negotiation and mediation. It does this in a relatively subtle manner (as opposed to a simulation/game directly pitting a husband and wife against each other in a divorce case, for example). If used for this purpose, it is recommended to set the stage as thoroughly as possible through suitable role assignment (see "Logistics"), mediator assignment (consider employing co-mediation by a male-female team), etc.

DEBRIEFING TOPICS

Begin the debrief by asking how many of the groups reached agreement; ask a couple of groups for the main points of their agreements (this is done mainly to allow participants still engrossed in the game to join the group, others to vent a bit, and to stress in general the joint-but-separate experience of the groups, transforming them back into one large learning group).

Provided are some recommendations for possible managing of the debrief session; this is not in any way meant to provide an exhaustive list of questions or discussion themes.

Early Training-Stage Debrief

1. Did the mediators explain the process to the parties in a clear manner? How did this affect the process?

2. What did the mediators do in order to help parties get all the necessary information on the table?

3. Were the mediators successful in building an atmosphere of trust around the table? How did they do this (or what could they have done, but did not)?

4. How did the mediators react in challenging situations (such as: parties interrupting each other, parties attacking each other, parties attacking the mediators, etc.)?

5. Do the parties feel that the mediators acted in a neutral and impartial manner? Did the mediators deal explicitly with issues of neutrality and impartiality? Can the mediators comment on ways in which they felt parties were trying to win them over to their side?

6. Through what general frame did the mediation process address the issue (for example: a consumerism issue, an argument about money, disappointment, etc.)? Did this frame prove a productive one in terms of allowing parties to come to grips with the past and look ahead to the future or in terms of their relationship with one another?

7. Did the mediators' feelings of familiarity with Pizzaroni's affect the way they handled the case? How?

8. What do the mediators view as the largest obstacle they had to face during this simulation?

Intermediate Training-Stage Debrief

1. Do the mediators feel they managed the process "by the book"—moving from one stage of the model they learned to the next in a conscious and controlled manner? Do they feel that the structured process they tried to manage got taken away from them every so often? How did they react?

2. Do the parties feel that their relationship shifted somehow at different stages of the mediation? What was the mediator's role in bringing this about (if any)? What did the mediators do in order to help parties face their problem constructively?

3. Did the conversation focus on the defined problem (payment for pizzas), or did the topic widen to include different relational issues? What was the mediators' role in the parties' adoption of this narrower or wider focus?

4. How did the process of problem solving and searching for options begin? Did the mediators take an active role in generating or evaluating options for agreement? What effect did this have on the process? What might have been done differently?

5. What effect did the "absent" party (the spouse/regular customer at Pizzaroni's) have on the conversation? Did the mediators attempt to focus the parties on their common interest in working things out for this party's sake? Did this work, or did it backfire in anyway?

6. Did the search for options (or the final agreement) focus on the elements that were very much on the table (e.g., a discount on the balance owed), or were attempts made to expand the pie? What was the mediator's role in this?

Gender Issues

1. Did it appear to the mediators that there was a gap in the parties' approaches to the conflict—one being cooperative and seeking to solve the problem jointly, and the other being of a more competitive nature? What do the parties feel about this?

2. Would the parties say that part of the dispute arose or persisted simply because the other party, from the opposite gender, couldn't comprehend what was bothering them?

3. Did the parties—overtly or subtly—attempt to co-opt a mediator of the same gender as themselves?

4. Did the mediators find it easier to connect with parties of the same gender as themselves?

5. Did the parties attempt to use the mediators in order to impose any type of thinking/dynamic/focus on the other?

6. Did the mediators attempt to utilize a gender-based connection with a party in order to achieve anything (such as a particular outcome, a particular way of framing or of thinking, etc.)?

FACILITATOR NOTES

What a Way To Meet

TYPE OF INITIATIVE

Conflict Simulation

SOURCE

Noam Ebner and Yael Efron, Tachlit Mediation Center, Jerusalem

PURPOSE

What a Way to Meet is designed for use in training aimed at skill-building in communication skills, conflict resolution, negotiation, or mediation. In no time at all, it plants participants solidly in the middle of a realistic and familiar interpersonal conflict setting, in which parties will either attempt to work together or risk the situation's escalating into a free-for-all. The simulation/game is structured so as to weigh the probabilities toward escalation kicking in at one point or another, allowing exploration of the dynamics of this element of conflict.

One key feature of this simulation/game is its quick set-up time and the simplicity of getting participants involved. In four brief paragraphs, requiring 1–2 minutes of quick reading and reflection, participants are ready for action. In fact, you've spent more time reading this overview than they will need to prepare themselves.

SCENARIO SYNOPSIS

Two drivers are headed home in heavy holiday traffic. One is a successful businessperson, driving a status symbol on wheels after the successful completion of an important deal; the other is considerably lower on the socioeconomic ladder and is driving an uninsured clunker. Due to a mistake, a misunderstanding, or a lack of attention by one or both of them (this is purposefully left unclear in the instructions), they crash, with both cars suffering damage. The meeting the simulation/game sets them up for is their initial interaction after the accident.

SUGGESTED RUNNING TIME

15–20 minutes for role-play, another 15–30 for debrief

PROPS NEEDED

1. Participant Instruction Form A and Form B (provided on following pages)

2. Debriefing Guide

GROUP SIZE

Minimum of 2 participants

DIRECTIONS

1. Divide participants into pairs.

2. Hand out roles: One participant plays the role of the Civic driver, and the other the role of the Mercedes driver.

3. Instruct participants to read the instructions, and imagine how they themselves would feel if this were a real-life situation. Many will be able to flash back to real-life situations they experienced.

4. When participants are ready, you can instruct them to begin by having them walk towards each other. An extra little bit of reality can be injected by having them conduct the simulation standing up.

5. Don't hesitate to "cut" the scene in the middle, before the conflict is resolved, if you feel that learning objectives have been met. When focusing on conflict escalation, the difficulty participants will experience in breaking out of character when the conflict is at its peak can have a tremendous effect!

VARIATIONS

1. Several groups can run simultaneously; try having pairs distance themselves from one another (so much as the training surroundings permit) because this simulation/game can get noisy.

2. You might assign an extra participant to one of the "cars" as a friend. This will allow you to see whether the 2-on-1 situation changed the dynamic, as well as the types of role these "extras" took on (advocating for their role-buddy, mediating, etc.)

3. You can assign a third participant to each pair as an observer. Give observers instructions regarding what to be on the lookout for. Observers can debrief the pair afterward and can assist you in the group debrief by describing situations and processes.

4. You can alter the scenario to include a third role—a pedestrian passing by, or a driver who stopped to make sure everything is ok. Depending on training goals, this participant can be instructed to play different types of roles (mediator, provocateur, advocating for one party, etc.)

5. You can have two participants play this out in a fishbowl in front of a class. Observers will not be able to control their urge to shout out escalatory advice, which often results in escalatory behavior.

FORMS

A. Instructions for the Civic driver

B. Instructions for the Mercedes driver

What a Way to Meet

Debriefing Guide

This simulation/game can be utilized for many learning objectives. Here are several of them, and some of the subjects you might wish to discuss with the participants, according to the goal of the exercise (training notes are italicized):

CONFLICT ESCALATION

You might want to cut the simulation/game short at the tip of the conflict spiral in order to allow participants to appreciate its effects.

- Ask each party how they feel with the situation and with each other. Allow them to blow off steam, and then comment on the amount of steam they accumulated just by playing a conflict *game*.
- What made the conflict escalate? Ask participants to try and remember particular moments.
- How did participants react to each other's escalatory moves?
- Did participants notice a particular "trigger"—something the other party did that made them see red?
- What might they have done to avoid these triggers?

DISPUTE RESOLUTION

Allow participants to continue negotiating until they have reached agreement or have terminated talks.

- What made reaching agreement difficult?
- What was missing in the negotiation? What assistance might participants have needed?
- Would participants have felt comfortable having a third party help you out? In what manner?
- Participants who have not reached agreement: What will you do now? Does this alternative plan of action seem as attractive to you now as it did when you broke off the discussion with the other?

COMMUNICATION SKILLS

- Did participants feel the other was listening to them? How could they tell?
- Were you (turning to individual participants), in fact, listening to your opposite?

When the answers to the previous questions conflict, ask:

- What did you do to *show* the other party you were listening?

Stress: Active listening, reflecting, body languages

- Ask participants to try and recall whether they asked each other questions or just made statements. If questions were asked, of what sort were they?

Stress: the difference between open-ended and closed questions, their uses and effects.

- How might participants have reframed uncooperative statements their opposite made?

NEGOTIATION

- What issues were each side interested in discussing? How could participants have attempted to jointly define the issues to be discussed?
- How would participants define their interests in this situation? How would they define the other party's interests?

Compare the two—stressing the difference between one party's interests and the other's perception of them.

- Ask participants to try to recall whether any use was made of standards (objective criteria), such as the law, traffic laws, etc.? How did this affect the negotiations?
- What are each party's alternatives? What can each participant do on their own, if agreement is not reached? How might this information affect the negotiations?
- What options did participants discuss while searching for a solution? What could have been done to promote their creative thinking? What could have been done to "expand the pie"?

FACILITATOR NOTES

What a Way to Meet!

Instructions for the Civic driver

You're driving along in your 1993 Honda Civic. You saved up for a year to buy it, and it allows you to get around in your endless marathon of home, work, and school. It's a holiday eve, and the road is crowded with people on their way home to family dinners; it seems like everybody has forgotten how to drive, and it takes all of your concentration just to avoid being hit.

You reach the intersection near your house. You're sure you have the right of way and that other drivers have a stop sign, so you drive right into the intersection. Suddenly you hear screeching brakes and a blaring horn. You see a large car that, having entered the intersection from your right, tries to brake and turn to avoid you. You also steer to avoid, but it is too late. You feel a sharp crash, and the car comes to a sudden halt.

It takes you a minute to recuperate, and then you climb shakily out of your car. You appear to be unhurt, but your heart sinks when you see that the front right side and fender of your car are smashed in, and the engine hood is peeled back and crumpled. Strange noises are coming from the still-running engine, but you have no idea what damage may have been caused to it.

Your car isn't insured, and you have no way to fund the repairs that seem necessary at first glance. Looking around in despair, you notice the other car is a fairly new Mercedes-Benz. The driver, who had walked around the car looking for damage, turns and walks your way.

Handle it!

FACILITATOR NOTES

What a Way to Meet!

Instructions for the Mercedes driver

You're on your way home in your car, late for dinner with your family. You've just sealed a major deal today with a new client and are feeling very satisfied with yourself. "What a deal! What a year!," you think to yourself, enjoying the drive despite the heavy holiday-eve traffic. You sure have earned this new Mercedes-Benz. . . .

You adjust the volume on the stereo and turn the seat-heater up a bit as you approach the intersection at the bottom of the hill. You don't see a stop sign, so you assume you have the right of way. You downshift and turn into the intersection.

Suddenly you catch a glimpse, in your side-view mirror, of a small white car flashing through the intersection. You honk your horn and jam down on the brakes, steering right to avoid being hit. You see the other car also steering to avoid and think you *might* just make it—but it's too late. You feel a sharp crash on your left and the air-bag bursts open. You keep your cool and bring the car slowly to a halt. You climb shakily out of the car. You appear to be unhurt, but your heart sinks when you see that the left side of your car is badly scraped, the front grill is crooked, and the Mercedes-Benz emblem is lying on the ground.

The other car, an old clunker of uncertain make, seems to be damaged pretty badly also. You see the driver get out and look at the smashed white vehicle.

Walk over and deal with it!

FACILITATOR NOTES

Who Am I?

TYPE OF INITIATIVE

Illustrate components of self (conscious, sub-conscious)

SOURCE

Dave Piltz, The Learning Key

PROPS NEEDED

One blue, green, and red index card per person; one writing utensil per person

GROUP SIZE

Any number

TIME

5 minutes for the activity; 10 minutes for debrief. You can connect the debrief to lecture Theory of conflict and/or self awareness.

STORY LINE

Let's do an activity that helps us understand what drives who we are and why we might act the way we do.

DIRECTIONS

Distribute a blue, green, and red index card to each participant. Start with the blue index card. Ask participants to write on the blue card the information they share freely with others when they first meet someone. It does not matter if the greeting is in a work environment or personal, social environment. Ensure the group it does not matter what they write down. It could be as simple as their name. As the facilitator, it is appropriate for you to participate in this activity as a model for the group.

Then ask everyone to place his or her blue index card to the side.

Next, invite everyone to take out their green index card. Assure participants that while they are with you today, they will never need to share what is on this card. After they write on this card, it will get folded up and put in their pocket. (It is very important to stress this point.) Remind them if they do not want anyone at home to see what they write on the card that they should destroy it before they go home. On the green index card, ask participants to write down something that they share about themselves after they get to know someone. Perhaps it has been several weeks or months since first meeting this person. What are the things they share with others at this point? Explain it does not matter what is written. They can write in code, with question marks or pictures, or whatever they feel comfortable doing. There is power in writing, so ensure that everyone puts something down.

As they are writing, reiterate that they do not have to share what they have written down. After they have finished, ask them to fold their card and put it in their pocket. If they do not have a pocket, ask them to sit on the card.

Now ask everyone to take his or her red index card. Again, assure them that while they are with you today, they will never need to share what is on this card. After they write on this card, it will get folded up and put in their pocket. (Again, it is very important to stress this point.) On the red index card, ask participants to write down something that they rarely share about themselves with others. In fact, it may be something they have never shared before.

As they are writing, reiterate that they do not have to share what they have written down. After they have finished, ask them to fold their card and put it in their pocket. If they don't have a pocket, ask them to sit on the card.

After everyone is finished, explain the following:

"It doesn't matter whether it is organizational or individual, but we live in the world of the blue index card—this is what we say and how we say it. However what drives the world of the blue index card is our green and red index cards." For effect, pull yours out and place them behind the blue index card.

Continue by saying: "Now, to be effective we don't need to uncover our red index cards at work—they are too personal. However if we want to be effective in the workplace (and at home) we need to discover ways to allow the green index cards to come out in safe, non-retributional ways—in ways that build awareness and understanding."

Continue by saying: "The difficult part, however, is that what constitutes a green card to one person is really a blue card to another." Use examples here like one co-worker went to the grocery store last night (hold up your blue index card), but the way they describe the experience was straight from an episode of the television show *Cops*. Anything that could happen happened. The other co-workers say to themselves: 'Wow—your friend was arrested last night? That's too much information—you shouldn't be telling me this at work.' (Hold up your green index card.)

DEBRIEFING TOPICS

- Why it is difficult to share green cards? Answers generally include: It's uncomfortable, it's a risk, I get in trouble, we don't do this in our personal lives so why would I do this in my work life, etc.
- What are the benefits of sharing green cards? Answers generally include: It builds bridges and awareness between others, we don't have to worry about what one is thinking because we know, etc.
- How do emotional triggers affect how we handle conflict with one another?

    Emotional triggers are things that set us off. It's easy to stay at the blue card level in life. It is a risk to go to the green card level. Allowing ourselves to share things at the green card level creates more valuable experiences.

This activity connects very well to the following theories/books:

Johari Window
Crucial Conversations/Crucial Confrontations
Emotional Intelligence

FACILITATOR NOTES

Who am I?

Your Piece of the Puzzle

TYPE OF INITIATIVE
Problem Solving

PURPOSE
To help a group see the importance of understanding the whole picture.

SOURCE
Lynette Voss, Heather Westbrook, Aletheia Schmidt, Shanna Conner

PROPS NEEDED
Two pieces of 8 1/2 × 11 paper, square *"Post-it"* note size paper, markers, and tape

GROUP SIZE
4–12

DIRECTIONS

Step 1

Create a master picture on an 8 1/2 × 11 piece of paper. This should be something that is fairly complex (a picture of someone's face is a good thing to use: see attached picture). Make sure to use a black-on-white drawing. Hard edges are best in helping participants to re-create this picture.

Step 2

After the master has been created, make a duplicate of it. This will be the copy you will cut up and hand to participants. Make sure to cut pieces evenly, in small squares, so when participants try to re-create their picture on a *Post-it* note, it is as close as possible to the original.

Step 3

Have participants replicate the markings of the unique square they are given on their *Post-it* note. Inform participants the picture needs to be drawn "to scale." (The small square from the 8 1/2" × 11" piece will be smaller than their "*Post-it*" note.)

Step 4

Have the group collectively put the picture together on a hard surface (floor, desk, or whiteboard works well). If you haven't used *Post-it* notes, you will need to supply tape.

IMPORTANT POINTS

Make sure to create two or three small cards that do not fit into the master picture. This is done on purpose with the intent of helping the group understand the point that everyone needs to have the correct information to solve the puzzle. If everyone does not have a piece of the same puzzle, the puzzle cannot be completed.

It might help to refer to **The Other Side** activity in this book and talk about having different perspectives. In conflict, you must see each of the small pieces, as well as the whole, in order to have complete understanding.

VARIATIONS

Use a product like The Community Puzzle™ to create your master design.

DEBRIEFING TOPICS

- How important was it for you to get your drawing "right"?
- How important was it for you to know what the full picture looked like?
- Were you more concerned with knowing where your piece went? Why or why not?
- How can you apply the learning from this activity back to the workplace?

Sample Picture

FACILITATOR NOTES

Zoom or Re-Zoom

TYPE OF ACTIVITY

Problem Solving, Communication activity, Discussions on Perspective

PROPS NEEDED

One *Zoom* book, with pages cut out and laminated. Typically, one page per participant (also see Variations). There are 30 pages in *Zoom* and 33 pages in *Re-Zoom*. The activity is based on the intriguing, wordless, picture books *Zoom* and *Re-Zoom* by Istvan Banyai, which consist of 30 sequential "pictures within pictures." The *Zoom* narrative moves from a rooster to a ship to a city street to a desert island and outer space. The *Re-Zoom* narrative moves from an Egyptian hieroglyphic to a film set to an elephant ride to a billboard to a train.

There are many variations of this activity. From a sequencing point of view, this is a good activity to do after your initial icebreakers and energizers.

DIRECTIONS

The challenge is for participants to get themselves lined up sequentially, so that their pictures tell a "story." And, they must do this without looking at each other's pictures. If you are using a portion of the book, make sure a continuous sequence is used.

PROCESS

- Distribute one page to each participant.
- Have players closely examine their picture for all the details. Let them know that they are NOT to show their picture to anyone else and are NOT allowed to look at anyone else's picture.
- Instruct players to line up in the correct sequence according to the picture they received.
- Participants will generally mill around talking to others to see whether their pictures have anything in common. Sometimes leadership efforts will emerge to try to understand the overall story.
- When they have done their best, allow them to reveal their pictures to the rest of the group and reposition themselves if they made any errors.

DEBRIEFING TOPICS

- How did the group first start solving the problem?
- Why was it hard to get the story together? (everyone had a piece, but no-one had the big picture)

- How many people stayed within their sub-group once they found someone who had similarities on their page? How is this like the real world? Do we tend to gravitate toward those who are similar to us?
- What type of communication was used?
- Imagine if, at the outset, the group had taken the time to let each person describe his/her picture to the rest of the group. What would have happened then? Would the solution have been found faster? What prevented such strategies from being considered?
- What kind of leadership was used? Who were the leaders? Why?
- What style of leadership might have worked best?
- How does one's perspective play into the success of this activity?
- What can we learn from this activity that will be helpful to the team?
- What real-life activities are similar to this activity?

DISCUSSIONS ON PERSPECTIVE

Perspective is one's "point of view"—the choice of a context for opinions or beliefs and experiences. Your perspective can be very different based on where you stand. In the Zoom activity, a page at the beginning of the storyline had a very different perspective than a page at the end of the storyline. Both pages were crucial to the success of the activity. In teams, people with different responsibilities have very different perspectives. Both are valuable and important to the team's success. They are both part of the big picture. How these perspectives are valued and communicated can impact the relationships of the team members.

The outcomes of this activity change dramatically with a few variations.

VARIATIONS

- For groups ranging from 25–32 people: Give each person one page of the book and tell them that this page is 'super glued' to their hand. They must always keep this picture in their possession. Any remaining pages may be passed around the group.
- For groups larger than 32: If you have a group of 35–40, you can double up a few people on one page.
- For groups larger than 50: If you have a group larger than 50 people, you could consider doing *Zoom* and *Re-Zoom* at the same time. Split your group into two subgroups and have them complete the activity separately. *Re-Zoom* is a more difficult storyline, so be prepared for the *Re-Zoom* group to take longer than the *Zoom* group.
- For smaller groups, take the first several pages of the book and set them aside. Then hand participants random pages of the book and lay some pages face down on the ground. The pages on the ground could be looked at 3 times for 20 seconds each.

- With 10–14 people you can take the first 10 pages of the book and set them aside. Hand the 14 participants random pages of the book and lay 8 pages face down on the ground. The pages on the ground can be looked at 3 times for 20 seconds. The task is to get themselves and the pages on the ground in order from the beginning of the book to the end of the book.
- Another variation is to use it for conference presentations dealing with community development. As people enter the room, greet them, introduce yourself, and hand them a page from *Zoom*. Ask them to find their place in the group based on their *Zoom* page. This typically leads to many great conversations about assumptions, connections in community, etc.
- Use as an icebreaker by handing each participant a picture on arrival. When everyone has arrived, explain that each person is holding part of a story, and the group task is to find out what the story is by putting their pictures in sequence.
- Use a time limit to increase difficulty and enhance focus on teamwork.
- Team performance can be measured (e.g., for a competition) by counting how many pictures are out of sequence.
- You can also take a few pages from *Re-Zoom* and put them into *Zoom*. Ask the group to determine which pages do not belong.

RECOMMENDATIONS

Carefully cut the pages out of the book and laminate them or use sheet protectors. We highly recommend protecting the pages, or it will be a one-time use activity. The activity takes anywhere from 30–45 minutes to complete. By the time someone handles a piece of paper that long it will be wrinkled, folded, rolled, or torn if it is unprotected.

Where to Find It/How to Make It:

Training Wheels, www.training-wheels.com or www.Amazon.com.

FACILITATOR NOTES

PART 6

Conflict Activities in a Youth Environment

When working with a youth population, having an environment that is fun, safe, and respectful can dramatically increase youth's interest and willingness to participate. Experiential activities can create an environment where individual and team growth can provide opportunities for youth to make positive choices, manage behaviors, gain self-confidence, and learn skills that are critical to their lifelong relationships and development.

The beauty of experiential activities is that they offer opportunities to deal with real situations in a low-threat environment. Rather than sitting around abstractly talking about a situation that *might* occur, activities provide situations that actually *do* occur. For example, during an activity called [Have You Ever], in which participants must find a new spot according to questions asked by a person in the middle of the circle, many participants 'pretend' that they do not see the empty spaces. Although it may appear that these students are sabotaging the game, thus making it boring for those rushing to the empty spots (and then waiting), they are used to sneaking around to get what they want (their individual needs/goals)/, their hidden agendas cause a group goal (having fun) to fall by the wayside.

By using this 'teachable moment' as a topic of discussion to compare the feelings and thoughts of all parties, the hidden agenda can be exposed. The students can then brainstorm ways to create a win-win situation in which all people can have their needs met, thus making the game fun and allowing all to have a chance in the middle. This is a simple yet important lesson about stating needs, as well as an exercise in conflict resolution (Frank, 2004, p. 34).[1]

For conflict resolution, experiential activities can create opportunities to develop an understanding of how and why conflict occurs and ways to manage conflict and anger. This is generally not a subject that is specifically taught in schools, and children can develop their conflict resolution skills from examples in the media or role models in their lives. The activities on the following pages will provide experiences in which participants learn and practice methods for resolving conflict in a non-violent way. The activities vary from creative strategies for managing personal conflict to issues of multicultural conflict and diversity. Exposure to these activities can deepen their awareness around accountability and responsibility for their actions during conflict situations. It will also give them an appreciation of their differences with others.

These activities can also empower youth to experience and practice how to resolve a conflict before it happens. The old adage "practice makes perfect" is true even for conflict and can help equip youth to deal with difficult situations.

While the initial activity is important to provide the framework for the discussion, the dialogue you have AFTER the activity is just as important—if not MORE important—than the activity itself. If you do not process through why you did the activity, the learning you had hoped the youth to get out of the activity may be lost. There are several processing activities in this book; however, for a more thorough selection of processing activities, please refer to Michelle Cummings' book co-authored with Jim Cain and Jennifer Stanchfield: *A Teachable Moment, a Facilitator's Guide to Activities for Processing, Debriefing, Reviewing and Reflection*. This book has over 130 different processing and debriefing activities to choose from. It also reinforces the importance of creating a safe environment for dialogue.

---

[1] Frank, L.S. (2004). *Journey Toward the Caring Classroom*. Oklahoma City, OK: Wood 'N' Barnes Publishing.

Sequencing

Keeping true to the metaphor of the title of the book, *Setting the Conflict Compass*, sequencing your activities is a lot like setting the declination of your compass when you get to a new area. With each conflict situation you encounter, you must choose the appropriate activities that will match the unique situation you are dealing with.

Sequencing of your activities is a very important piece of experiential education. If you introduce activities that are above the functioning capability of your participants, it can cause more damage than good. In order to create effective reflection, it is important to start with introductory level activities and then proceed to more difficult challenges. Groups need to share simple experiences together before introducing them to activities that have a higher emotional risk. As facilitators it is important to start with activities that are appropriate for the needs of the group, the group's background, and/or their stage in group development.

Sequencing of activities begins with assessing client readiness for each activity. It ends with the activities being placed in an order that makes sense to participants. You wouldn't want to start with a Trust activity and then move into an Icebreaker activity. This would not make sense to the participant if you ask them to trust the other participants before they even knew their names.

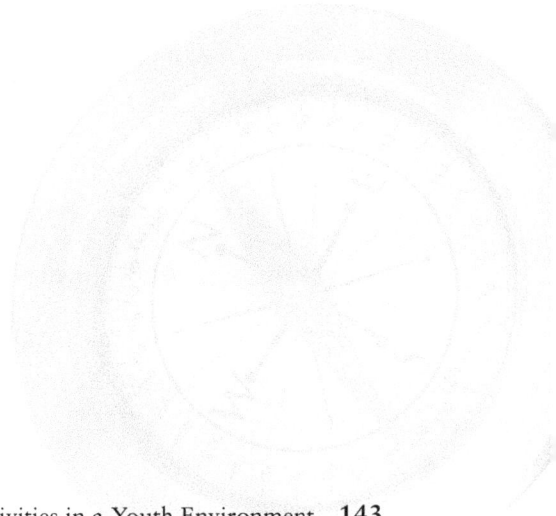

Sample 8-Week Sequence

The following information is not a set curriculum, but it is an example of an 8-week course that was implemented into an elementary school. This Bullying Prevention Program was implemented into a Montessori school where they have multiple grade levels in one classroom. There were fourth-, fifth- and sixth-grade students participating in the same program at the same time. The program was implemented in one-hour segments every Monday for 8 weeks. There were approximately 30 students participating in the program.

Week 1

Activity #1 **Handshakes,** 15 minutes

Questions asked:

- First handshake, Lumberjack: Discuss with your partner an example of bullying you have encountered in your classroom.
- Second handshake, Salmon: Discuss with your partner an example of a time when you might have bullied someone in your class or outside of your class.
- Third handshake, Cappuccino: Discuss with your partner one thing you know you can do to prevent bullying from happening in your class.
- Fourth handshake, Dairy Cow: Discuss with your partner a positive way you handle conflict.

Activity #2 **Protector Destroyer,** 10 minutes for the activity, 15 minutes for the debrief. Activity done in 3 stages: Stage 1 Protector/Destroyer, Stage 2 Protector/Bully, and Stage 3 Victim/Bully with the participants as the Protector.

Activity #3 **Pokerface,** 5 minutes for the activity, 15 minutes for the debrief.

Week 2

Activity #1 **Have You Ever** with **Stop N Go Poly Spots,** 15 minutes

- Red Light: What is something I can do to stop bullying in my class?
- Yellow Light: What is something I need to be careful of in regard to bullying?
- Green Light: What is something I do really well to prevent bullying from happening?

Activity #2 **Dots,** 5 minutes for the activity, 15 minutes for the debrief.

Activity #3 **Privilege,** 10 minutes for the activity, 15 minutes for the debrief. Debrief the group with the *Body Part Debrief* activity.

Week 3

Activity #1 **Back to Back,** 4 partner exchanges. 15 minutes for activity.

Questions asked:

* Discuss with your partner whether you think incidents of bullying have decreased in class since the beginning of this program.
* Discuss with your partner something you have done or could do to stop bullying in your class.
* Discuss with your partner something you need to be careful of in class in regard to bullying.
* Discuss with your partner something you do really well to prevent bullying from happening in class.

Activity #2 **Cross the Line,** 15 minutes for the activity, 30 minutes for debrief.

Week 4

Activity #1 **Rejection,** 10 minutes for the activity, 15 minutes for the debrief.

Activity #2 **In Group Out Group,** 20 minutes for the activity, 15 minutes for the debrief. Debrief the group using the activity **Traffic Debrief.**

Week 5

Activity #1 **Blind Shapes,** 5 minutes for the activity, 10 minutes for the debrief.

Activity #2 **Inside Outside Cards.** 15 minutes for crafting, 20 minutes for the debrief.

Activity #3 **Shuffle Left, Shuffle Right,** 10 minutes for the debrief.

Week 6

Activity #1 **Push Off,** 5 minutes for the activity, 10 minutes for the debrief.

Activity #2 **Multicultural Picture Cards,** 45 minutes for the activity.

Week 7

Activity #1 **Card Mixers,** 10 minutes

Activity #2 **Get Into Your Groups,** 5 minutes for the activity, 15 minutes for the debrief.

Activity #3 **Conflict Animals,** 20 minutes for the activity, 10 minutes for the debrief.

Week 8

Activity #1 **Pocket Processor,** 10 minutes on Line activity, 20 minutes on Consensus Activity in small groups.

Activity #2 Action Planning and Goal setting with **Pocket Processor** Consensus Activity results from the class.

Research Findings

The following information is a research study completed by Jeff Strickland, the current assistant director of student activities for Regis University in Denver, CO. He shadowed Michelle Cummings of Training Wheels while she implemented the sample 8-week sequence found on the preceding pages. This is a portion of his research findings.

CHAPTER I

LITERATURE REVIEW

Introduction

"Jonesboro, Arkansas; West Paducah, Kentucky; Springfield, Oregon; and Littleton, Colorado, are just a few of the American towns and cities that have experienced the horror of school violence . . ." (Garrett, 2001, p.1). These tragic school shootings that claimed the lives of students and teachers who were shot down within the walls of their own schools were unbelievably perpetrated by students. From these tragedies has emerged the looming question, "why?" What was happening in the lives of these young people that would result in their extreme actions? Why would they want to hurt other kids their own age? What would make them so angry at teachers and staff in their schools? How could they take it to the point of killing others from their own communities? Their actions caused so much grief and pain, not only to others, but in many cases the taking of their own lives left their families bewildered and confused. Parents, educators and other students are looking to schools, to experts and asking the questions, how could this happen? How can such a danger be within schools? How is it being addressed and is it enough?

After these tragedies, there has been much focus on the lives of the perpetrators. Many myths have been shattered such as the natural assumption and desire that the perpetrators were just "bad people, bad kids", and instead it has been learned that their lives were very complex. In most situations, it has been found that behind the horrific actions were very troubled and hurt young people. All have been described as loners with an absence of friends. It has been reported that these same students were actually victims of bullying in their own school experiences. Secret Service has found that school shooters typically were chronically bullied (Espelage & Swearer, 2004). These incidents have drawn national attention to the topic of school violence and bullying and renewed research in these areas. There has grown a great commitment to eliminate bullying in schools.

Current research indicates that the levels of bullying and school violence are creating multiple problems within schools throughout our nation and the world (Garrett, 2001; Piskin, 2002). This produces a number of problems such as: concentration problems in the classroom, children missing school, academic struggles, and in extreme cases producing anti-social behavior resulting in tragedies like assault or school shootings (Garrett, 2001; Piskin, 2002).

The results of bullying are tragic for both the victim and the perpetrator. Both parties produce social and financial drains upon society. Primary age children who were labeled by their peers as bullies required more support as adults from government agencies. As adults these bullies had more court convictions, more alcoholism, and developed more antisocial personality disorders and used more mental health services than the average citizen. By age 24, 60% of identified bullies have a criminal conviction. For the victims, children who are repeatedly victimized sometimes see suicide as their only escape (Bullying B'ware Productions, 2005). Prior to 2000, as a nation, there seemed to be reluctance to recognize the problem of school violence and to create responses to make the school environment safer and more productive for our children. Since that time, as evidenced by the development of new programs and initiatives within schools, government support and community changes, the culture is changing (Hazler & Miller, 2001).

LITERATURE REVIEW

Leading researchers in the topic of bullying define it as the repeated exposure to negative behavior by a student or group of students to inflict harm toward an individual, who is perceived to be weaker (Olweus & Limber, 1999; Dake, Price, & Telljohann, 2003). Bullying can include hitting, kicking, punching, threats, continuous teasing, name calling, lying or spreading false rumors, being left out of groups, property damage, or loss of money or possessions on threat of harm.

For these actions to be considered bullying, an imbalance of power must exist. This can be either a physical, emotional, or intellectual imbalance (Piskin, 2002). Through research about the topic of bullying, the evidence suggests the following about bullying: bullying is one of the most underrated and enduring problems in schools today; schools are a prime location for bullying; the majority of bullying occurs in or close to school buildings; and most victims are unlikely to report bullying (Bauman & Del Rio, 2006; Espelage & Swearer, 2003; Furlong, Morrison, & Greif, 2003; Olweus, 1993). In the United States approximately 20% of students report having been bullied (Hazler & Miller, 2001; Leff, Power, Costigan, & Manz, 2003).

Four Contributing Factors Leading to Bullying

According to Olweus (1993) there are four problems that contribute to the issues of bullying in schools. The first is lack of awareness and knowledge by adults as to what constitutes bullying and how to best intervene and support students involved. The second problem centers on these same concepts but from confusion or lack of comprehension from a student perspective, and the third problem is student skill and practice in dealing or avoiding a bullying situation. The fourth issue involves the locations where bullying typically occur and the kind of supervision in those areas.

Adult Identification and Intervention in Bullying

It has become evident that adults are unsure of how to identify and intervene with instances of school bullying. There are some programs and training in place to address the issue of bullying; however, many adults are either not aware or not prepared to deal with the realities of bullying (Rigby, 2001; Smith, Pepler & Rigby, 2004). Since many adults do not know how to intervene in bullying situations, bullying is often overlooked. This happens because teachers have difficulty determining if bullying is occurring or if it is only rough and tumble play. Another problem could be that students are careful about where and when engaging in these activities and do it outside of a teacher's supervision. Only 25% of students report that teachers intervene in bullying situations, while 71% of teachers believe they always intervene. This leads to bullying often being tolerated and ignored by adults such as parents and teachers (Skiba & Fontanini, 2000).

Student Identification and Intervention in Bullying

The second aspect of bullying is that students themselves do not understand how to intervene or deal with instances of school bullying. Students who watch instances of bullying feel the effects of it even though they are not the target of the behavior. Eighty-three percent of students indicate that watching bullying makes them feel uncomfortable (Pepler & Craig, 2000). They often don't want to get involved because they may not want to be the next victim, but they know what they are seeing is wrong. They don't want to be looked down on by the bully or other bystanders, or they may actually be supporting the bully (Sullivan, Cleary & Sullivan, 2004).

Student Skill in Responding to Bullying

The third contributing problem is that students haven't developed the skills necessary to avoid becoming a bully or a victim. According to Rigby (2001) bullies often lack necessary social skills and have little or no experiences cooperating with others. They also have not typically had opportunities to exercise power in a socially acceptable way, and they lack impulse control. In speaking about the victims of bullying, Rigby (2001) explains that they lack conflict resolution skills. Helping students learn to resolve the conflicts on their own can lead to a dramatic increase in their self-esteem which makes them less vulnerable to bullies.

Location and Supervision

It is well documented that bullying and victimization happens when students are in school settings that are unstructured, such as playgrounds and lunch rooms (Hazler & Miller, 2001; Olweus, 1993; Leff et al., 2003). In addition, some educators feeling the pressure to increase academic performance determine recess to be taking away from valuable classroom time and disrupting children's academic focus (Pellegrini & Smith, 1993). However, there has been little evidence to support these assertions (Leff, et al., 2003). Between these two concerns, there has been some momentum over the last decade to administrators cutting down on the amount of recess time available to school aged children (Blatchford, 1995; Leff, et al., 2003). Between 1990 and 1995, 56% of primary schools and 44% of secondary schools decreased the length of recess, citing a need to increase teaching time to meet new academic requirements and to reduce behavior problems in the school (Blatchford, 1995; Leff, et al., 2003).

Reducing recess opportunities has negative consequences for students. Recess has been shown to provide students with appropriate outlets for energy, which increases their focus on academic work (Pellegrini & Bjorklund, 1996). There has been additional concern that kids are not that active now when they do have free time. There are less of the time-honored playground games being played (Blatchford, 1995). Blatchford (1995) also argues that there needs to be a balance between managing student actions and allowing children to develop and practice friendship skills and social experiences through unstructured play.

One positive attribute of recess is that it helps children to develop social competence. Social competence is defined as students being able to adjust to the strain of dealing with school culture and peer relationships (Pellegrini & Glickman, 1990). Also, physical activity can help students in the development of gross and fine motor skills. Rough and tumble play can help children to learn social problem-solving techniques and develop social norms (Pellegrini, 2001). Olweus (1993), an expert in bullying prevention, advocates for positive recess time while also noting that it is only effective when there is appropriate adult supervision and students have allies established within their peer group.

He states:
An additional way to counteract bullying is to provide a well-equipped and more attractive outdoor environment that invites positive activities. It is likely that some students bully more when they are bored; the bullying may become a way of making school life somewhat more exciting. Further, a well-laid-out and well planned playground may make it more attractive for adults to participate in the students' activities. (p. 73–74)

POSITIVE YOUTH DEVELOPMENT

Positive youth development (PYD) is a term used to describe the approach of finding and developing each youth's strengths, skills, and natural abilities instead of focusing on their weaknesses. It carries a belief that youth are ". . . resources to be developed not problems to be managed" (Roth, Brooks-Gunn, Murray, & Foster, 1998, p. 427). Benson (1990) was the first to use the term Positive Youth Development in his book, *The Troubled Journey: A Portrait of 6th–12th Grade Youth*. In building upon the concept of positive youth development, subsequent researchers have identified five indicators of thriving individuals. The five C's are competence, confidence, connection, character, and caring or compassion (Lerner, Almerigi, Theokas, & Lerner, 2005a). Research is starting to suggest that a sixth indicator should be added which is contribution (Lerner, Lerner, Almerigi, Theokas, Phelps, Gestsdottir et al., 2005b).

Competence has been described as a positive attitude about one's abilities in a number of domains including social, academic, cognitive, and vocational. Social competence as described earlier in this paper deals with conflict resolution and the ability to deal with social situations. Academic competence is specifically measured through grades, attendance, testing and assessments. Cognitive competence revolves around an individual's ability to make decisions. Lastly, vocational competency describes the standard of work habits and career choices (Lerner, 2004; Roth & Brooks-Gunn, 2003).

Confidence expresses one's sense of self-worth or self-efficacy. It reflects what one generally thinks about oneself. Connection refers to the positive relationships a person has with individuals or organizations such as schools or the community as a whole. Character deals with one's respect for societal norms or their perception of what is right or wrong. And lastly, caring and compassion describes a person's consideration of others feelings or needs (Lerner, 2004; Roth & Brooks-Gunn, 2003). The sixth C, contribution, is portrayed as using the first five C's and doing something positive with them in your community (Lerner et al., 2005b).

The factors mentioned earlier in this paper that contribute to bullying such as student identification of bullying, social competence, and self esteem are deficits in a child's development. Positive youth development and its focus on finding and developing each youth's strengths, skills, and natural abilities instead of focusing on their weaknesses provides a philosophical umbrella of concepts that are also the backbone of most anti-bullying programs.

Experiential Education

Experiential education falls within the scope of positive youth development as it encourages students to explore their environment and learn from their own experiences. Experiential education is exemplified by the Chinese Proverb: "Tell me and I will forget. Show me and I may remember. Involve me and I will understand." (Association of Experiential Education, n.d.). Experiential education philosophy suggests that learning happens when educators use purposefully planned direct experiences that engage the learner. This leads to a deeper understanding and comprehension of the material being taught (Association of Experiential Education, n.d.; Hunt, 1990; Gass, 1993).

Although it may seem like a new concept to put experience and education together, it has been discussed for quite some time. Plato and Aristotle both connected experience and education, in the form of virtues, in their philosophy of education (Hunt, 1990). Plato referred to the process in which craftsmen and artisans involve their children from an early age in observation of their craft for years before beginning to learn the skills of the trade (Hunt, 1990). Aristotle specifically talked about teaching moral virtues and that in order to learn virtues it is important to live those virtues (Hunt, 1990).

It was, however, John Dewey, who is described as the modern father of experiential education (Neil, 2005). He was generally thought of as a supporter of "progressive education," which allowed students' freedom of education in contrast to "traditional education" where the focus was on content and memorization (Neil, 2005). However, Dewey argued against total freedom or student derived learning and believed that structure was important to avoid the possibility of mis-educative or non-educative experiences (Hunt, 1990; Neil, 2005). These mis-educative or non-educative experiences happen when students don't understand how to structure their experiences to help them build a frame of reference.

Experiential education is a term that includes a number of approaches to education such as: adventure education, outdoor education, environmental education, service learning, leadership development, internships, schools and colleges, and civic engagement programs. These different types of educators have found that experiential education is a foundation of learning. For the purpose of this study, the programs we will discuss fall in the adventure education realm.

Adventure Education

As mentioned, there are many mediums that use experiential education, and adventure education is one of them. Adventure education or adventure-based education uses the philosophy of experiential education through developing teamwork and group skills by using games, problem- solving activities, or outdoor activities (Rohnke, 1989). Adventure activities do not necessarily need to take place in the outdoors. They are often used in traditional classrooms, gymnasiums, and other adapted spaces.

Kurt Hahn, a German educator who escaped Nazi Germany, started using adventure education in the British Navy during World War II when he realized that the older sailors were surviving at higher rates than the younger, stronger sailors. He created Outward Bound as a training program for the British Navy. Its goal was to give sailors experience at facing challenges (perceived risk) and overcoming them psychologically, physically, and mentally. It also gave them the chance to work together as a team and develop some tools so then in real danger, they knew how to respond to it and be successful (James, 2000; Richards, 1990).

Once the war was over, Hahn started the Outward Bound School where his new focus was working with high school students and focusing on his ideals of developing moral and physically fit individuals (James, 2000; Richards, 1990). Adventure education started growing and expanding from there as the merit of this type of learning developed into numerous other programs such as adventure therapy, corporate training and leadership initiatives (Gass, 1993; Schoel, Prouty, & Radcliff, 1989). Some common aspects of adventure education include small group sizes, group or individual challenges, problem-solving and decision making opportunities, facilitated in a non-intrusive manner, and short in duration. However, the biggest similarities these programs have are that they take their participants out of their comfort zone and place them into physically and mentally challenging situations (Hatti, Marsh, Neill, & Richards, 1997).

Adventure programs have self reported data that it builds skills in the areas of team building, community building, self efficacy, self esteem, confidence building and better communications skills (Davis-Berman & Berman, 1989; James, 2000). Hatti et al. (1997) also found a moderately positive effect of adventure education in areas of self-concept, locus of control, communication and leadership. This study was based on a meta-analysis of 96 empirical outcome studies. These results were similar to Cason and Gillis (1994) findings in their meta-analysis of 43 studies focused on adolescents. Additionally, in more recent years as the field has been growing and developing, hard data reveals the level of skill building in each area. Because there is overlap between the skills adventure programming may develop and the skills that are proven to decrease bullying, anti-bullying programs based upon an experiential foundation have begun to be built around the United States.

OVERVIEW OF THE DEVELOPMENT OF BULLYING PREVENTION PROGRAMS

Researchers have been studying the issue of bullying for thirty plus years. Because bullying used to be considered "a part of growing up", programs on how to respond and remediate to bullying didn't develop until the last ten to twenty years (Furlong, Morrison, & Greif, 2003). Olweus, an innovative researcher, from the University of Bergen, Norway, began studying the problem of bullying much earlier than anyone else: as early as the late 60's and early 1970's. He created and implemented a bullying prevention program in the early 1980's. His research was timely due to a tragic incident that happened in Norway in 1982 when three 10–14 year old boys committed suicide because of being bullied by peers. This event created a national outcry demanding that something must be done about bullying. Olweus's program was then implemented throughout Norway (Olweus, 1993). Olweus (1993) explains in detail his whole school approach to the issue of bullying in his book *Bullying at School: What we know and what we can do.*

Olweus studied his own program in large scale measure with impressive decreases in bullying, and most current anti-bullying programs are designed upon facets of his philosophy of a whole school response to bullying. Olweus's whole school program requires a high level of commitment and resources that not all schools can or do choose to undertake. As a highly developed program, the whole school approach has a variety of "vehicles" it uses to address bullying such as teacher education, parent involvement, peer accountability, etc. Some schools adopt a few of these vehicles and in addition, other methods have been created such as presentations, videos, board games, special groups, etc.

The Whole School Approach Program

Olweus Bullying Prevention Program

The Olweus Bullying Prevention Program is a whole school approach to intervening in bullying. The philosophy focuses on systematic, intentional changes to school culture, parental and community involvement, teacher training and student support. These changes include: school wide measures, classroom measures, and individual measures. What Olweus terms measures are experiences which are intended to address the issue of bullying at the school (Olweus, 1993; Olweus & Limber, 1999).

School Wide Measures

School wide measures are changes that are made at the school wide level. That could include: taking the Olweus bully/victim questionnaire in a school conference day, supervision in the outdoor environment, hotline, a general PTA meeting, and teacher groups for the development of the social milieu of the school (Olweus, 1993). Current research states that successful programs in reducing bullying and school violence consist of a whole school approach where there is a complete change in school culture and an increase in investment of students, educators and the community (Espelage & Swearer, 2003; Horne, 2004; Olweus, 1993; Olweus & Limber, 1999; Piskin, 2002). In his system, one aspect he focuses on is supervision in the outdoor environment. He begins by advocating for more adult presence during recess and free times, but he states that even more needs to be done. The adults need to intervene in bullying situations even if they are unsure if it is bullying or only aggressive play. To do this they need to be trained to recognize bullying situations and a plan needs to be developed on how to intercede in these situations (Olweus, 1993). Unfortunately, many teachers and aides who are assigned the duty of recess often dislike the responsibility and only intervene when necessary or when asked directly by a student (Lewis, Colvin, & Sugai, 2000; Peplar, Craig, & Roberts, 1998; Anderson-Butcher, Newsom, & Nay, 2003). It is important to make recess a fun, positive and safe environment not only for students but for staff as well. This will lead to adults taking on a more active role during this important developmental time.

Classroom Measures

Classroom measures are intended to make changes at the impact level. The Olweus program suggests: having class rules about bullying, using praise, having clear sanctions, utilizing class meetings, using cooperative learning and common positive activities and having class PTA meetings (Olweus, 1993; Olweus & Limber, 1999).

Individual Measures

Individual measures are intended to make changes by focusing on the specific students involved in these incidences. They are the interventions that address the issue directly and in the moment.

They include: having serious talks with the bully, having talks with the victim, talking with the parents. It's also important to let the parents of the bully know what they should do as well as the parents of the victim. He also suggests the use of imagination, creating discussion groups for parents of bullied or bullying students and possible change of class or school for these individuals (Olweus, 1993; Olweus & Limber, 1999).

The research of Olweus's whole school approach program yields positive results. In his first study of the program, his research was with approximately 2500 children over a period of twenty months. Not only did he find significant reductions in bullying, but he found that there were still considerable decreases in bullying situations two years following the program. Two further studies of the same size and scope but at different districts revealed similar results. Additionally, two studies within the United States by school districts who have adopted the Olweus Program have also shown decreases in bullying (Olweus, 1993; Olweus & Limber, 1999). Within the United States, some well known and successful whole school approach programs are *Bully Proofing your School* created by Creating Caring Communities (Plog, n.d.), and *Steps to Respect* which was put together by the Committee for Children (2001). These programs use the basic concepts of the Olweus Bullying Prevention Program in the creation of their systems.

Adventure Models

Research shows two programs that attempt to address the issue of bullying by using an adventure model. The first is Project Adventure's Peaceable Playground model. The second is the Training Wheels Bullying Prevention Field Guide, which is more focused on facilitation techniques but attempts to address the issue in similar methods.

Peaceable Playground Model

The Peaceable Playground Model is one program that attempts to deal with the issue of playground bullying issues, created by Project Adventure in 1999 (Kilty, 2001). The goal was to address the social development needs of students and concerns about aggressive play at recess. The program was developed as an optional activity in which students could elect to participate during the lunch time recess period and was facilitated by students, parents, and educators (Kilty, 2001). The premise was that games help kids learn identity development, conflict resolution, positive peer interaction, and good sportsmanship. When kids have less opportunity to practice these concepts, it is a lost opportunity to teach them these positive skills (Blatchford, 1995).

The program, using the whole school approach involved parents as an integral aspect. This involvement sent a community wide message that bullying is not tolerated and parents can be powerful role models when it comes to positive behaviors (Kilty, 2001; Garrett, 2001; O'Connell, Pepler, & Craig, 1999; Olweus,1993).

Parents and educators participate in a three day training program that teaches group management skills, activity facilitation, and basic conflict resolution skills. After the training parents and educators work in pairs and facilitate activities to students during recess periods. After the first year of the program students begin to take over the main responsibility of facilitating the program. Older students run the program for younger students, i.e., fourth graders facilitate activities for the first graders who share their recess time. Parents and educators become a support network for the students, empowering them to set the tone against bullying in their school (Kilty, 2001).

A description of the activities used in the Peaceable Playground Model can be found in the Project Adventure book *Adventures in Peacemaking* (Kreidler & Furlong, 1996). The book outlines the basics on how to handle conflict within a program and adventure facilitation. The activities in the book are divided up into five core concepts of peacemaking. They are: cooperation, communication, expressing feelings, appreciating diversity, and conflict resolution. They also suggest some ideas for culminating events for each peacemaking program (Kreidler & Furlong, 1995). The testimonial below displays the effects of this model:

> Toward the end of our day together, the students were journaling on a large sheet in the classroom. Two students were sitting side by side, drawing and talking with one another. We checked in with the teacher to see how she felt the day had gone. Pointing to the two students, she said, "If nothing else, that made it all worth it. They haven't talked to each other since S . . . was killed. They would not be in the same room together and almost left this morning when they found out they were in the same group. We asked them to please just try it." The two students the teacher was referring to were the best friend of the murdered student and the leader of the gang that allegedly had beaten him to death. I watched them closely, moved by the peaceful scene they had created, trying to comprehend what they were feeling. As they drew on the group journal sheet, they talked quietly and intently about what happened. Apologizing, empathizing, relating. We all took a deep breath and watched as two young men worked through their anger, fear and uncertainty in ways that made sense. It was a powerful moment for all of us. (Kilty, 2001, p. 12)

Training Wheels Bullying Prevention Field Guide

Cummings (2005) created a field guide using adventure activities called *Bullying Prevention Field Guide: Experiential activities specializing in anti-bullying*. Cummings is the founder of Training Wheels, an organization dedicated to training teachers and facilitators to use a variety of skills and topics by using experiential activities. Cummings has trained teachers in various settings on how to use her program in schools around the country. The field guide addresses what bullying is, why it happens, how to recognize it, who it involves, and how adventure can be used to address it. Cummings (2005) identifies ten strategies that represent "best practices" in bullying prevention and intervention:

1. Focus on the social environment of the program.

2. Assess bullying in your school/program.

3. Obtain staff and parent buy-in and support for bullying prevention.

4. Form a group to coordinate the program's bullying prevention activities.

5. Provide training for the staff in bullying prevention.

6. Establish and enforce school rules and policies related to bullying.

7. Increase adult supervision in "hot spots" for bullying.

8. Intervene consistently and appropriately when you see bullying.

9. Devote some program time to bully prevention.

10. Continue these efforts. (p. 13)

The Training Wheels *Bullying Prevention Field Guide* encourages teachers to spend time discussing each one of these points. Then, the next step of the program focuses on the implementation of activities that teach skills to prevent and/or intervene in bullying situations. These activities are categorized into get to know you activities, problem solving activities, processing activities, trust activities, and diversity activities. Each is designed for students to get to know one another better. This can happen personally, culturally, and/or socially. *The Bullying Prevention Field Guide* summarizes this in a quote by Chris Cavert "The more I know about you the less likely I am to hurt you." (Cummings, p. 28, 2005)

While there are common elements between bullying prevention and adventure education, there are few empirical studies to support the link between adventure programming and its effectiveness to reduce bullying. Therefore, the purpose of this study was to investigate how a bullying prevention program using adventure activities is perceived by its participants. The program was designed to help students to recognize and learn how to decrease instances of bullying that they may encounter. This study focused on how adventure activities enhanced student skills in responding to bullying situations. The specific research question for this study was "What are participants' perceptions of the effectiveness of an anti-bullying adventure-based program?"

CHAPTER II METHODS

Bullying is a growing issue in our world today. To further explore interventions utilizing adventure activities as a method of teaching bullying prevention techniques, this chapter describes in detail the study that was conducted. It discusses the participants, school, program, data collection and analysis process.

Participants

Students and teachers

The participants in this study were children in one class comprised of 4th, 5th, and 6th grade students. The class consisted of 13 males and 16 females. Among the students, 86% were described as Caucasian, 13% Hispanic, and 3% African American. All participants participated in an in-school anti-bullying program using adventure education as the medium. Participants were from a convenience sample. Additional participants included the teacher, teacher's assistant, and the principal of the school. All three were Caucasian.

The Training Wheels Program for this study was facilitated by Michelle Cummings, founder of Training Wheels Group. Training Wheels is a company offering professional training in facilitating adventure based team building activities. Training Wheels also sells resources needed to facilitate these activities in the form of publications, props, and other equipment. Cummings wrote the *Bullying Prevention Field Guide* used in the study. She holds a Master's in Experiential Education from Minnesota State University at Mankato. She speaks at over 25 local, national and international conferences a year, and she has authored several books.

School

The Smith Academy is a public Montessori charter school in the larger metro area of Colorado. According to the International Montessori Index (n.d.), Montessori practices of teaching were developed by Dr. Maria Montessori. It is a method of teaching where students are allowed to develop and institute their own curriculum or process of learning. Students operate individually in an intentional environment where students choose how they will work. The teaching structure encourages focused concentration and hands on exploration as an important educational learning tool. These priorities are opposed to the more traditional form of teaching that emphasizes teacher authority and more sedentary group learning (The International Montessori Index, n.d.). The Montessori Method compliments the tenets of experiential education, which is the foundation of adventure programming, where students learn by experiencing the environment around them.

Training Wheels Anti-Bullying Program

The Training Wheels anti-bullying program was offered once a week for eight weeks. The in-school program was conducted during the first period of the day, which was an hour and a half in length. The program met for six weeks in a row and then there was a three week break due to standardized testing. The last two sessions were completed after the testing was finished.

The kids helped set up the room by removing the desks and creating a large space in the middle of the classroom. The group then circled up and received an introduction of the session's program. The program was activity based with a discussion at the end of each activity. The activity or activities typically lasted for an hour and the remainder of the time was spent on reflection and/or discussion led by the main facilitator. Teachers, researcher and students all participated in the discussions. Teachers sometimes participated in the activities depending on their availability. The topics ranged from defining bullying to deepening relationships with other students to situational games exploring relative concepts of bullying. The activity sequence used for the 8 week program is laid out at the beginning of this chapter.

PROCEDURE

Permission was gained from the school system through discussion with the principal. School system consent was gained through the school district consent form. Parents of the participants were asked if their child could participate in the study. Participants were asked to read and sign the assent form that described the procedure and risks involved with their child participating in the study. Participants were informed that participation was completely voluntary and they could end their participation at any time they chose. They also were informed that they would not benefit from being a part of this study and they would experience minimal to no harm from participation. If they agreed and signed the consent form, then they were asked a series of questions about their knowledge of bullying, their perception of how often bullying occurs in their school, what their current school policies are, and how they recognize and intervene in bullying situations.

Data Collection

Of the 29 students in the class 10 returned the parental consent forms to participate in the interviews. Of the 10 students 9 participated in the study due to the remaining student being absent the day interviews were conducted. The interviews were semi-structured and approximately 6-10 minutes in length. A semi-structured interview is guided by a list of questions; however, the exact wording and order of questions are determined by the course of the conversation between the interviewer and interviewee (Merriam, 1998). The interviews were tape recorded and transcribed. Semi-structured interviews were also conducted with the head teacher, assistant teacher and principal. The information was used to determine how teachers and teacher's aides identify and intervene in bullying situations observed in their schools.

Researcher's Personal Stance

I became interested in bullying prevention programs after being hired to run an experientially based after school program geared towards helping students understand how to deal with bullying and school violence in an appropriate way. I trained 12 high school students to facilitate adventure activities specifically designed to build skills in the areas of: *cooperation, appreciating diversity, expressing feelings, communication, and conflict resolution.* These 12 students then conducted a weekly program with 5th graders for the course of the school year. It was a powerful program, and it left me interested in knowing more.

My interest in adventure activities began as a child. I grew up camping, hiking and spending time in the backcountry. In high school, I participated in a wilderness class that I found to be very fun; however, it was in college that I had a paradigm shift when I became involved in recreation courses and realized the possibility to create a career path within that field. I became passionate about adventure education by practicing it myself and then the desire grew to share that experience with others. From my professional work I have seen that adventure activities have a powerful impact on individuals, when facilitated by an experienced trainer. This impact is particularly rewarding when seeing children use adventure to learn and change. I became intrigued with studying and measuring the effect that adventure activities have for change within bullies and victims.

Because of my passion for adventure education, there is a risk of bias about my viewpoint that adventure education is a positive tool to reduce bullying. However, my purpose for studying this topic was to examine whether my anecdotal observations of change through personal work experience have measureable results within a structured study.

Trustworthiness of Data

Qualitative research is often gauged by terms such as trustworthiness, accuracy, consistency and plausibility (Blumenfeld-Jones, 1995). The technique used to establish trustworthiness was triangulation which uses multiple sources of data to confirm the findings (Merriam, 1998). This was accomplished by interviewing students, the teacher of the class, and the school principal to compare results from the program. Teachers were asked about their perceptions of the student learning that took place through the program and how they see those perceptions playing out in the hallways of their school. Questions were focused on specific behavior by students using the skills they learned during the program. As well as using a "peer examination", which Merriam (1998) describes as having experts review the findings as they become known to determine the accuracy of the interpretation of the data.

Data Analysis

Participant's responses to individual interview questions were analyzed using two distinct yet overlapping processes of analysis derived from grounded theoretical perspective: open and axial coding (Strauss & Corbin, 1998). Open coding is the process of developing categories of concepts and themes derived from the data. In this study, open coding was used to analyze interview transcripts by reviewing each interview transcript multiple times and making notes about what they might mean. Additionally, open coding involves the process of conceptualizing, defining categories, and developing categories of results in terms of their properties and dimensions. Axial coding facilitates building connections within categories. The goal is to systematically develop and relate categories. This step includes the process of sorting out the relationships between concepts and sub concepts with the ultimate goal to discover the ways that categories relate to each other. Through the axial coding process, a researcher's goal is to answer the questions of who, when, where, why, and how with what consequences (Strauss & Corbin, 1998).

CHAPTER III

RESULTS

The specific research question for this study was "What are participants' perceptions of the effectiveness of an anti-bullying adventure-based program?" The program was designed to intervene and help students to recognize and learn how to decrease instances of bullying that they may encounter. After data analysis three themes were identified, along with several subthemes, which described the students' perceptions of the effectiveness of an adventure program on enhancing their skills in responding to bullying situations. The themes include: (a) a differentiated understanding of bullying, (b) perceptions of change, and (c) the importance of the method.

CONCLUSIONS

Discussion

As the world is more focused on the negative effects of bullying on victims and bullies, increased attention and questions have arisen about the most effective ways to counter bullying in school systems (Olweus, 1993). As schools grapple with how to positively affect student behavior with reasonable cost and resources, researchers are examining current programs and strategies to give insight into the best practices (Olweus & Limber, 1999).

The literature about bullying is clear on the types of learning that decreases bullying including adult identification and intervention with bullying, student identification and intervention with bullying, student skill in responding to bullying and focusing on the location and supervision of common bullying areas (Olweus, 1993, Olweus & Limber, 1999). The missing link is how do students best learn these concepts.

With regard to the research question, "What were participants' perceptions of the effectiveness of an anti-bullying adventure-based program?", the results of the study were that it helped (a) students get to know one another better, (b) it empowered them in bullying situations, and (c) the adventure activities helped students to be more engaged in the material thus increasing learning potential.

Student responses gave credence to Chris Cavert's observation, "the more I know about you the less likely I am to hurt you" (Cummings, p. 28, 2005). Students reported that the activities forced them to interact outside of their comfort zone. This allowed students to explore relationships with students they would not normally interact with. It allowed them to step away from their circle of friends and helped them to find commonalities and insight into other students. This supports the research that adventure activities help groups build group cohesion and reduces alienation (Glass & Banshoff, 2002; Cross, 2002). In addition, students need to have established allies within their peer group (Pelligrini & Glickman, 1990), and students getting to know each other better provided that connection. Students reported that not only were they less likely to bully people because they began to get to know them, but they discussed taking it one step further to even standing up for other students.

The second finding was that the adventure activities helped the students feel empowered to intervene in situations they may not have been able to before. This may be due to the fact that they knew one another and had investment in one another as individuals or the fact that they had opportunity to consider how to handle these situations and to practice in a safe and controlled environment. The reality of the games provided a training for them to speak up, which translated into more confidence in real life situations as opposed to a game. The discussions and debriefs after each activity helped students to consider different outcomes of the situations they faced and allowed them to consider how they would handle future situations differently. This describes one of the key elements of experiential education which is reflection is critical to the learning process and learning must have present as well as future significance (Kraft & Sakofs, 1985).

Students were also empowered to intervene because they were practicing and building their skill level. Research shows that to decrease bullying, students need to improve their competence in the following categories: social skills, cooperation with others, conflict resolution, and impulse control (Kreidler & Furlong, 1995). In addition, an overall growth in self esteem makes students less vulnerable to being a victim of bullying or becoming a bully (Rigby, 2001).

The third finding was that the games kept students engaged in the material giving them an opportunity to look at people and situations from a new perspective thus increasing learning potential. The safe environment created by the facilitator and group allowed them to explore these concepts in a deeper but non-threatening way. Because students felt so engaged, it provided anecdotal support that adventure activities are a helpful tool in helping students with the issue of bullying. Being engaged in the material and knowledge of bullying is important due to the complexity of bullying itself. These complexities include types or levels of bullying and the different contexts of bullying situations. It is helpful for students to learn about these intricacies of bullying at a young age due to the severity of the consequences of bullying on both victims and bullies (Garrett, 2001; Piskin, 2002).

IMPLICATIONS FOR PRACTITIONERS

It is really important for teachers and facilitators to understand that there is a lot going on in the classroom that they are not able to observe or their observations are limited and they may not be aware of the entirety of a situation. Olweus' research stated similar results in that teachers felt they were aware of and intervened in most bullying situations; however, students' perceptions were that teachers intervened only occasionally (1993). The data analysis seemed to indicate that teachers do respond to most physical and emotional instances of bullying but social bullying was harder to identify and harder to respond to without making things worse for the victim. With this knowledge, it stresses how important it is to give students the tools to help them deal with these problems themselves and to create a positive culture of groups who will band together to address these problems collectively. It also gives further credence to research in the field that emphasizes more parent, teacher, and community presence at schools.

Another implication from this study was how the experiential component of this type of bullying prevention program was beneficial for both genders, but the learning was different for each group. Students expressed that the boys learned more about bullying from the hands on activities than previous teachings that may have been more traditional (lecture, presentation, discussion), while the benefit to girls was the empowerment of getting to know the boys better and practicing their interactions with them. This could be really important to practitioners in planning to provide bullying intervention information in multiple ways to fully address each group's needs.

For more information about this research, please contact Jeff Strickland.

REFERENCES

Anderson-Butcher, D., Newsome, S., & Nay, S. (2003). Social skills intervention during elementary school recess: A visual analysis. *Children and Schools, 25*(3), 135–146.

Association for Experiential Education. (n.d.). *What is Experiential Education?* Retrieved February 2, 2009, from the Association for Experiential Education: A community of progressive educators & practioners: http://www.aee.org/about/whatIsEE.

Bauman, S., & Del Rio, A. (2006). Preservice teacher's responses to bullying scenarios: Comparing physical, verbal, and relational bullying. *Journal of Educational Psychology, 98*(1), 219–231.

Benson, P.L. (1990). *The troubled journey: A portrait of 6th–12th grade youth.* Minneapolis, MN: Search Institute.

Blatchford, P. (1995). The state of play in schools. *Child Psychology & Psychiatry Review. 3*(2) 58–67.

Blumenfeld-Jones, D. (1995). Fidelity as a criterion for participating and evaluating in narrative inquiry. *Qualitative Studies in Education, 8*(1), 25–35.

Bullying Beware Productions, retrieved October 13th, 2005, from the Bully B'ware website: http://www.bullybeware.com/moreinfo.html.

Cason, D., & Gillis, H.L. (1994). A meta-analysis of outdoor adventure programming with adolescents. *The Journal of Experiential Education, 17,* 40–47.

Committee for Children. (2001). *Steps to Respect: A bullying prevention program.* Seattle, WA: Author.

Cross, R. (2002). The effects of an adventure education program on perceptions of alienation and personal control among at-risk adolescents. *The Journal of Experiential Education, 25*(1), 247–254.

Cummings, M. (2005). *Bullying prevention field guide: Experiential activities specializing in anti-bullying*. Littleton CO: Training Wheels.

Cummings, M. (In press). *Setting the Conflict Compass: A Facilitator's Guide to Activities for Conflict Resolution*. Dubuque, IA: Kendall Hunt Publishing Co.

Dake, J., Price, J., & Telljohann, S. (2003). The nature and extent of bullying at school. *Journal of School Health, 73*(5), 173–180.

Davis-Berman, J., & Berman, D. S. (1989). The wilderness therapy program: An empirical study of its effects with adolescents in an outpatient setting. *Journal of Contemporary Psychotherapy, 19,* 271–281.

Espelage, D., & Swearer, S. (2003). Research on school bullying and victimization: What have we learned and where do we go from here? *School psychology review, 32*(3), 365–383.

Espelage, D., & Swearer, S. (Eds.). (2004). *Bullying in American schools: A social-ecological perspective on prevention and intervention*. Mahwah, NJ: Lawrence Erlbaum.

Furlong, M., Morrison, G., & Greif, J. (2003). Reaching an American consensus: Reactions to the special issue on school bullying. *School Psychological Review, 32*(3), 456–470.

Garrett, A. (2001). *Keeping American schools safe: A handbook for parents, students, educators, law enforcement personnel and the community*. Jefferson, NC: McFarland and Company, Inc.

Gass, M.A. (Ed) (1993). *Adventure Therapy: Therapeutic applications of adventure programming*. Dubuque, IA: Kendall Hunt Publishing Co.

Glass, S.J. & Benshoff, J.M. (2002). Facilitating group cohesion among adolescents through challenge course experiences. *The Journal of Experiential Education, 25*(2), 266–277.

Hazler, R. & Miller, D. (2001). Adult recognition of school bullying situations. *Educational Research, 43*(2), 133–146.

Hatti, J., Marsh, H.W., Neill, J.T., & Richards, G.E. (1997). Adventure education and outward bound: Out-of-class experiences that make a lasting difference. *Review of Educational Research, 67,* (1), 43–87.

Horne, A.M. (2004). Bully buster: A psychological intervention for reducing bullying behavior in middle school students. *Journal of counseling and development. 82*(3), 259–268.

Hunt, J.S. (1990). Philosophy of adventure education. In J.C. Miles & S. Priest (Eds.), *Adventure Education* (pp. 119–128). State College, PA: Venture Publishing.

James, T. (2000). *Kurt Hahn and the aims of Education*. Retrieved January 18, 2009 from Kurt Hahn.org website: http://www.kurthahn.org/writings/writings.html.

Kraft, R, & Sakofs, M. (1985). *The theory of experiential education*. Boulder, CO: Association for Experiential Education.

Kilty, K. (2001). Where do the children play? *Zipeline, 43,* 12–16.

Kreidler, W.J., & Furlong, L. (1995). *Adventures in peacemaking: A conflict resolution guide for school-aged programs.* Hamilton, MA: Project Adventure.

Leff, S., Power, T., Costigan, T., & Manz, P. (2003). Assessing the climate of the playground and lunchroom: Implications for bullying prevention programming. *School Psychology Review, 32*(3), 418–430.

Lerner, R.M. (2004). *Liberty: Thriving and civic engagement among American youth.* Thousand Oaks, CA: Sage.

Lerner, R.M., Almerigi, J.B., Theokas, C., & Lerner, J.V. (2005a). Positive youth development: A view of the issues. *Journal of Early Adolescence, 25*(1), 10–16.

Lerner, R.M., Lerner, J.V., Almerigi, J., Theokas, C., Phelps, E., Gestsdottir, S., et al. (2005b). Positive youth development, participation in community youth development programs, and community contributions of fifth grade adolescents: Findings from the first wave of the 4-H study of positive youth development. *Journal of Early Adolescence, 25*(1), 17–71.

Lewis, J., Colvin, G., & Sugai, G. (2000). The effects of pre-correction and active supervision on the recess behavior of elementary student. *Education and Treatment of Children, 23,* 109–121.

Merriam, S., (1998). *Qualitative research and case study applications in education: Revised and expanded from case study research in education* (2nd ed.). San Francisco, CA: Jossey-Bass.

The International Montessori Index (n.d.) Retrieved November15, 2008, from Montessori: The international Montessori index website: http://www.montessori.edu.

Neill, J. (January 26, 2005). *John Dewey, the modern father of experiential education.* Retrieved April 4, 2009, from http://wilderdom.com/experiential/ExperientialDewey.html.

O'Connell, P., Pepler, D., & Craig, W. (1999). Peer involvement in bullying: insights and challenges for intervention. *Journal of Adolescence.* 22, 437–452.

Olweus, D. (1993). *Bullying at school: What we know and what we can do.* Cambridge MA: Blackwell Publishing.

Olweus, D., & Limber, S. (1999). *Blueprints for violence prevention program: Bullying prevention program.* Boulder, CO: Institute of Behavioral Science, University of Colorado.

Pellegrini, A.D. (2001). Rough-and-tumble play from childhood through adolescence: Development and possible functions. In P.K Smith & C.H. Hart (Eds.) *Childhood Social Development* (pp. 438–453). Malden, MA: Blackwell Publishers Ltd.

Pellegrini, A.D., & Bjorklund, D.F. (1996). The place of recess in school: Issues in the role of recess in children's education and development. *Journal of Research in Childhood Education, 11,* 5–13.

Pellegrini, A.D., & Glickman, C.D. (1990). Measuring kindergartners' social competence. *Young Children, 45,* 40–44.

Pellegrini, A.D., & Smith, P.K. (1993). School recess: Implications for education and Development. *Review of Educational Research, 63,* 51–67.

Pepler, D., & Criag, W. (2000). Making a difference. Retrieved November 29th, 2005, from Bullying.org website: http://www.bullying.org/public/frameset.cfm.

Peplar, J., Craig, M., & Roberts, L. (1998). Observations of aggressive and non-aggressive children on the school playground. *Merrill-Palmer Quarterly, 44,* 55–75.

Piskin, M. (2002). School bullying: Definition, types, related factors, and strategies to prevent bullying problems. *Educational Sciences: Theory and Practice,* 2(2), 555–562.

Plog, A. (n.d.). Creating Caring Communities. *Research base of bully proofing your school.* Retrieved April 10, 2009 from http://www.bullyproofing.org/index.php?s=16.

Richards, A. (1990). Kurt Hahn. In J.C. Miles & S. Priest (Eds.), *Adventure Education* (pp. 67–74). State College, PA: Venture Publishing.

Rigby, K. (2001). *Stop the bullying: A handbook for schools.* Philadelphia, PA: Jessica Kingsley Publisher Ltd.

Rohnke, K. (1989). *Cowstails and cobras II.* Dubuque, IA: Kendall Hunt Publishing Company.

Roth, J.L., & Brooks-Gunn, J. (2003). What exactly is a youth development program? Answers from research and practice. *Applied Developmental Science, 7,* 94–111.

Roth, J.L., Brooks-Gunn, J., Murray, L., & Foster, W. (1998). Promoting healthy adolescents: Synthesis of youth development program evaluations. *Journal of Research on Adolescence, 8,* 423–459.

Schoel, J., Prouty, D., & Radcliff, P. (1989). *Islands of healing: A guide to adventure-based counseling.* Hamilton, MA: Project Adventure, Inc.

Skiba, R., & Fontanini, A. (2000). Bullying Preventions: What works in preventing school violence. *Early Identification and Intervention.* Retrieved March 20, 2005, from Indiana University, Indiana Education Policy Center website: http://www.indiana.edu/~safeschl/publication.html.

Smith, P., Pepler, D., & Rigby, K. (2004). *Bullying in schools: How successful can interventions be?* Cambridge, United Kingdom: Cambridge University Press.

Strauss, A.C., & Corbin, J.M. (1998). *Basics of Qualitative Research: Techniques and procedures for developing grounded theory.* Thousand Oaks, CA: Sage Publications Inc.

Sullivan, K., Cleary, M., & Sullivan, G. (2004). *Bullying in secondary schools.* Thousand Oaks, CA: Corwin Press, Inc.

Bullying Prevention

WHAT IS BULLYING?

Bullying is aggressive behavior that is intentional and that involves an imbalance of power or strength. Typically, it is repeated over time. A child who is being bullied has a hard time defending him or herself.

Bullying can take many forms

- Physical bullying: hitting, punching, or kicking
- Verbal bullying: teasing, name-calling, spreading rumors
- Nonverbal bullying or Emotional bullying: intimidation through gestures or social exclusion
- Cyber bullying: sending insulting messages by e-mail or text messaging.

There is not a single cause of bullying among children. Individual, family, peer, school, and community factors can place a child or youth at risk for bullying his or her peers.

Prevalence of Bullying

- Studies show that between 15–25% of U.S. students are bullied with some frequency ("sometimes or more often") while 15–20% report that they bully others with some frequency (Melton et al., 1998; Nansel et al., 2001).
- Recent statistics show that while school violence has declined 4% during the past several years, the incidence of behaviors such as bullying, has increased 5% between 1999 and 2001 (U.S. Dept. of Ed., 2002).
- In surveys of third through eighth graders in fourteen Massachusetts schools, nearly half who had been frequently bullied reported that the bullying lasted six months or longer (Mullin-Rindler, 2003).
- Research indicates that children with disabilities or special needs may be at a higher risk of being bullied than other children (see Rigby, 2002, for review).

Bullying and Gender

- By self-report, boys are more likely than girls to bully others (Nansel et al., 2001; Banks 1997).
- Girls frequently report being bullied by both boys and girls, but boys report that they are most often bullied only by other boys. (Melton et al., 1998; Olweus, 1993).
- Verbal bullying is the most frequent form of bullying experienced by boys and girls. Boys are more likely to be physically bullied by their peers (Olweus, 1993; Nansel et al., 2001); girls are more likely to report being targets of rumor-spreading and sexual comments (Nansel et al., 2001). Girls are more likely to bully each other through social exclusion (Olweus, 2002).

Consequences of Bullying

- Stresses of being bullied can interfere with student's engagement and learning in school (NEA today, 1999).
- Children and youth who are bullied are more likely than other children to be depressed, lonely, anxious, have low self-esteem, feel unwell, and think about suicide (Limber, 2002; Olweus, 1993).
- Students who are bullied may fear going to school, using the bathroom, and riding on the school bus (NEA, 2003).
- In a survey of third through eighth graders in fourteen Massachusetts schools, more than 14% reported that they were often afraid of being bullied (Mullin-Rindler, 2003).
- Research shows that bullying can be a sign of other serious antisocial and/or violent behavior. Children and youth who frequently bully their peers are more likely than others to get into frequent fights, be injured in a fight, vandalize or steal property, drink alcohol, smoke, be truant from school, drop out of school, and carry a weapon (Nansel et al., 2003; Olweus, 1993).
- Bullying also has an impact on other students at school who are bystanders to bullying (Banks, 1997). Bullying creates a climate of fear and disrespect in schools and has a negative impact on student learning (NEA, 2003).

Children Who Bully

Children who bully tend to have average or above-average self-esteem. Other characteristics may include:

- Impulsive, hot-headed personalities
- Be easily frustrated
- Lack of empathy
- Difficulty conforming to rules
- Positive attitudes toward violence (Olweus, 1993)
- Boys who bully tend to be physically stronger than other children

Family Risk Factors for Bullying

Children who bully are more likely than their non-bullying peers to live in homes where there is:

- A lack of warmth and involvement on the part of parents
- Overly-permissive parenting (including a lack of limits for children's behaviors)
- A lack of supervision by parents
- Harsh, physical discipline
- A model for bullying behavior

Peer Risk Factors for Bullying

- Children and youth who bully are more likely to have friends who bully and who have positive attitudes toward violence.

Common Myths about Children Who Bully

"Children who bully are loners"

- In fact, research indicates that children and youth who bully are not socially isolated.
- They report having an easier time making friends than children and youth who do not bully.
- Children and youth who bully usually have at least a small group of friends who support or encourage their bullying.

"Children who bully have low self-esteem."

- In fact, most research indicates that children and youth who bully have average or above-average self-esteem.
- Interventions that focus on building the self-esteem of children who bully probably will be ineffective in stopping bullying behavior.

WHY DO KIDS BULLY OTHER KIDS?

There are all kinds of reasons why young people bully others, either occasionally or often. Here are a few reasons that kids have given for why they bully others:

- Because I see others doing it.
- Because it's what you do if you want to hang out with the right crowd.
- Because it makes me feel stronger, smarter, or better than the person I'm bullying.
- Because it's one of the best ways to keep others from bullying me.

Whatever the reason, bullying is something we need to address. Whether we've done it ourselves, or whether friends or other people we know are doing it, we all need to recognize that bullying has a terrible effect on the lives of young people. It may not be happening to you today, but it could tomorrow. Working together, we can make the lives of young people better.

ARE YOU BEING BULLIED?

Bullying is a widespread problem among young people today. There are lots of kids all over the world that get bullied each day. Some kids are bullied because of the color of their skin; others for their religion. There is no one reason why people bully others.

Here are a few tips on what you can do if you are being bullied.

Always tell an adult. Find an adult that you can trust who will do something about it. Examples might be a teacher, school counselor, parent, youth minister, neighbor, or coach. It may be hard to tell them at first, but you will feel better knowing that you have someone on your side that can help you. If you tell an adult and they do not do anything about it, tell someone else. No one has the right to bully you, and it should be stopped.

Stay in a group. People who bully tend to pick on kids who are by themselves. It's easier, and they are more likely to get away with their bad behavior.

If it feels safe, try standing up to the person who is bullying you. Even if it's a simple, "Hey, cut it out!" or "Leave me alone!" Say or do something that lets the bully know that you can stand up for yourself. This doesn't mean you should fight back or bully them back. Kids who bully like to see you upset, so be as calm as possible. Always tell an adult if someone is bullying you.

Join clubs or take part in activities where you'll meet other kids. The more friends you have, the less likely you are to be bullied. This goes back to the 'Stay in a group' tip above. Bullies tend to pick on people who are considered loners and off by themselves.

WHAT **NOT** TO DO IF YOU ARE BULLIED:

Don't . . .

- Think it's your fault. No one deserves to be bullied.
- Fight back or bully a person back. This probably won't make the situation any better, and it might get you into big trouble.
- Keep it to yourself and just hope that the bullying will go away. Don't try to ignore bullying and hope that it will stop—or hope that the bully will start picking on someone else. Often, bullying won't stop until other kids or adults get involved, so be sure to report bullying.
- Stop school or avoid clubs or sports because you're afraid. Missing out on school or activities that you enjoy isn't the answer.
- Seclude yourself from others. Bully's like to pick on people who have isolated themselves.
- Quit things you enjoy doing to avoid being bullied. Take friends with you to do those activities. Kids who bully are less likely to bully you if you are in a group.

DO YOU BULLY OTHERS?

Do you bully others? Good question! Here are a few questions to ask yourself:

- Have you ever used your size to intimidate someone else?
- Have you ever used your popularity to intentionally leave someone out?
- Have you ever physically hurt someone to get your way?
- Have you ever spread a rumor about someone that was hurtful in conversation, whether in a note or through e-mail or text messaging?
- Have you ever had someone else hurt someone you don't like?
- Have you and your friends ever intentionally kept one or more kids from hanging out with you? For example, at your lunch table at school, during sports, or during other activities.
- Have you ever teased someone in a mean way by calling them a name, making fun of their appearance, or the way they talk, dress, or act?
- Have you ever been part of a group that did any of these things—even if you only wanted to be part of the crowd?

If you said *yes* to any of these questions, you have bullied someone! Being aware of the fact you might bully others is the first step to changing your behaviors. Bullying is serious business. It causes young people a lot of pain, and it can affect their ability to do well in school as well as their general happiness.

References

Ahmad, Y. & Smith, P.K. (1994). Bullying in schools and the issue of sex differences. In *Male Violence,* J Archer (Ed). NY: Rutledge.

Banks, R. (1997). *Bullying in schools* (ERIC Report No. EDO-PS-97-170.) University of Illinois, Champaign, Ill.

Bosworth, K., Espelage, D.L., & Simon, T. (1999). Factors associated with bullying behavior in middle school students. *Journal of Early Adolescence,* 19, 341–362.

Cairnes, R.B., Cairnes, B.C., Neckerman, H.J., Gest, S.D., & Gariepy. J.L. (1988). Social networks and aggressive behavior: Peer support or Peer rejection? *Developmental Psychology,* 24, 815–823.

Chase, B. (March 25, 2001). Bully proofing our schools: To eliminate bullying, first we must agree not to tolerate it. Editorial. www.nea.org/publiced/chase/bc010325.html.

Cohen, R. (2002, February). Stop mediating these conflicts now! *The School Mediator: Peer Mediation Insights from the Desk of Richard Cohen.* Electronic newsletter, School Mediation Associates. www.schoolmediation.com.

Limber, S.P. (2002). *Addressing youth bullying behaviors.* Proceedings from the American Medical Association Educational Forum on Adolescent Health: Youth Bullying. Chicago, IL: American Medical Association. www.ama-assn.org/ama1/pub/upload/mm/39/youth bullying.pdf

Limber, S.P. (2004, Winter). What works—and doesn't work—in bullying prevention and intervention. Student Assistance Journal. 16–19.

Melton, G.B., Limber, S., Flerx, V., Cunningham, P., Osgood, D.W., Chambers, J., Henggler, S., & Nation, M. (1998). "Violence among rural youth." Final report to the Office of Juvenile Justice and Delinquency Prevention.

Mullin-Rindler, N. (2003). *Findings from the Massachusetts Bullying Prevention Initiative.* Unpublished manuscript.

Nansel, T.R., Overpeck, M.D., Haynie, D.L., Ruan, W.J., & Scheidt, P.C. (2003). Relationships between bullying and violence among US Youth. *Journal of American Medical Association,* 285, 2094–2100.

Nansel, T., Overpeck, M., Pilla, R.S., Ruan, W.J., Simmons-Morton, B., & Schmidt, P. (2001). Bullying behaviors among US youth. *Journal of American Medical Association,* 285, 2094–2100.

National Education Association. (1995). "Youth risk behavior survey data results." www.nea.org.

National Education Association. (2003a). "National bullying awareness campaign." www.nea.org/schoolsafety/bullying.html.

National Education Association. (2003b). "Parents role in bullying prevention and intervention." www.nea.org/schoolsafety/bullyingparentsrole.html.

National Education Association. (2003c). "School safety facts." www.nea.org/schoolsafety/ssfacts.html.

National Education Association. (2003d). "Youth violence intervention and prevention." www.naspoline.org/advocacy/youth_violence.html.

NEA Today. (1999). *Easing the strain of students' stress*. Departments: Health. September 1999. NEA Washington, DC. www.nea.org/neatoday/9909/health.html.

Olweus, D. (1993). *Bullying at school: What we know and what we can do*. Cambridge, MA: Blackwell Publishers, Inc.

Olweus, D., Limber, S., & Mihalic, S. (1999). *The Bullying Prevention Program. Blueprints for Violence Prevention*. Boulder, CO: Center for the Study and Prevention of Violence.

Rigby, K. (2002). *New perspectives on bullying*. London: Jessica Kingsley Publications.

Roland, E. (1989). A system oriented strategy against bullying. In E. Roland & E. Munthe (Eds). *Bullying: An international perspective*. London: David Fulton Publishers.

Smith, P.K., & Sharp, S. (1994). *School bullying: Insights and perspectives*. London: Routledge.

Stop Bullying Now, www.stopbullyingnow.hrsa.gov.

U.S. Department of Education, National Center for Education Statistics, *The Continuation of Education 2002*, NCES 2002-025, Washington DC: US. Government Printing Office, 2002. http://nces.ed.gov/

Best Practices in Bullying Prevention

A review of bullying prevention programs and feedback from educators in the field led us to suggest ten strategies that represent best practices in bullying prevention and intervention.

1. Focus on the social environment of the program. In order to reduce bullying, it is important to change the social climate of the program and the social norms with regard to bullying. This requires the efforts of everyone in the program environment—directors, staff members, administrators, counselors, facilitators, parents, and children.

2. Assess bullying in your program. Adults are not always very good at estimating the nature and prevalence of bullying in their program. As a result, it can be quite useful to administer an anonymous questionnaire to kids about bullying.

3. Obtain staff and parent buy-in and support for bullying prevention. Bullying prevention should not be the sole responsibility of any single individual at an organization. To be most effective, bullying prevention efforts require buy-in from the majority of the staff and from the parents. However, bullying prevention efforts should still begin even if immediate buy-in from all isn't achievable. Usually, more and more supporters will join the effort once they see what it's accomplishing.

4. Form a group to coordinate the program's bullying prevention activities. Bullying prevention efforts seem to work best if they are coordinated by a representative group from the program.

5. Provide training for the staff in bullying prevention. All administrators and staff at an organization should be trained in bullying prevention and intervention. Specialized training can help staff members to better understand the nature of bullying and its effects, how to respond if they observe bullying, and how to work with others in your program to help prevent bullying.

6. Establish and enforce rules and policies related to bullying. Developing simple, clear rules about bullying can help to ensure that kids are aware of adult expectations: that they not bully others and that they help kids who are bullied. Organization rules and policies should be posted and discussed with kids and parents. Appropriate positive and negative consequences should be developed.

7. Increase adult supervision in "hot spots" for bullying. Bullying tends to thrive in locations where adults are not present or are not watchful. Adults should look for creative ways to increase adult presence in locations that kids identify as "hot spots."

8. Intervene consistently and appropriately when you see bullying. Observed or suspected bullying should never be ignored by adults. All staff should learn effective strategies to intervene on-the-spot to stop bullying. Staff members also should be designated to hold sensitive follow-up meetings with kids who are bullied and (separately) with kids who bully. Staff members should involve parents whenever possible.

9. Devote some program time to bullying prevention. Kids can benefit if staff set aside a regular period of time (e.g., 20–45 minutes each week) to discuss bullying and improving peer relations. This book is packed full of activities to do in that time slot! These meetings can help staff to keep their fingers on the pulse of kids' concerns, allow time for discussions about bullying and the harms that it can cause, and provide tools for students to address bullying problems.

10. Continue these efforts. There should be no "end date" for bullying prevention activities. Bullying prevention should be continued over time and woven into the fabric of your program environment.

*This information is based, in part on: Limber, S.P. (2004, Winter). What works—and doesn't work—in bullying prevention and intervention. *Student Assistance Journal,* 16–19.

Source: modified from: http://www.stopbullyingnow.hrsa.gov/indexAdult.asp?Area=bestpractices

Activities Section

All Mixed Up

This activity is a lot like the popular game of Scrabble™ and is a great way to get people working together.

TYPE OF INITIATIVE

Icebreaker/Problem Solving

SOURCE

Modified from 4-H Teambuilding Facilitation Manual, 2002 Penn State University

GROUP SIZE

6–20

PROPS NEEDED

You will need at least 30 index cards, the 3 × 5 size works well, but we prefer the larger 5 × 7 size, as it is much easier to see them from across the room. Cards that are brightly colored add to the fun. You can also use plain computer paper if you so desire. Multiple writing utensils, such as colored pencils, markers, or crayons, are also required. Lastly, you will need an open area to lay down the cards.

PURPOSE

All Mixed Up is a great icebreaker. This activity creates opportunities for conversations with a focus on solving a task.

DIRECTIONS

- Begin by giving each player a 3 × 5 card (or other chosen paper material) and a marker. Ask everyone to write one vowel and one consonant on the card they have. These letters should be kept in confidence until instructed to reveal one side or another.
- In the first round, instruct the group to create as many two- or three-letter words as they can. Once you have joined a word, you must stay with that group until we move into the next round.
- For round two, increase the length of the word to four or five letters. Consider having a pile of extra letters in the middle of the room and let the group know that prior to any round they may exchange their sheet or card for a new one.

- Continue to play until you have words that are at least six letters in length. These groupings must form a word. The word must have one letter per participant. When forming a word, it is important for the participants to know they can use either side of their card but not both sides at the same time.
- After a minute or so, allow participants to exchange cards with those that have not yet joined a word, or allow them to exchange cards from the pile of extra words.

VARIATION

Using the same set of cards and letters, ask the large group to again break into smaller groups and then arrange their cards into real words. The word needs to be at least three letters in length. Every word must be attached in some way to another word—like a big crossword puzzle. You can give out some wildcards, but everyone in the group must agree on the wildcard letter.

DEBRIEFING TOPICS

- What value did we put on certain letters?
- Did some letters get ignored while others we prized no matter what?
- How is that relevant to conflict resolution of bully awareness?
- At what point in your life have you been the popular letter "e" and when were you the letter "x"?

FACILITATOR NOTES

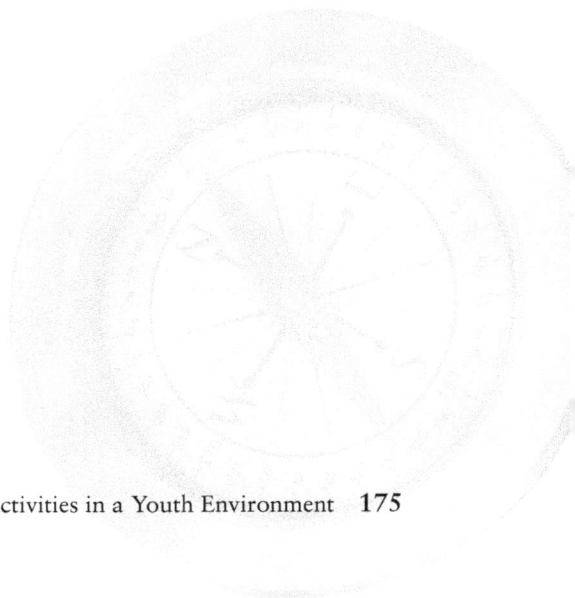

As If

TYPE OF INITIATIVE
Icebreaker

SOURCE
Relayed to us by Chris Cavert who learned it from "Steve the Aussie" at the 2006 National Challenge Course Practitioner Symposium

PROPS NEEDED
None

GROUP SIZE
2–100

DIRECTIONS

Divide your group into pairs. Begin this activity by letting participants know that you will give them a relationship role to play for the upcoming interaction. Have the pairs stand about 15 feet apart from one another. Have them determine which partner will be the "greeter" and which partner will play out the "role." Each interaction is approximately 20–30 seconds in duration. Then announce the first interaction.

Ask your group to greet another person in the room **AS IF** you are:

* best friends

Let this interaction go on for 20–30 seconds. Afterward, briefly process what happened in this interaction, what some of the feelings were, and the general mood of the interaction. Then proceed with another role. Here are some examples of other roles you could use:

- cousins
- someone you don't hang out with normally
- your teacher
- the author of your favorite book
- a friend you had a conflict with
- someone you saw being a bully on the playground
- the President of the United States
- a classmate you are intimidated by
- a famous musician
- someone who does not speak English (or the dominant language of the group)
- a favorite actor or actress

You can come up with as many different AS IF scenarios as you wish. This is a great follow-up activity to the Handshakes activity.

When introducing this exercise, tell the group that there may be periods of uncomfortable interaction, or there may be periods of joy, anger, or frustration. You will find that the way people greet one another is open to an incredible amount of interpretation. For example, just about everyone greets their best friend with a hug or a handshake, and it typically involves some shouting and a lot of asking "what's up?" However, a greeting between someone you saw bully someone else can vary greatly. Some people will confront the behavior, while others will ignore it. By the time we see folks introducing themselves to the President, we observe many different approaches . . . some are thrilled, others are rude, and some pretend to be violent. My response is "really?" That is REALLY how you would great the President? My comments following this activity are always the same, and they typically go something like this: "Would you agree that everyone we greeted today is human? Is it safe to say that all humans deserve the same respect in terms of being polite to one another? This activity provides examples of how our attitude and belief systems affect our ability to be respectful of one another. Does that make sense?"

Also, allowing the participants to practice how to greet someone they have had a conflict with can be good experience for the future. Have the pairs greet one another as they normally would when they are in a conflict with someone. Then have them practice a second time how they would *like* to greet someone they are in a conflict with. Sometimes practicing a desired behavior in an uncomfortable situation can help in a later instance when a conflict arises.

DEBRIEFING TOPICS

- What did you notice?
- Who was uncomfortable with some of the early "as if" situations?
- What about the later introductions?
- What did you notice about non-verbal body language with the different roles?
- How did your attitude change during the exercise?
- Would you agree that everyone we "greeted" today is human? Is it safe to say that all humans deserve the same respect in terms of being polite to one another?

FACILITATOR NOTES

Award-Winning Drama

Conflict in the Movies

TYPE OF INITIATIVE
Discussion and Drama

PURPOSE
Participants will brainstorm different conflict situations in movies and process through the reality of the ending.

SOURCE
Adapted from an idea given in a workshop.

PROPS NEEDED
Imagination

GROUP SIZE
2–20

DIRECTIONS
The movies are full of drama, and so are conflict situations! Kids are naturally drawn to movies, drama, and books. Much of literature is focused on a point of conflict for the character in a story. Movies are sometimes criticized for having "Hollywood endings," in which conflict is resolved in an unrealistic way in order to provide a happy ending. Not all conflict is resolved with happy endings. If children are allowed to practice how they would resolve a conflict, it will help them when an actual conflict arises.

- Have students brainstorm a list of their favorite movies.
- Assign students to choose one movie and rewrite the ending so that the conflict is not resolved, or it is resolved in what they believe to be more realistic. Host classroom "Oscars" the next day, allowing students to choose the best one or two new endings. Divide the class into groups according to the number of Oscar winners selected, and have students write scripts for their new movie endings and then perform them.
- After each performance, discuss the questions that follow.

DEBRIEFING TOPICS

- What was the point of conflict, and was it resolved with a Hollywood ending?
- Which ending was more true to life?
- Which provided a more important lesson?
- How can we apply the lessons of stories that seem very far removed from reality?

As an extension, students may want to read the novel *Violet and Claire*, by Lia Block. The plot revolves around their ambition to make a movie, which comes to represent the world as they wish it to be.

FACILITATOR NOTES

Batten Down the Hatches

TYPE OF INITIATIVE

Conflict resolution, reaching win-win solutions, consensus

SOURCE

Laurie Frank, Goal Consulting

PROPS NEEDED

A list of household items like the one shown here

LEVEL

Grades 6 and higher

SOURCES

This activity is from the book, *Journey Towards the Caring Classroom*, by Laurie Frank. This is an adaptation of a classic Values Clarification exercise. See also "Stranded!" in *Cowstails and Cobras* by Rohnke.

LIST OF SUPPLIES

Matches
Five gallons of gasoline
Tent with stakes and poles
Case of dog food
Rain coat for each person
10-pound bag of oranges
Charcoal grill
Charcoal
Package of toilet paper

Car keys
Flashlight with new batteries
Suitcase with a change of clothes for each person
Winter coat for each person
Five boxes of Pop Tarts®
Gallon of milk
Weather radio
Three pounds of cheese

© 2004 Laurie Frank

Family photo album   Jack knife
Video game   Box of 10 candles
Road atlas of the United States   Cell phone
Five gallons of water   Emergency flares

DIRECTIONS

1. Tell the group that they are living in southern Florida, and there has just been news of a large hurricane heading their way. The evacuation notice has just gone out. They have 15 minutes to gather up everything they need before leaving. Due to limited space, they can only take 15 items with them, not including people and pets. The family consists of two kids, parents, and the family dog, Juno.

2. Give each person a list of supplies. Have participants rank their top 15 items.

3. Divide them into groups of 4–6.

4. Review the idea of win-win solutions and reaching consensus.

5. Ask each group to reach consensus and list at least their top 5 items. If they get that far, then have them continue to rank the other 10.

6. Have each group report their top 5 to 15 items to the group.

VARIATION

For older students: Instead of giving them a list, have them each come up with their own top 10 to 15 items. Then come to consensus on which 10 to 15 items to take.

EXTENSIONS

•   Discuss issues and instances where the students might be unwilling to be flexible. These can be issues of principle or values that are near and dear to them.

DEBRIEFING TOPICS

•   Which items were easy to agree on? What were some of your disagreements about?
•   How did you reach a consensus on the items? What strategies did you use?
•   Did you feel that you arrived at win-win solutions? Why or why not?

Consensus activities like this can really be a struggle for some people. Many times it is relatively easy to choose the 15 items to keep; the interesting part is attempting to rank those items. Here are a few hints that might make the reaching of consensus a little easier:

1. Avoid arguing. Try to present ideas logically.

2. Listen to others. They may just convince you to change your mind.

3. It isn't necessary to win or lose. If agreement stalls, look for the next best alternative.

4. Don't agree just to avoid conflict. Yield only if other sides make sense.

5. Avoid conflict-reducing tactics. Don't flip a coin to decide. Look for the win-win through compromise.

6. Disagreements are healthy. Everyone has a different opinion. Work through disagreements and, possibly, you'll find a great solution.

FACILITATOR NOTES

ADAPTATIONS FOR STUDENTS WITH DISABILITIES: BATTEN DOWN THE HATCHES

Cognitive Disabilities	• Have fewer items to consider. • Do not insist on consensus for all things. Have students agree on a few and talk about why they picked these items.
Orthopedic Impairment	• No major modifications necessary.
Hearing Impairment	• No major modifications necessary. • Have interpreters available to facilitate communication if necessary.
Visual Impairment	• Have the list of supplies written in Braille. • Have 3-D representations of each item.

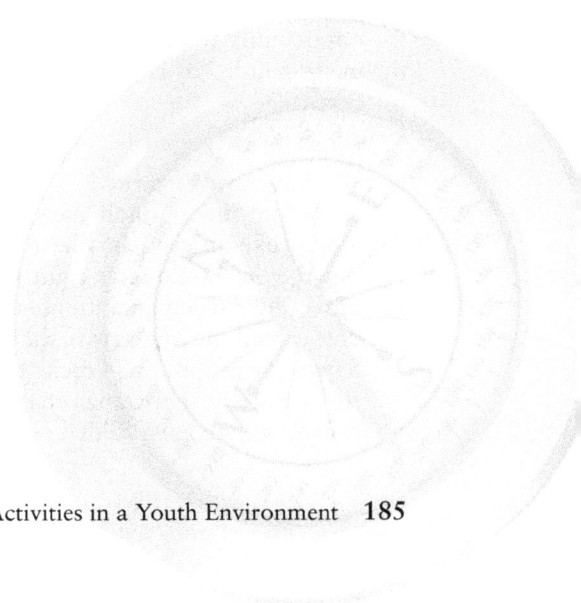

The Blind Men and the Elephant

by John Godfrey Saxon

TYPE OF INITIATIVE

Perspective

SOURCE

http://en.wikipedia.org/wiki/Blind_Men_and_an_Elephant (downloaded on 12/18/06)

PROPS NEEDED

You will need at least one copy of the Blind Men poem and one blank sheet of paper for each participant. You will also need multiple writing utensils, such as pencils, markers, crayons, or colored pencils.

GROUP SIZE

1–40

A NOTE FROM MIKE

When I was teaching middle school, I was constantly looking for exercises that engaged more than one learning style . . . something that appealed to the kids that needed something visual. The Blind Men and The Elephant accomplished this. This exercise gave kids (and adults alike) the opportunity to explore differences in perspective without having to be analytical or "find the missing link," as is the case in so many of the perspective puzzles we use.

DIRECTIONS

- Begin by giving instructions for how to fold the paper. First, fold it in half the long way (like a hotdog), then in half the short way (like a hamburger), and then in half the short way again (like an even smaller hamburger) . . . now unfold completely. When you open the paper, you should have eight rectangles.
- Have the participants number each rectangle from 1 to 8 starting in the upper-left-hand corner and moving across the paper.
- Say to the group: "As I recite the following poem to you, one stanza at a time, please draw the picture of that stanza that develops in your mind's eye. There are eight stanzas to the poem; one for each folded rectangle on your piece of paper."

The Blind Men and the Elephant

It was six men of Indostan, to learning much inclined, who went to see the elephant (Though all of them were blind), that each by observation, might satisfy his mind.

The first approached the elephant, and, happening to fall, against his broad and sturdy side, at once began to bawl: "God bless me! but the elephant, is nothing but a wall!"

The second feeling of the tusk, cried: "Ho! what have we here, so very round and smooth and sharp? To me tis mighty clear, this wonder of an elephant, is very like a spear!"

The third approached the animal, and, happening to take, the squirming trunk within his hands, "I see," quoth he, "the elephant is very like a snake!"

The fourth reached out his eager hand, and felt about the knee: "What most this wondrous beast is like, is mighty plain," quoth he; "Tis clear enough the elephant is very like a tree."

The fifth, who chanced to touch the ear, Said; "E'en the blindest man can tell what this resembles most; Deny the fact who can, This marvel of an elephant, is very like a fan!"

The sixth no sooner had begun, about the beast to grope, than, seizing on the swinging tail, that fell within his scope, "I see," quothe he, "the elephant is very like a rope!"

And so these men of Indostan, disputed loud and long, each in his own opinion, exceeding stiff and strong, Though each was partly in the right, and all were in the wrong!

VARIATION

This activity can also be done in small groups. Each group will get eight large sheets of paper or poster board. The process is the same—read the stanza and then ask the group to draw what they see. You will need to allow a few minutes for the small groups to discuss what they "see" when they hear the stanza. Have the group draw one picture per sheet. At the conclusion of the drawing portion, hang the illustrations on the wall.

DEBRIEFING TOPICS

- What was the premise of the exercise?
- Who was right? Why or why not?
- What did the "blind men" learn?
- How could they have resolved their conflict?
- In your life, have you ever been part of a group that was in a similar situation? What did you do about it?

FACILITATOR NOTES

Blind Shapes

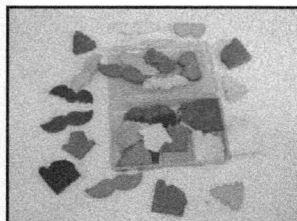

SOURCE

A Teachable Moment, pp. 196–197.

TYPE OF INITIATIVE

Problem Solving

PROPS NEEDED

Wooden, colored shapes; one piece for each participant. There should be 4–5 pieces that are similar in shape but different colors. One piece should be unique by shape and unlike the other pieces; it should have a similar color to other pieces in the set. We like to use a star shape for the unique piece, as it is easy to distinguish what it is without looking.

GROUP SIZE

10–100 people

DIRECTIONS

- This activity begins with the facilitator holding a bag filled with a variety of wooden shapes.
- Within the bag, most shapes come in a variety of colors.
- Participants are invited to each take a piece, but they cannot look at it, nor can they show this piece to anyone else. They are allowed to hold this piece, feel the shape, talk about it, describe it, and otherwise try to share information about their piece, but they *cannot look at it*.

- The facilitator provides the following minimal instruction to the group: "Find your people." Simply stated, everyone is looking to find the other group members that are holding a piece of wood similar to theirs.
- After a few minutes, the facilitator calls out "one more minute" and encourages everyone to find their people. At the end of this minute, everyone freezes location, and the facilitator allows them to look at their piece.

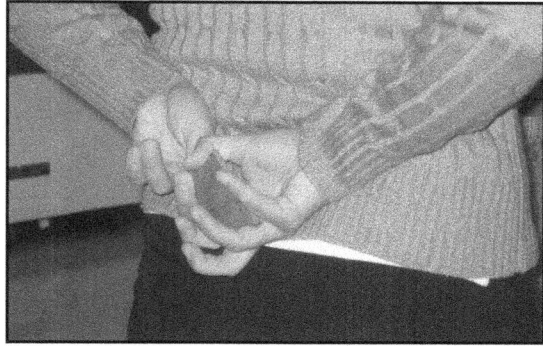

- Some groups form easily, as their shapes are easy to describe. Others are a bit more difficult to sort out. Some groups have other shapes mixed in (that's OK). And then there is the case of our one and only 'star' in the group. Here is a person with star qualities, but, unfortunately, there is only one star in the bag.
- The facilitator now begins the reviewing component of this activity, and asks, 'Where are my square shapes? Where are my triangles?'
- Next the facilitator can ask the 'star' participant to talk about their experience of trying to fit into other groups and trying to find their place in the group. What did it feel like to not fit in anywhere? Did other people push you away because you weren't like them? How did that feel?
- Finally, the facilitator can ask all the red team members to hold up their piece of wood. "Aren't these some of 'your people'?" Group members reply "yes, but we couldn't see their color." Which creates another teachable moment—aren't there people right now in your group that are part of 'your people,' but you just don't know that yet? What can you do to find them? What things do you have in common with others in this group that you have not discovered yet? Conflicts can often take place between people that are 'different' from each other. How can we foster an environment of acceptance and learning with this group? A discussion related to inclusion, invitation, and connection is suitable here, followed by the facilitator's command, "now you have one more minute . . . find your people . . . and make sure no one is left behind!"

DEBRIEFING TOPICS

- Identify where each shape is: Where are my houses? Where are my cats? Where are my trees? Etc.
- Where is my lone star? What was it like trying to fit in? How did others treat you? Did you join another group just so you could fit in?
- Ask the participants to look at the color of their wood shape. "If you have a red piece, please hold it up." Then ask, "Now aren't these some of your people, too but you just didn't know it? What do you have in common with others in this group that you have not discovered yet?"
- What is a common thread between all of the pieces? They are all made of wood. We have something in common with each person in this group.

- What does it feel like to not fit in? Was it easy to push people away or exclude people because they weren't like you?
- Are people that do not fit in well more likely to become a target of bullying?
- Can you think outside the box and come up with a common characteristic, such as, "All of the pieces are made of wood"?

FACILITATOR NOTES

Body Part Debrief

SOURCE

A Teachable Moment, pp. 59–62
Trademarked activity of Training Wheels. Created by Michelle Cummings.

TYPE OF ACTIVITY

Processing

PROPS NEEDED

Tossable items shaped like body parts

GROUP SIZE

1–20

PURPOSE

The Body Part Debrief activity is a great activity for both new and experienced facilitators. It is simple enough that groups of any age will understand it. The body parts have a 'coolness factor' to them that fosters a safe environment for people to talk. If you are having a hard time getting participants to share or reflect, this activity will help solve that problem.

The basic concept for this activity is that you have different balls or objects that are shaped like body parts. Each part can represent a metaphor related to that part. Many of the parts can have metaphors that relate to conflict, bullying, or other issues that arise in your group. For example:

Eye

- Could represent something new that you saw in yourself or someone else.
- What vision do you have for yourself/the group?
- What qualities do you see in yourself?
- Describe some of the warning signs you saw before the conflict happened.
- How did you see yourself perform within the group?
- Have you ever seen or witnessed bullying in your school?
- Do you keep an eye out for bullies? How?

Stomach

- Could represent something that took guts for you to do.
- What pushed you outside your comfort zone?

- What sick feelings have you felt before?
- What is your gut reaction to conflict?
- Was something hard for you to stomach?
- What does your gut do when someone starts to bully you?

Brain

- Could represent something new that you learned about yourself, a teammate, or the group.
- What thoughts do you have on conflict resolution?
- What did you learn through your experience?
- What have you learned about bullying that would prevent you from hurting someone else?
- Do people think consciously when bullying others? Why or why not?

Heart

- Could represent a feeling that you experienced.
- What things come from the heart?
- Name a few feelings that may happen during a conflict.
- What means a lot to you?
- How do you think bullies feel when they are bullying others?

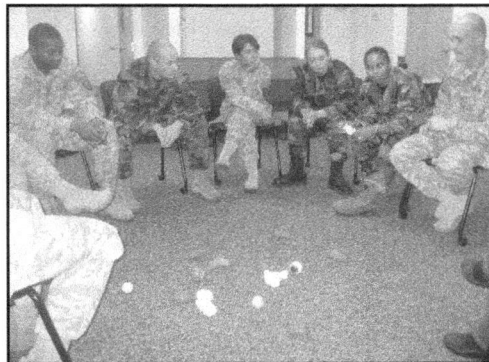

Hand

- In what way did the group support you?
- Could represent someone you think deserves a hand for a job well done.
- How did you lend a hand during the activity? Have you ever had a hand in bullying someone? In escalating a conflict?
- Have you ever physically used your hand in a bullying manner?

Ear

- Could represent something you listened to.
- What was a good idea you heard?
- How can being a good listener help dissolve a conflict?
- Could represent something that was hard to hear—did someone call you a bad name or make fun of you?
- When you hear bullying, what should you do?

Smiley face

- Could represent something that made you smile or laugh.
- What are some of your positive attributes?
- What are some positive attributes of the group?
- How can we look at conflict as something positive?

Foot

- What direction would you like to see yourself/the group go?
- Have you ever stuck your foot in your mouth and said something you wished you wouldn't have?
- Have you ever intentionally 'kicked' someone when they were down?
- How can we kick the cycle of harboring resentment as opposed to resolving a conflict in a healthy way?

Bone

- What strengths do you have?
- Have you ever come close to a breaking point?
- Have you ever felt emotionally broken by a bully?
- What are some of your breaking points when you are in conflict with someone?

Spine

- What is the backbone of your family or friends?
- What took a lot of backbone to do?
- Does standing up for yourself against a group of bullies take a lot of strength?

Nose

- Did you stick your nose into someone else's business?
- What really stunk about your performance? What would you have changed?
- Have you ever prevented someone from being bullied by 'sticking your nose' in someone else's business?
- Was this the right thing to do? Why?
- Have you ever escalated an argument between two people by 'sticking your nose' in the conflict?

World

- Although it's not a human body part, it is a living and breathing body. Use it to talk about how your actions affect others.
- What happens if we do not take care of our resources? Resources can be friends, family, our community, etc.
- Talk about the bigger picture of bullying in your program.
- How can looking at the big picture help resolve a conflict?

DIRECTIONS

There are many ways to use these metaphors. Here are a few of our favorites:

- Describe each part and then leave them in the center of the circle. Ask participants a question such as, "How do you feel about conflict?" Invite participants to think about which metaphoric part they would like to share with the group that relates to your question. Ask them to come forward and pick a ball that relates to their feeling. Depending on the time you have allotted for sharing, participants can share as much or as little as they want. Encourage each participant to share at least one time.
- Use each piece for a targeted metaphoric debrief to resolve a conflict.
- Present each ball and explain the different metaphors they could use to talk about when they receive that ball. Frontloading this activity can give the participants an idea of what to do. Once you describe a ball, toss it randomly to someone in the group. Then, as you describe the other balls, the person that received the first ball will have time to think about what they want to share. Once all of the balls are distributed within the circle, go back to the person that received the first ball. Ask them to share their thoughts with the group and then have them toss the ball randomly to someone else in the group. Move onto the second person you threw a ball to, etc. You can use as many balls as you would like; however, more than four balls can confuse the order in which people are supposed to talk.

FACILITATOR NOTES

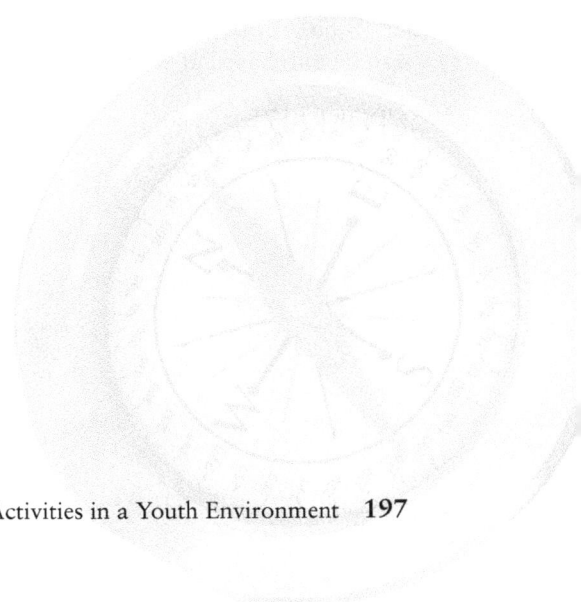

Building Our House

TYPE OF INITIATIVE

Processing

SOURCE

unknown (this exercise was first shared with Mike Anderson in the late 1990s at Bradford Woods)

PURPOSE

In the classroom, this activity allows students to share a bit about themselves in a thoughtful and controlled manner. The students choose their level of disclosure and draw or write on puzzle pieces as much or as little as they wish about the questions asked. Visually, a wall of "houses" creates conversation between students. These opportunities allow students to share more about themselves with others.

PROPS NEEDED

A blank universal puzzle called The Community Puzzle™. You will need one puzzle piece for each participant. Each puzzle piece is 4″ × 4″. If you give each student four puzzle pieces, it increases their work/drawing area to 16″ × 16″.

The Community Puzzle™ consists of large, blank universal puzzle pieces that go together in any order. Each person decorates their own puzzle piece in their own style. Puzzle pieces are interchangeable and fit together in any order. You may add more pieces for larger projects or groups. The standard Community Puzzle has 24 center pieces and 24 border pieces for a total of 48 pieces per puzzle. Center pieces measure 4″ × 4″. Border pieces are 2″ × 4″. The puzzle can be purchased at www.communitypuzzle.com

GROUP SIZE

1–40

DIRECTIONS

- Begin by distributing one piece of the Community Puzzle to each member of the group. The particular number of puzzle pieces does not matter as long as each participant receives at least one.
- Ask each participant to draw the skeleton of a house with:
  a. A foundation (the stronger the foundation the stronger the house)
  b. A chimney with smoke billowing out of it
  c. Windows (perhaps lots of windows)
  d. A door (maybe you feel like having a house with double doors)
  e. Next to the house, draw a big tree with roots and branches.

Make it YOUR house!!!

1. In the foundation, write your strengths. More than one is preferred; we all have many strengths. Your strengths may not be apparent to others. This is your chance to share and validate them.

2. Along the sidewalls of the house, write the names of two of the strongest influences in your life: people that give or have given you support in your life. These influences may be people that you have interacted with or a situation you have been involved with.

3. On the roof, write something that you are proud of. Are you proud of a personal accomplishment, like completing a marathon, or are you proud of the way you handled a family crisis?

4. In the windows, write what you are comfortable letting others "see." What characteristics or traits do you have that you are willing to share with others?

5. In the door, write a habit or personal quality that you would like to work on or improve (THIS IS NOT A PHYSICAL QUALITY). Do you have a short fuse? Are you too relaxed and do not react when you should?

6. In the chimney, write what you do to release pent up tension or to relax. How do you blow off steam? Do you go for a run? Do you read? Do you travel?

7. In the roots of the tree, write what keeps you "growing" or gives you life—is it work, family, or hobbies? Be specific.

8. In the branches of the tree, write what you see for your future. Where do you want to be ten years from now? Think of your future in terms of a "Keynote Address." What would you like the audience to know about your accomplishments?

VARIATION

Have the group create one large house together. Each person can contribute to the creation of the house design and share their personal contributions. The first step is for the team to assemble the blank puzzle. Have one person sketch the skeleton of the house and the rest of the group can decorate the house.

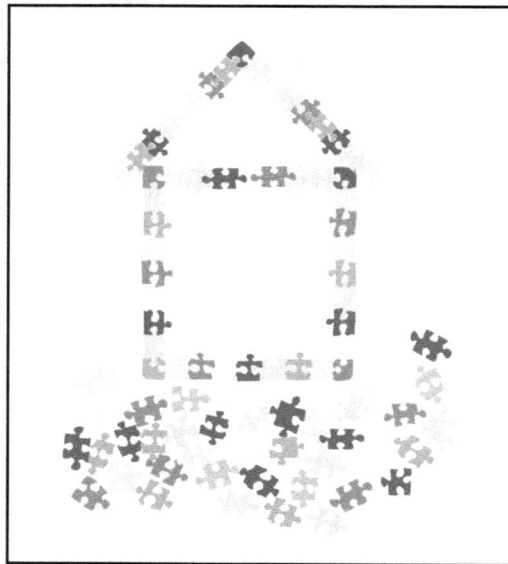

Image © 2010 JupiterImages Corporation.

VARIATION

Give each participant a large piece of poster paper, newsprint, or butcher paper. Deliver the same activity without using the puzzle. After each round, ask for volunteers to share a few of their insights.

DEBRIEFING TOPICS

- Take time to read each person's puzzle. Can you find similarities? Can you find differences?
- What is unique about your house?
- Do you see places where you can be an influence in another's life? Will you take that chance?
- What are some habits or personal qualities that you would like to improve?
- What are some ways you blow off steam?
- What are some of the things you listed that you are proud of?

FACILITATOR NOTES

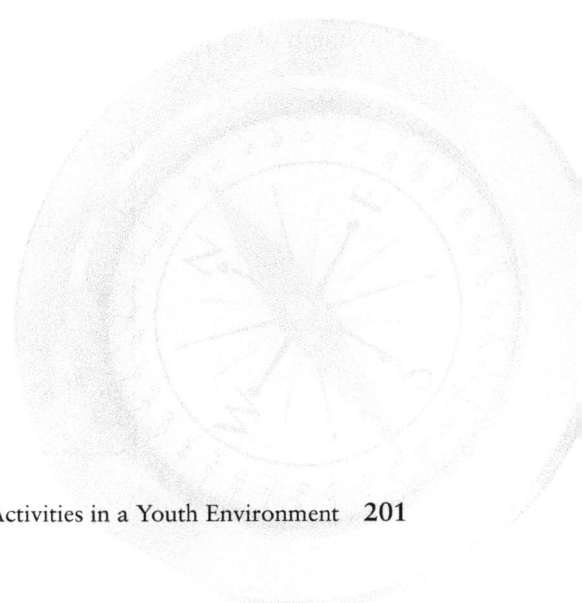

Buzz Ring

Talking in Circles

SOURCE

Introduced by Pat Rastall; further developed by Michelle Cummings

SOURCE

A Teachable Moment, pp. 67–68

PURPOSE

This physics phenomenon will have your participants talking about the 'Buzz Words' of conflict in a unique way.

TYPE OF INITIATIVE

Problem Solving, Processing

PROPS NEEDED

One buzz ring

GROUP SIZE

Maximum of 15 people per ring.

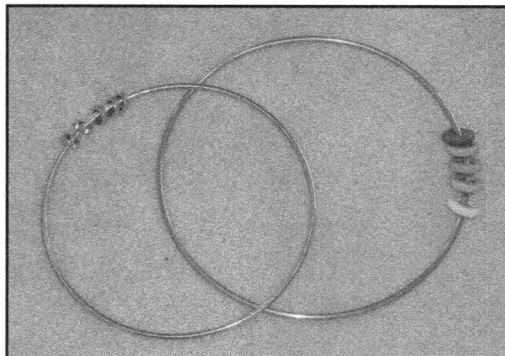

DIRECTIONS

- To begin this activity, identify the "buzz" words that your group may encounter during a conflict. For example, your group may come up with the words: communication, respect, positive language, trust, and conflict.
- Explain to the group that it takes a lot of effort to keep communication, respect, positive language, trust, and conflict working together simultaneously. Like most group work, it takes time and practice to master a new skill. Explain to the group that you are going to start the buzz ring and give them a task that is quite difficult to accomplish. Explain that you are not certain if they will be able to successfully complete the activity but would like to see how they do. Then start up your buzz ring.
- The object is to pass the buzz ring around the circle without stopping any of the rings from buzzing. As previously stated, this is a difficult task, and the majority of groups will not be successful their first attempt.
- While the group is passing the ring around, you can talk about the buzz words and what they will encounter throughout your program.
- If someone in the group makes the rings stop, process it immediately. This person is feeling some embarrassment, disappointment, stress, and may feel that they have let the group down. First, encourage them to get the rings going again. If they are unsuccessful, ask the group the following questions: "Has anyone ever done this before? Is it acceptable to the group that we do not have to be perfect the first time we attempt new tasks? How many people hoped that someone else would be the first to stop the rings before it was their turn?"
- At this point you can have the group set goals based on the number of mistakes they want to allow in one pass of the ring. Then help the group get the rings going again.
- Verbal encouragement from the facilitator helps in the group success. Encouraging statements include: "It's a simple hand-over-and motion. Communicate with the person next to you when you are ready to release the buzz ring into their possession."
- Encourage the group to celebrate after the ring makes it all the way around the group.

DEBRIEFING TOPICS

There are several things to bring up as you process this activity. Here are a few examples:

- Was anyone nervous to be the one receiving the ring? Why? Examples they may give may include not wanting to fail in front of the group or not wanting to let the group down by making a mistake. This opens up a great opportunity to talk about how those issues might come up throughout the program as the group works together. It is also good to point out that most people have not handled a buzz ring before, so being willing to try new things in front of the group is important. It encourages risk taking and emphasizes how small failures enable us to have success in the end.
- Starting the program with this activity creates a safe environment for participants to talk about any fears they may have about the day. Ending the program with this activity lets the group see how much they have learned together as a group.

- Sometimes if the rings stop in the process, a participant will give a good effort to get the rings going again but only get three of the five rings buzzing and then continue passing it around. This gives you a good avenue to talk about how difficult it can be to keep all five of the buzz words they came up with (communication, respect, positive language, trust, and conflict) going at one time. Can we have trust if we do not have respect at the same time? Some great dialogue around conflict can develop from this.
- Another way to use the buzz ring is to ask who in the group is good at multitasking. After those people admit (or do not admit!) to the skill, pass the buzzing ring around the circle and ask each participant to tell the group three things about themselves while keeping the rings buzzing. This is difficult for even great multitaskers!

SPECIFIC DEBRIEFING QUESTIONS

- Were you nervous to receive the ring? Why?
- What did your body do as the ring got closer to you?
- Did you hope that someone else made a mistake before the ring got to you?
- Has anyone ever tried this before? Is it acceptable to make mistakes the first time you try new tasks?
- In what ways can we as a group create an atmosphere of support and respect so people feel comfortable trying new things?
- How difficult is it to be successful at (the buzz words they chose) trust, teamwork, communication, bullying . . . at the same time?
- Was it risky to try something new in front of this group?
- How likely would you be to try something new in front of someone who had bullied you in the past?

SEQUENCING

The Buzz Ring can be implemented in many different ways. Here are a few suggestions:

1. Start and end the training with the Buzz Ring.

   Sequencing the Buzz Ring at the beginning of a program can set the tone for what you want to accomplish with the group. Giving them a task that is difficult to achieve, allows them to think metaphorically, creates some performance anxiety, and has the potential to push them outside their comfort zone is a wonderful first step when talking about the hard topic of conflict. Dealing with conflict is critical to successful teams and people and often takes a step-by-step approach to resolve. Being successful at the Buzz Ring activity is also a step-by-step sequence. Oftentimes we are not 100% successful at our attempts. The sequence of starting the program with the Buzz Ring allows the group to have the initial experience with the ring itself.

Ending the program with the Buzz Ring allows the group to have other experiences during the day of working together, effective communication, and more conversation about how to deal with conflict and each other. The more practice we have at resolving conflict and working together, the better we will be at it. Experience has shown that groups that end the program with the Buzz Ring have a higher success rate at completing the task with little to no errors. You will be amazed at how well groups do with this.

2. Use the Buzz Ring as a stand-alone activity.

The Buzz Ring activity works well as a stand-alone activity for many reasons. Because the buzz ring is such a unique tool participants often buy-in quickly due to the 'coolness factor' of what it physically does. Multiple learning styles are utilized—auditory, visual, and kinesthetic—so right away you have engaged a large percentage of your audience.

3. Debrief the Day: Pass the Buzz

Using the Buzz Ring as a wrap-up at the end of a training or workshop can be an effective way to encourage participants to 'Pass the Buzz' about what they learned.

At the end of the training, invite participants to form a circle. Present the buzz ring and start it buzzing. Then ask: "How do we keep the buzz going from this workshop?"

While keeping the buzz ring in motion, model a response by saying, "I learned more about the conflict styles of my co-workers. I'm going to use this knowledge to approach individuals differently if I have conflict with them (or whatever else may be appropriate from the workshop content)." Then pass the buzz ring to the next person in the circle.

When the next person gets the ring, he/she states what he/she will take from the workshop and passes the buzz ring to the next person. This pattern continues around the circle until the ring gets back to the facilitator.

If the ring stops buzzing as it goes around the circle, the person has to restart the buzz and mentions what might be an obstacle that could stop the buzz. After sharing this, they proceed with the initial question.

The fascination with the buzz ring combined with the reflection helps participants leave with a smile and an action plan.

GETTING THE BUZZ RING STARTED

Getting the rings to start can be tricky, and practicing ahead of time is a must. There are multiple ways to start the rings so finding your 'style' just takes some practice to figure out which system works best for you. Some place their palm down on the still rings and give them a good spin. By turning the large ring at the same time, the rings start buzzing. Others will slap straight down at the rings and turn the large ring at the same time to get them buzzing. Practice to see which method works best for you.

HERE ARE SOME BASIC INSTRUCTIONS

1. Hold the large metal ring in either hand.

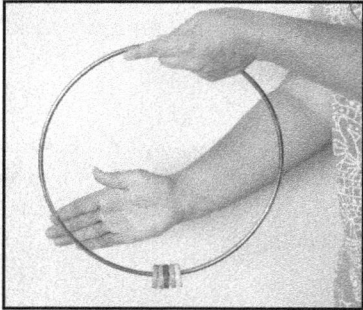

2. Use the other hand to spin-out the washers.

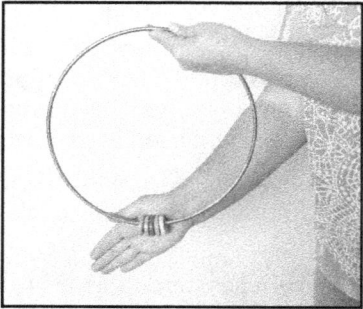

3. After the washers begin "spinning," quickly use both hands to smoothly rotate the large metal ring toward you.

The washers should continue to spin as long as you rotate the large ring.

WHAT ARE THE PHYSICS BEHIND THE BUZZ RING?/HOW DOES THE BUZZ RING WORK?

The buzz ring is really just five little tops of unusual design strung on a metal ring. Do you remember how tops appear to start "wobbling" as they slow down? This rotation of the spin axis is called precession and causes the ring to press on one side of the hole in the spinning top. The contact point between the ring and the top can be thought of as a gear that changes the motion of the upward-moving ring into the top's spinning motion.

WHERE TO FIND IT

Training Wheels, www.training-wheels.com 888.553.0147

FACILITATOR NOTES

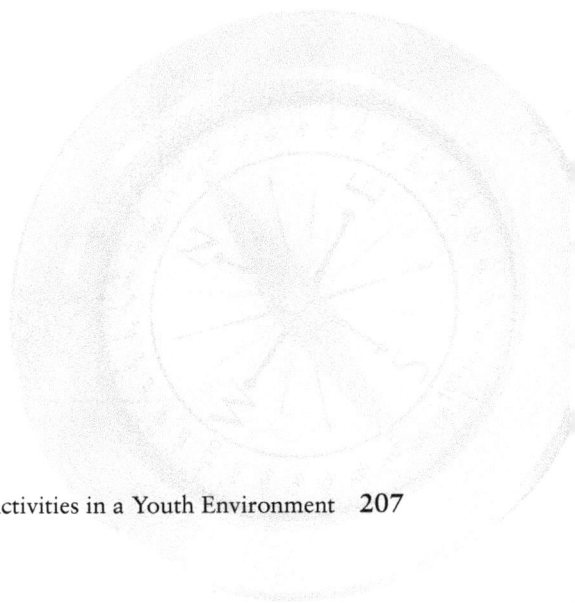

Change Debrief

TYPE OF INITIATIVE

Processing tool

SOURCE

Michelle Cummings. This activity was created out of an Internet story that circulated. Origin unknown. Michelle added parts to the activity to add more metaphor to the group application.

PROPS NEEDED

Objects shaped as an egg, a carrot, a coffee bean, a rock, and an ice cube. Props could be pictures of each item, the item itself, or stress relievers in the shape of each item.

GROUP SIZE

1–20

DIRECTIONS

Here is a truly unique tool to help organizations and individuals deal with change.

Set these parts out in front of your group, and ask them to describe their actions when put in a "hot water" situation. Frontloading the metaphors that accompany each part is important to the level of depth participants will share.

Egg

- In "hot water" situations, are you like an egg?
- Do you look the same on the outside but turn hard on the inside?
- How easy is it for you to put your "game face" on when talking to teammates about a decision that, on the inside, you are quite unhappy about?
- If an egg is left in boiling water too long, it will crack or explode.

Carrot

- What happens to a carrot when placed in boiling water?
- A carrot will turn soft and change itself dramatically as an effect of the hot water. Do you turn to mush and do whatever the "hot water" wants you to do when faced with a change?

Coffee Bean

- Are you like the coffee bean; do you change the "hot water" situation?
- Do you get energized about new changes or try to influence how the changes get implemented?

Rock

- When a rock is placed in a pot of boiling water, it will sink to the bottom and not change. What do you do with the "rocks" in your team—those that refuse to change while the change is happening around them?
- How does this change style encourage conflict within a team?

Ice Cube

- How are you like the ice cube? Do you try to diffuse the hot water situation? Are you a small ice cube that attempts to cool things down and then become overwhelmed with the situation and melt back into it? Or are you a large ice cube that really affects the hot water situation and sticks with it to diffuse it?

Oftentimes, individuals will go through each stage in a changing environment. Use the parts as a 'timeline' to describe a person's journey through the change.

DEBRIEFING QUESTIONS

- What do you think is your typical change stage when first faced with a new change?
- Does this stage encourage or prevent a conflict with others?
- How do you approach others who have different perspectives and opinions about the change?
- Describe the positive aspects of knowing what change stage each individual is in.

VARIATION

Here is a story that could be a good topic of discussion to use with The Change Debrief.

IN THE TEST KITCHEN OF LIFE

A young woman was complaining to her father about how difficult her life had become. He said nothing, but took her to the kitchen and set three pans of water to boiling. To the first pan, he added carrots; to the second, eggs; and to the third, ground coffee. After all three had cooked, he put their contents into separate bowls and asked his daughter to cut into the eggs and carrots and smell the coffee. "What does this all mean?" she asked impatiently.

"Each food," he said, "teaches us something about facing adversity, as represented by the boiling water. The carrot went in hard but came out soft and weak. The eggs went in fragile but came out hardened. The coffee, however, changed the water to something better."

"Which will you be like as you face life?" he asked. "Will you give up, become hard, or transform adversity into triumph? As the 'chef' of your own life, what will you bring to the table?"

WHERE TO FIND IT/HOW TO MAKE IT

Training Wheels sells a set of stress reliever parts for this activity. There are five parts packaged in a tidy 7 × 9-inch mesh envelope. The stress relievers are all made of polyurethane. Latex free. Visit www.training-wheels.com for more information.

You can also source all of these items from your kitchen and back yard. We recommend hard boiling the eggs before you bring them to your group!

SUGGESTION

If you are trying to encourage everyone to be like the coffee bean and be energized about the new changes, you could send everyone home with a bag of coffee beans encouraging them to be energetic change agents.

FACILITATOR NOTES

Choice and Consequences

TYPE OF INITIATIVE

Conflict resolution, making informed choices

PROPS NEEDED

Index cards with a choice written on each one, pen/pencil for each group of 3 to 4

LEVEL

Grades 2–5

SOURCE

Journey Towards the Caring Classroom, by Laurie Frank.

DIRECTIONS

1. Divide participants into small groups of 3 to 4, and have each group sit together.

2. Give each group one index card with a choice written on it and a pencil. Here are some examples of choices:

   - Helping a friend with his or her homework.
   - Sassing to the principal.
   - Asking your elderly neighbor if she needs help shoveling snow.
   - Yelling loudly in the car when someone is driving.
   - Not wearing a seatbelt.
   - Wearing a seatbelt.
   - Picking up litter when you see it on the sidewalk.
   - Seeing a younger kid who is crying and finding out what is wrong.
   - Throwing things at moving cars.
   - Doing all your homework.
   - Volunteering at the neighborhood or community center.
   - Seeing an argument between your friends and walking away.

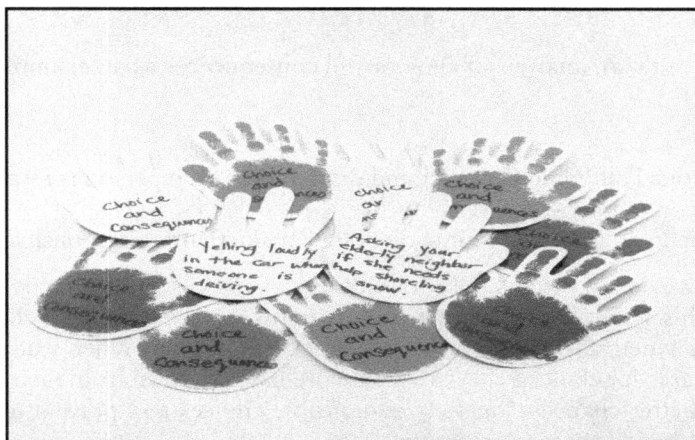

3. Have each group brainstorm as many consequences of that choice as they can think of. Give them a reasonable amount of time to complete that task. Remind them that there may be positive and negative consequences.

4. Have each group share three ideas from their list.

5. Discuss which of the choices from this list could be described as responsible, and which ones could be described as irresponsible.

6. Next, pass out two index cards to each group.

7. Ask them to come up with one responsible choice and one irresponsible choice. Write one on each card.

8. Periodically choose one of the cards to discuss as a whole class. What are the possible consequences of the choice? Why is it responsible or irresponsible?

DEBRIEFING TOPICS

- On the board write "Responsible choices" and brainstorm possible consequences of that. Do the same with "Irresponsible choices."
- If being responsible is a choice, how do you know when you are making a responsible choice? An irresponsible choice?
- Share a responsible and irresponsible choice you have made in your life to show that everyone does it. Then ask, "What do you think I learned from my irresponsible choice? From my responsible choice?"
- Is it possible to change irresponsible choices to responsible ones? How?
- What are some choices you make every day?
- How do you know these are choices?

VARIATION

As a class, first do an analysis of choices and consequences as an example.

EXTENSIONS

- Revisit your Full Value Contract and discuss how each person is responsible to each other and the community.
- Ask students to journal about choices they make that are responsible or irresponsible.

Many times we do not discuss the consequences of choices with students until they have made a bad one. This activity offers an opportunity to discuss the making of choices and the ensuing consequences when students are in a rational frame of mind. When students are subsequently held accountable for choices, they are then more likely to learn from their situations. They may also have a better chance of making responsible choices and preventing some conflicts and disagreeable situations from occurring.

FACILITATOR NOTES

Cognitive Disabilities	<ul><li>Have fewer items to consider.</li><li>Use examples from their daily routines.</li></ul>
Orthopedic Impairment	• No major modifications necessary.
Hearing Impairment	<ul><li>No major modifications necessary.</li><li>Have interpreters available to facilitate communication if necessary.</li></ul>
Visual Impairment	• No major modifications necessary.

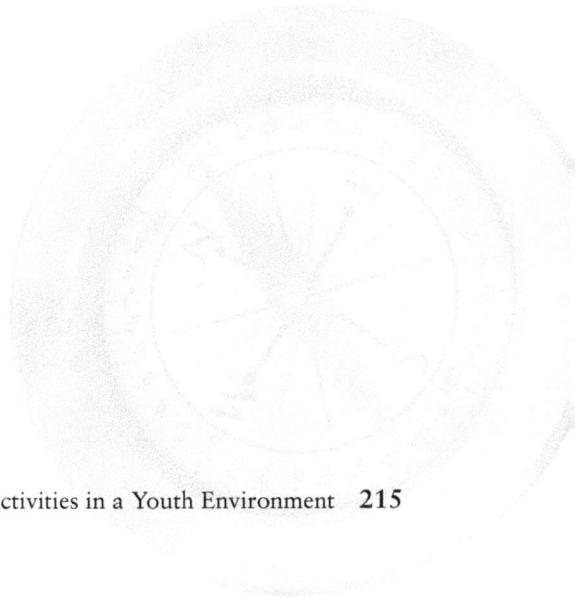

Conflict Animals

TYPE OF INITIATIVE

Debriefing tool and Conflict Resolution tool

SOURCE

The idea for this activity came from *Resolving Interpersonal Conflicts*, Chapter 8, pp. 254–257. The initial concept of these "conflict styles" (animals metaphor) came from Johnson & Johnson (1981) and was adapted from *Group Dynamics in the Outdoors: A Model for Teaching Outdoor Leaders* by Maurice L. Phipps of Western State College of Colorado, Wilderness Educator in The Wilderness Education Association Curriculum Guide, which was edited by David Cockrell. It was further developed by Michelle Cummings and Mike Anderson.

PROPS NEEDED FOR VARIATION #1

Pictures of or physical models of the following animals: turtle, shark, bear, fox, and owl.

PROPS NEEDED FOR VARIATION #2

Pictures of or physical models of the following animals: turtle, shark, bear, fox, owl, camel, bull, lion, mouse, panther, parrot, rabbit, cobra, chicken, elephant, horse, and mule. You will also need blank index cards and writing utensils for each participant.

VARIATION 1

Directions

Place the five animals in the center of the group (turtle, shark, bear, fox, and owl). Begin the conversation about conflict styles by asking your participants to share with you what they know (stereotyping) about the animal in question. It is important that you also know some basic biological information about each animal.

Once the group shares enough information, you can ask the participants to place themselves into those roles according to how they typically deal with conflict. Some questions to ask might include: Would you like to work for a "shark"? Do you know a "turtle" in your workplace or classroom? Who do you know that is an "owl"?

After a short discussion, place the animals around the room. Ask everyone to move to the location in the room with the animal that best represents their own conflict style. You could also put chart paper and markers in these same areas and have participants write down the similarities and differences in interpretation of each animal's qualities. The rule of feet applies at all times. If a participant feels that they need to move to another location, they are allowed. When each group is finished, encourage them to partner up with someone that was not in their conflict style group and discuss the information the small groups developed.

THE COMPETING SHARK (FORCE)

Forces and tries to make opponents accept his/her decisions; often threatening and intimidating

- Sharks use a forcing or competing conflict management style
- Sharks are highly goal-oriented
- Relationships take on a lower priority
- Sharks do not hesitate to use aggressive behavior to resolve conflicts
- Sharks can be autocratic, authoritative, uncooperative, threatening, and intimidating
- Sharks have a need to win; therefore others must lose, creating win-lose situations
- Advantage: If the shark's decision is correct, a better decision without compromise can result
- Disadvantage: May breed hostility and resentment toward the person using it
- Appropriate times to use a shark style:
  - when conflict involves personal differences that are difficult to change
  - when fostering intimate or supportive relationships is not critical
  - when others are likely to take advantage of noncompetitive behavior
  - when conflict resolution is urgent; when decision is vital in crisis
  - when unpopular decisions need to be implemented

FACILITATOR NOTES

THE AVOIDING TURTLE (WITHDRAW)

Withdraws from the conflict; hides until it is safe to emerge

- Turtles adopt an avoiding or withdrawing conflict management style
- Turtles would rather hide and ignore conflict than resolve it; this leads them to be uncooperative and unassertive
- Turtles tend to give up personal goals and display passive behavior, which creates lose-lose situations
- Advantage: May help to maintain relationships that would be hurt by conflict resolution
- Disadvantage: Conflicts remain unresolved; overuse of the style leads to others walking over them
- Appropriate times to use a turtle style:
  - when the stakes are not high or issue is trivial
  - when confrontation will hurt a working relationship
  - when there is little chance of satisfying your wants
  - when disruption outweighs benefit of conflict resolution
  - when gathering information is more important than an immediate decision
  - when others can more effectively resolve the conflict
  - when time constraints demand a delay

THE ACCOMMODATING TEDDY BEAR (SMOOTH)

Avoids the conflict when possible; ignores his/her own goals and resolves conflict by giving in to others

- Teddy bears use a smoothing or accommodating conflict management style with an emphasis on human relationships
- Teddy bears ignore their own goals and resolve conflict by giving into others; unassertive and cooperative, which creates a win-lose (bear is loser) situation
- Advantage: Accommodating maintains relationships
- Disadvantage: Giving in may not be productive; bear may be taken advantage of
- Appropriate times to use a teddy bear style:
  - when maintaining the relationship outweighs other considerations
  - when suggestions/changes are not important to the accommodator
  - when minimizing losses in situations where outmatched or losing
  - when time is limited or when harmony and stability are valued

THE COMPROMISING FOX (COMPROMISE)

Sly, sneaky, tricky, and able to persuades others to give up part of their most important and valued positions

- Foxes use a compromising conflict management style; concern is for goals and relationships
- Foxes are willing to sacrifice some of their goals while persuading others to give up part of theirs
- Compromise is assertive and cooperative; result is either win-lose or lose-lose
- Advantage: Relationships are maintained and conflicts are removed

- Disadvantage: Compromise may create less-than-ideal outcome and game playing can result
- Appropriate times to use a fox style:
  - when important/complex issues leave no clear or simple solutions
  - when all conflicting people are equal in power and have strong interests in different solutions
  - when there are no time restraints

THE COLLABORATING OWL (PROBLEM SOLVER)

Known throughout children's books as the wise old owl . . . the owl views conflicts as problems to be solved; confronting the sitations and seeking solutions that will satisfy both parties

- Owls use a collaborating or problem-confronting conflict management style that values their goals and relationships
- Owls view conflicts as problems to be solved; works to find solutions agreeable to all sides (win-win)
- Advantage: Both sides get what they want and negative feelings are eliminated
- Disadvantage: Takes a great deal of time and effort
- Appropriate times to use an owl style:
  - when maintaining relationships is important
  - when time is not a concern
  - when peer conflict is involved
  - when trying to gain commitment through consensus building
  - when learning and trying to merge differing perspectives

The chart below illustrates, depending on the importance of the result, which conflict style we might utilize in any given situation . . . the value of the goal versus the relationship is often the determining factor.

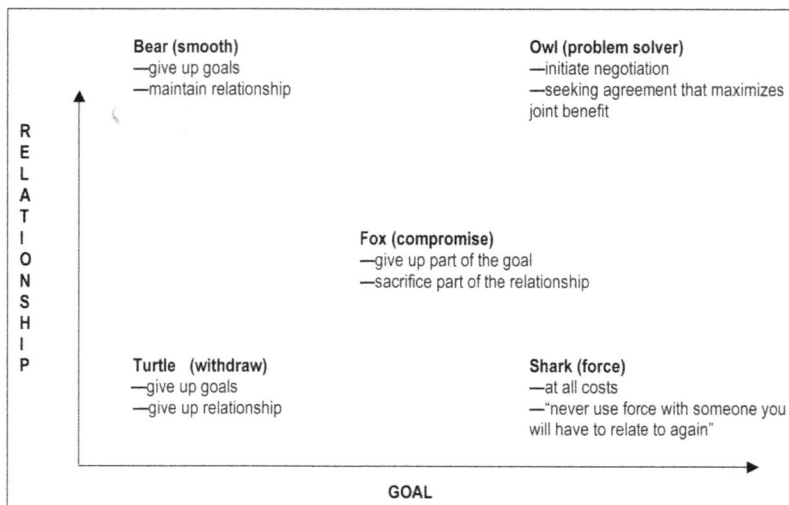

Bear (smooth)
—give up goals
—maintain relationship

Owl (problem solver)
—initiate negotiation
—seeking agreement that maximizes joint benefit

RELATIONSHIP

Fox (compromise)
—give up part of the goal
—sacrifice part of the relationship

Turtle (withdraw)
—give up goals
—give up relationship

Shark (force)
—at all costs
—"never use force with someone you will have to relate to again"

GOAL

VARIATION 2

Directions

Place a large collection of animals in the center of the group. Begin the conversation by asking your participants to share with you how each animal deals with conflict. Go through each of the animals you have in the center of the group. During the discussion ask the participants to be thinking about which animal conflict styles match their own conflict styles. Encourage them to think of other animals not represented by the props you have in the center and add them to the discussion.

After this discussion, pass out one index card and a few writing utensils to each participant. Ask them to pick three or four of the animals whose conflict styles match their own. Invite them to morph these three or four animals into one and draw it on their index card. Then ask them to re-name their new animal with a combination of the three animals. For example: If a participant chooses a tiger, a horse, and a dog for their three animals, they might draw the body of a horse with the arms of a tiger and the tail of a dog. They might name this new animal a 'Hors-ger-og.'

Give plenty of time for each participant to complete their index card. Offer assistance to those that appear to struggle with the concept. After everyone has completed their card, invite them to share their card and their conflict style with the group.

Here are some examples of different animals and their conflict styles:

- **Turtle (withdraw)**—Withdraws from the conflict; hides until it is safe to emerge
- **Shark (force)**—Forces and tries to make opponents accept his/her decisions; often threatening and intimidating
- **Bear (smooth)**—Avoids the conflict when possible; ignores their own goals and resolves conflict by giving into others
- **Fox (compromise)**—Sly, sneaky, tricky, and able to persuade others to give up part of their most important and valued positions
- **Owl (problem solver)**—Known throughout children's books as the wise old owl . . . the owl views conflicts as problems to be solved, confronting the situation and seeking solutions that will satisfy both parties
- **Camel**—Carries others' burdens without taking care of their own needs first
- **Bull**—Hits the issue head-on when provoked. Certain triggers ignite anger.
- **Lion**—Very proud, works within a group; King of the jungle. Another metaphor to work with is the "cowardly lion"; those that tuck their tail and run when faced with conflict.
- **Mouse**—Very timid, runs from conflict, easy target.
- **Panther**—Slinks around in the background, stalks his prey, and pounces for the kill.
- **Parrot**—Repeats everything that is heard. Often annoying and loud.
- **Rabbit**—Runs and hides from any kind of conflict.
- **Cobra**—Deadly and dangerous when provoked. Can be charmed by some and submit to those in authoritative positions.

- **Chicken**—Everyone has heard the phrase, "You're just being a Chicken!" when referring to someone who is shying away from a situation or opting out because they are scared. Chickens tend to flee from conflict and frighten easily.
- **Elephant**—The strongest animal on earth, has an amazing memory, yet when faced with small restrictions, such as a rope around their foot, it paralyzes them from moving forward.
- **Horse**—Can be tamed to do whatever their manager wants them to do. Very loyal when treated properly. When faced with conflict it rears back and attempts to protect itself. Able to handle a great deal of weight and workload.
- **Mule**—Very stubborn. Will not move forward unless given something positive in return.

FACILITATOR NOTES

Conflict Resolution Thumball™

TYPE OF INITIATIVE

Icebreaker, Problem Solving, Processing tool

PURPOSE

Here is a truly unique tool to help organizations and individuals resolve a conflict.

PROPS NEEDED

Conflict Resolution Thumball™

GROUP SIZE

1–100; small groups of 10 people per ball is recommended

DIRECTIONS

Here is a truly unique tool to help organizations and individuals resolve a conflict. There are 32 different conflict resolution or peer mediation questions pre-printed on the panels of the ball. The ball is made of soft material.

- Invite your group to sit or stand in a circle.
- Ask participants to toss the Thumball™ to a teammate. This teammate should catch it, look under their thumb, and respond to the question found there.

Participant responses can vary each time you play. Here are a few suggestions:

- Respond to the panel under your thumb by answering for yourself.
- Respond by asking another player to answer.
- Predict the answer another player would give.

Once a group has played together several times, you can add the challenge of recalling an answer provided by another player on a previous day. You may also ask them to recall an answer given by another participant that may be helpful in solving a new conflict.

Sample questions found on the Conflict Resolution Thumball™:

1. What is one thing you could have done differently?

2. How would you like to see the conflict resolved?

3. How did you approach the other party?

4. Describe your initial reaction to the conflict.

5. Is there old stuff you are using to fuel this fire?

6. In the grand scheme of things, how important is this conflict?

7. Are you trying to cast blame?

8. What are you doing that is blocking the resolution of this problem?

VARIATION

Read the group a conflict scenario and then ask them to toss the ball around and respond to the questions based on how they would try and resolve the conflict.

VARIATION

This is a wonderful processing tool for one person. If you are going through a conflict of some kind, toss the ball in the air and look under your thumb to reflect on the question silently. The 32 questions are well thought out and may give you insight on how to solve your own inner conflict.

WHERE TO FIND IT/HOW TO MAKE IT

The Conflict Resolution Thumball™ is a custom design of Michelle Cummings. You can purchase the Conflict Resolution Thumball™ from the Training Wheels website at www.training-wheels.com. You could make a similar ball by writing conflict resolution questions using a permanent marker on a beach ball or other soft, tossable sphere.

FACILITATOR NOTES

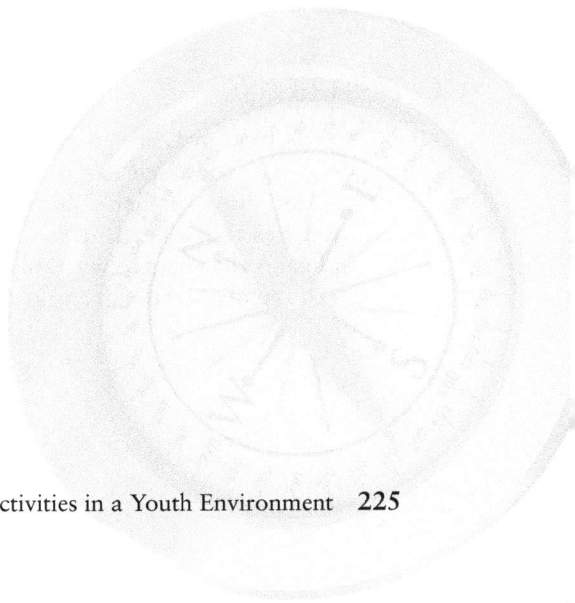

Consensus Cards

Kelly Johnston Smith came up with the concept of Consensus Cards while working with a group of fifth graders. They had a hard time understanding the concept of the Consensus Thumbs (pg 198) system of consensus, so she came up with Consensus Cards.

TYPE OF INITIATIVE

Consensus tool and Conflict Resolution

SOURCE

Kelly Johnston Smith

SOURCE

A Teachable Moment, pp. 78–79

PURPOSE

Consensus Cards are a decision-making tool designed for use with participants who need to come to consensus on an issue. Most groups will take a vote and identify majority-rules voting as consensus. Individuals need a way to make their voice heard, and the group needs a way to easily check for individual responses.

PROPS NEEDED

Set of Consensus Cards; one card for each participant

GROUP SIZE

4–30

DIRECTIONS

- Consensus cards are palm-sized cards with three colored circles arranged like a stop light on it. The top circle is red, next is yellow, followed by green at the bottom. On the back, the definition of each color is printed: red indicates I do not agree with this plan, yellow indicates that I need more information/I have a question before proceeding, and green indicates that I agree with this plan.
- Each member of the group receives one consensus card.

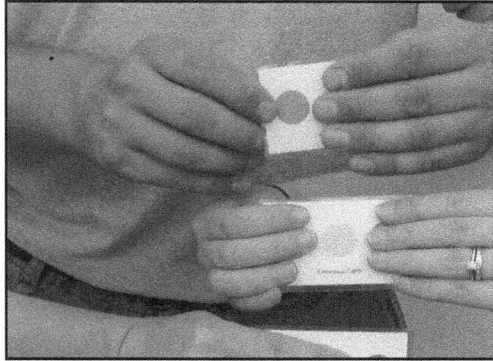

- Once a proposal is given to the group, each member votes by holding up his/her card with two of the three colors covered by his/her hand. If everyone is green, the group can go forward with the proposal. If anyone is yellow, the group must respond to the person's need or request before continuing. If anyone is red, the person is given the opportunity to explain his/her resistance and offer a compromise. This visual voting system allows the group to quickly hear from each person, and the use of the stoplight colors is familiar to them.
- Consensus cards work best when initially introduced as a decision-making tool for a group decision with minimal consequences. For example, you might ask the group to decide on one picture card that would metaphorically describe an activity they have just completed. Introduce the consensus cards for them to use to find out if everyone is in agreement. You can then continue to have the group use the cards throughout the day for increasingly difficult decisions.
- Sabotage: If a participant simply answers red to any proposal, in order to delay the group process, the facilitator/teacher needs to intervene appropriately. One way to do this is to require anyone voting red to give the group an alternative suggestion or plan. As is the case with many consensus-building tools, consensus cards allow participants to voice their concerns without blocking the progress of the group.

WHERE TO FIND IT/HOW TO MAKE IT

These cards are very simple to make using clip art. Business card stock is the perfect size, especially for small hands. Print the three colored circles on one side and the directions for each color on the back. Laminating the cards will give you a tool for a lifetime!

You can find a set of these cards for retail sale at Training Wheels, www.training-wheels.com.

FACILITATOR NOTES

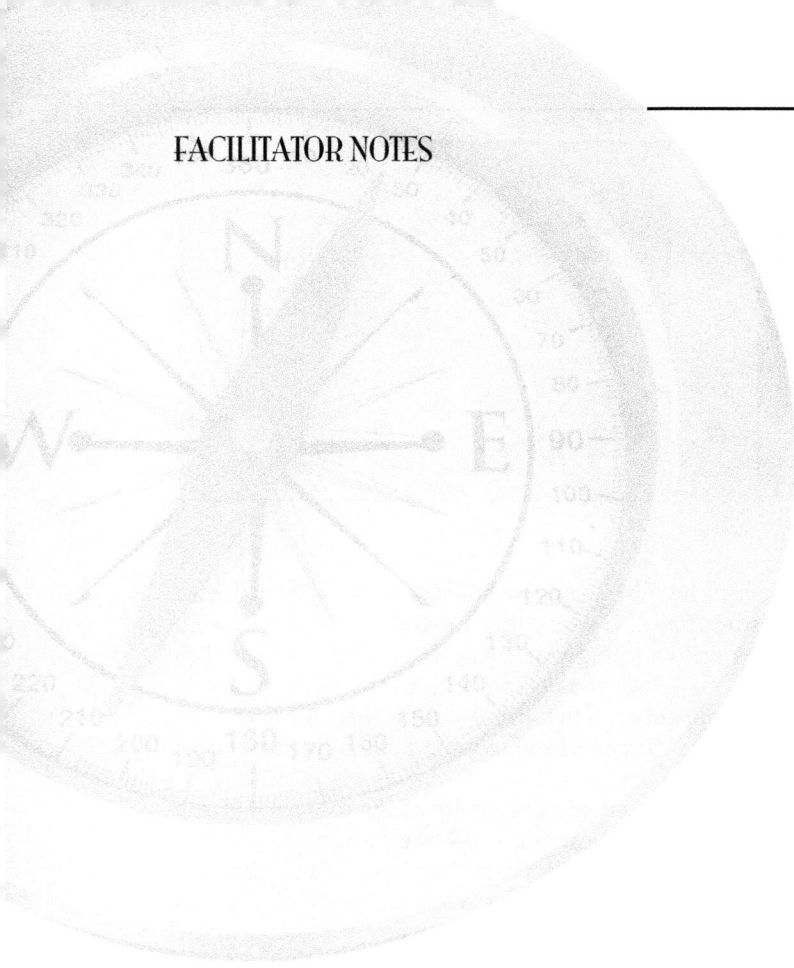

Consensus Thumbs

Thumbs Up, Thumbs Sideways, Thumbs Down

This facilitator favorite was difficult to credit to a single source, so thanks to everyone who contributed. Have thumb, will process!

Published in *A Teachable Moment,* pp. 80

TYPE OF INITIATIVE

Consensus tool, Conflict Resolution or Processing activity

PURPOSE

To aid participants in consensus voting. See Consensus Cards for more consensus activities.

PROPS NEEDED

One thumb per participant

GROUP SIZE

4–20

DIRECTIONS

- Define consensus for the group.
- Next, demonstrate the three positions of the thumb and what each position means.

    Thumbs Up: I agree with the decision

    Thumbs Sideways: It wouldn't be my first choice, but I will fully participate and support the group.

    Thumbs Down: I do not agree. We need to discuss further.

- Help the group understand that consensus is achieved when there are no participants with a thumbs down. If there is someone displaying Thumbs Down you have majority rules, not consensus. Oftentimes when the majority rules you have a larger number of participants in favor of the group decision, and a few that are not bought into the process because they are not 'on board.' This can often lead to behavior issues when there are participants not bought into what the rest of the group is doing.

- Explain to the group that if someone chooses the Thumbs Down position, they must give a suggestion to the group that would enable them to move to a Thumbs Sideways or a Thumbs Up position. Then the group would vote again on the new suggestion. Consensus is achieved when everyone in the group is in a Thumbs Sideways or Thumbs Up position.

DEBRIEFING TOPICS

- How did the Consensus Thumbs process aid your decision?
- How does this process help avoid conflict?
- What is most helpful to you when using consensus thumbs?
- How can you use this tool at home with your family?
- Would a tool like this be helpful in a group to resolve conflict?

FACILITATOR NOTES

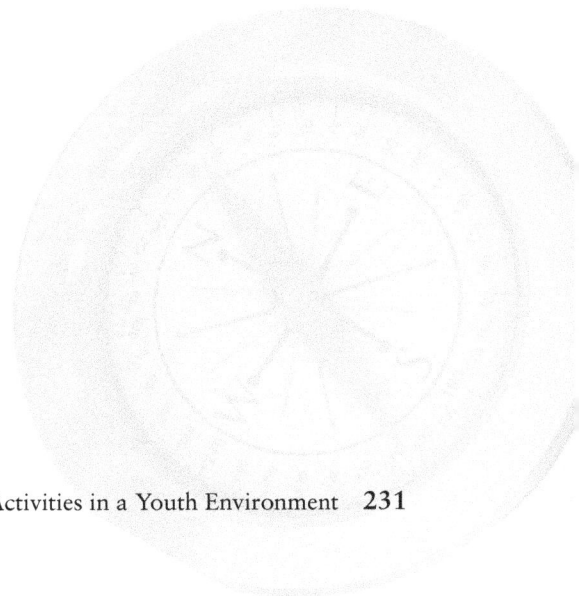

Conversation Cards©

Facilitators know that one good question is often enough to get a group of people talking, sharing, and connecting. Conversation Cards is a tool designed to stimulate conversation, get to know others on a deeper level, and to explore issues of risk, trust, and emotional safety within a group.

SOURCE

Lisa Blockus-Brown

TYPE OF INITIATIVE

Conversation Starter, Self-disclosure and discovery

SOURCE

A Teachable Moment, pp. 82

TYPE OF INITIATIVE

Conversation Starter, Self-disclosure and discovery

PROPS NEEDED

Set of conversation cards

GROUP SIZE

1–20

DIRECTIONS

- The Conversation Cards concept is simple: a series of thought-provoking questions are written on cards and are then divided into categories organized around level of risk and self-disclosure.
- The low-risk category includes general questions about likes, dislikes, and other safe topics. This category is high on fun and a great way to get participants better acquainted. An example of a question in this category is "what is your favorite holiday?"
- Medium-risk questions go a bit beyond surface conversation and get people to reveal a little more about themselves. An example of a conversation starter in this category would be "what three words would you most like said about you?"

- The high-risk category includes questions that require a fair amount of personal reflection, self-awareness, and a sense of vulnerability with the group to give a genuine response. "What is something that you wish your friends or family better understood about you?" is an example of the kinds of questions included in this category.

Over 200 college students (ages 17–21) around the country—along with professional college personnel administrators, adventure education facilitators, and counselors—took part in evaluating the questions and sorted them into the three levels of perceived risk. Use has shown that these questions foster great discussion and discovery among high school students as well.

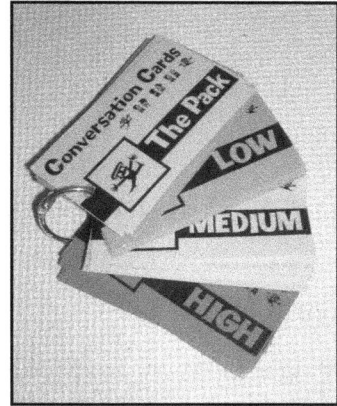

Conversation cards have proven to be a versatile tool to bring people together. People have used the cards informally around a campfire, over a meal, in the car, and as a break during a business meeting. The cards can also be used as a part of a formal activity with specific outcomes and goals. One structured activity to try is to place the cards in three piles based on the risk level. Each individual takes a turn by drawing a card from ANY pile. The participant then reads the question and shares his/her answer. Try several rounds of this and watch the risk-taking level in the group go up as they become more connected and more willing to share.

WHERE TO FIND IT

Training Wheels, www.training-wheels.com

FACILITATOR NOTES

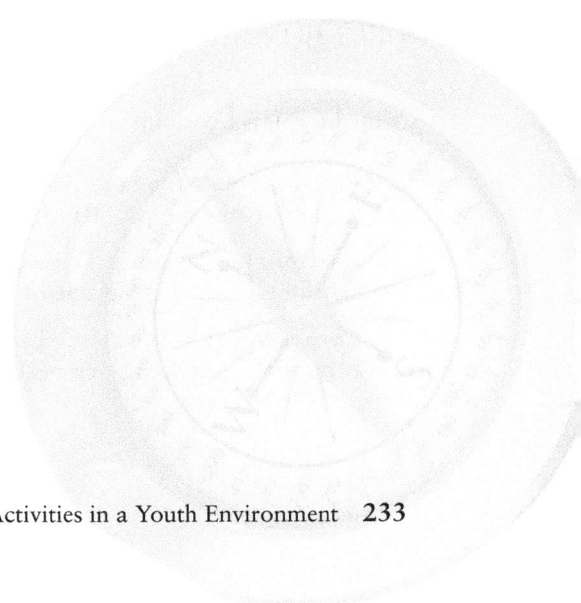

Cross the Line

TYPE OF INITIATIVE

Diversity, Behavior Awareness, Empathy

SOURCE

Making the Peace and Michelle Cummings

PROPS NEEDED

Two ropes or masking tape, large room (big enough for entire group)

GROUP SIZE

4–100

PURPOSE

This activity is one of the more powerful activities in this book. In everyday speech when someone has "crossed the line" it usually means that they have gone too far or stepped over a boundary. These scenarios are breeding grounds for conflict. This activity will allow participants to reflect on times when they have demonstrated a behavior (or one demonstrated toward them) that crossed the line.

TIME NEEDED

20 minutes for activity; 30–45 minutes to debrief

DIRECTIONS

Step-by-Step Procedure:

1. Put two ropes (or tape lines) parallel to one another in the center of the room on the ground. Place them 8–10 feet apart and span the length of the room.

2. Ask your participants to line up on one side of the rope you placed on the ground. Everyone should be on the same side of the room, facing the line.

3. Introduction to the activity: Explain to the group that this activity involves people's feelings. It requires four things; respect, sensitivity, silence, and not judging others.

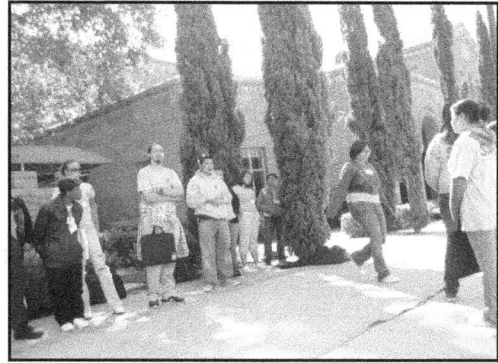

Specifically describe these four things with the participants.

- **Respect:** Being respectful means that you will refrain from intruding upon or interfering with someone's experience.
- **Sensitivity:** This means you will be aware of and responsive to the feelings of others. Let them know that they might experience strong feelings during this activity—sadness, anger, guilt, etc.
- **Silence:** The activity should be done in silence to create a safe environment for individuals to cross the line. If laughing or side comments were allowed, it may inhibit a participant's willingness to share.
- **Not Judging Others:** You have the choice to cross the line or not cross the line—even if the prompt pertains to you. It is important not to judge others because of this rule. An individual may choose not to cross the line, even if the prompt is truthful for them. It may be tempting to form an opinion about someone else in the room from circumstances presented in the activity.

4. Verbalize to the group that this activity is about individual choices, not their friends, or the people standing next to them.

5. Once you have covered the "rules" to the activity, you may ask the group if they feel they are ready to begin. Once they are able to be quiet, respectful, and sensitive, they may cross the line.

6. Explain to the group that you will read a statement out loud. If that statement is true for them or if they identify with that group, they may cross the line. Explain that they should walk across to the other rope, step across the line, turn around, face the other participants on the other side of the line, and pause there. Give an example; "if you are a male, please cross the line"; "if you are wearing tennis shoes, please cross the line." After the participants have crossed the line, you say out loud, "Notice how it feels to cross the line; look who is with you, look who is not with you, and cross back over."

7. Allow for a few seconds of reflection time before you begin your next prompt.

The goal of this activity is to help break down the barriers between people that perpetuate acts of unkindness. Participants become aware that others face many of the same insecurities, fears, and challenges that they do. They learn that showing your feelings does not make you a weak person; rather, it takes courage. They learn that other individuals can be appreciative and supportive when they reveal those feelings. Be careful not to be judgmental or shaming in this activity. Be supportive and accepting. All participants will most likely have a reason to cross the line. Many participants will need your support in realizing that they may be modeling behaviors that they have seen or are passing along treatment they have received. With help and guidance children and adults can change such hurtful behaviors.

Debriefing Questions for Cross the Line

Please sit and discuss these questions in your small group.

1. What are some feelings that came up for you during this activity?

2. Why was it so important to be quiet, respectful, and sensitive?

3. What was the hardest part for you?

4. What did you learn about yourself? About others?

5. What do you want to remember about what we've just experienced?

6. Based on this experience, are there any changes you will make in the way you treat others?

Cross the Line Prompts for School Groups

- Cross the line if you've ever been teased or called a bad name or made fun of.
- Cross the line if you've ever been picked last in games or sports or left out of an activity all together.
- Cross the line if you've ever been called a mean name or put down just because you're a girl.
- Cross the line if you've ever been judged or teased because of the color of your skin.
- Cross the line if you've ever been teased because of your religious background.
- Cross the line if you have ever bullied someone in your class.
- Cross the line if you have been bullied by someone in this class.
- Cross the line if you've ever been teased about your accent or your voice or told that you couldn't sing.
- Cross the line if you or anyone in your family has a disability that you cannot see.
- Cross the line if you're a male and you've ever been told you shouldn't cry, show your emotions, or be afraid.
- Cross the line if you've ever felt alone, unwelcome, or afraid.
- Cross the line if you have intentionally hurt someone's feelings.
- Cross the line if you've ever felt pressure from your friends or an adult to do something you didn't want to do and felt sorry for it afterward.
- Cross the line if you've ever stood by and watched while someone was hurt and said or did nothing because you were too afraid.
- Cross the line if you have ever started a rumor about a classmate that was untrue.
- Cross the line if people routinely mispronounce your name.
- Cross the line if you have ever been teased because of the part of the world or country you or your family comes from.
- Cross the line if you have ever been the only person of your race/ethnicity in a classroom.

Debriefing Topics

- What are some feelings that came up for you during this activity?
- Why was it so important to be quiet, respectful, and sensitive?
- Why was it important not to judge others?
- What was the hardest part for you?
- What did you learn about yourself? About others?
- What did you want to remember about what we've just experienced?
- How does it make you feel when you are getting teased for something that you cannot help?
- Why do you think other people tease?
- Talk about the cycle of teasing, name calling, etc. How can you put an end to this cycle?
- Why is it important to be allies to each other?
- How can we avoid treating others poorly in our class?

These prompts are examples. You may customize a list of prompts that fit the needs or issues within your group.

Cross the Line Prompts for Camp

- Cross the line if you've ever been teased or called a bad name or made fun of.
- Cross the line if you've ever been picked last in games or sports or left out of an activity all together.
- Cross the line if you've ever been called a mean name or put down just because you're a girl.
- Cross the line if you've ever been judged or teased because of the color of your skin.
- Cross the line if you've ever been teased because of your religious background.
- Cross the line if you have ever bullied someone at camp.
- Cross the line if you have been bullied by someone at camp.
- Cross the line if you or anyone in your family has a disability that you cannot see.
- Cross the line if you're a male and you've ever been told you shouldn't cry, show your emotions, or be afraid.
- Cross the line if you've ever felt alone, unwelcome, or afraid.
- Cross the line if you have intentionally hurt someone's feelings.
- Cross the line if you've ever felt pressure from your friends or an adult to do something you didn't want to do and felt sorry for it afterward.
- Cross the line if you've ever stood by and watched while someone was hurt and said or did nothing because you were too afraid.
- Cross the line if you have ever started a rumor about someone at camp that was untrue.
- Cross the line if people routinely mispronounce your name.
- Cross the line if you have ever been teased because of the part of the world or country you or your family comes from.

Debriefing Topics

- What are some feelings that came up for you during this activity?
- Why was it so important to be quiet, respectful, and sensitive?
- Why was it important not to judge others?
- What was the hardest part for you?
- What did you learn about yourself? About others?
- What did you want to remember about what we've just experienced?
- How does it make you feel when you are getting teased for something that you cannot help?
- Why do you think other people tease?
- Talk about the cycle of teasing, name calling, etc. How can you put an end to this cycle?
- Why is it important to be allies to each other?
- How can we avoid treating others poorly at camp?

These prompts are examples. You may customize a list of prompts that fit the needs or issues within your group.

FACILITATOR NOTES

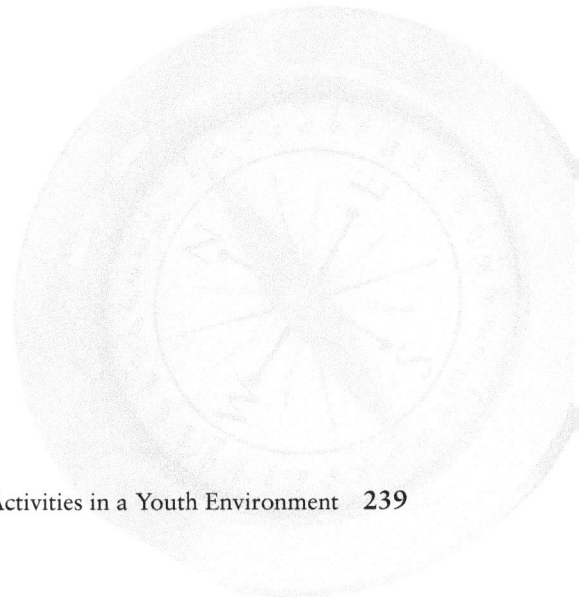

Deck of Card Debrief

TYPE OF INITIATIVE

Processing tool

SOURCES

Playing With a Full Deck, pp. 99.
A Teachable Moment, pp. 172.
Reflective Learning, Sugerman, Doherty, Garvey, Gass, pp. 66.

PROPS NEEDED

A jumbo deck of playing cards, primarily non-face cards and those between one (ace) and five are best.

GROUP SIZE

4–100

PURPOSE

The benefits of this activity are that it is less threatening for participants to speak to just one person at a time rather than the whole group. Sometimes participants are more open if they aren't speaking to their facilitator. Remember good processing can happen even if the facilitator is not present to hear it! This is a useful activity not only for processing a specific experience but also as a closing activity for a session or program day.

DIRECTIONS

Variation #1

Designate a meaning to each suit within the deck of cards. For example, hearts could represent feelings, spades could represent situations individuals had a difficult time with, diamonds could represent successes, and clubs could represent something they noticed about one of the other group members.

Shuffle the deck and deal each individual a hand (up to eight cards). For each card, the individual shares with the group an example of what the suit represents. The numbers on the cards and face cards can be involved also. For example, Jacks are wild cards that can be traded for another card in the deck, and the numbers on the cards represent how many thoughts that individual may share with the group, etc. You may want to "stack the deck" with specific cards or adapt the rules so that the person who draws a "10" does not have to share 10 items—that could get a bit lengthy!

Variation #2

At the completion of the activity, the facilitator passes out a playing card to each participant. The suit of each card describes the category of your response, and the number shown on the card identifies the number of ideas you need to share on this subject. For example, a four of spades suggests mentioning four things related to new thoughts that you dug up during the activity.

- Hearts: generate conversations about something from the heart.
- Clubs: describe things that grow (new ideas, new thoughts, a new point of view)
- Spades: are used to dig in the garden and describe planting some new ideas or things that you dug up during the activity.
- Diamonds: are gems that last forever. What are some of the gems of wisdom you gathered during this activity?

CONFLICT CATEGORIES FOR DISCUSSION

- Hearts: Describe some feelings you might have if you are in a conflict with someone. Describe some feelings you might have if you were being bullied. How do you think it feels to be a bully?
- Clubs: Describe a time when you resolved a conflict with aggression. How would you change the way you responded? Generate conversations about ways that you've seen people bullied.
- Spades: How do bullies dig themselves a hole when they are mean to others?
- Diamonds: Describe a time when you have handled a conflict with a teammate in a positive way. Describe some positive attributes of standing up for yourself against a bully.

FACILITATOR NOTES

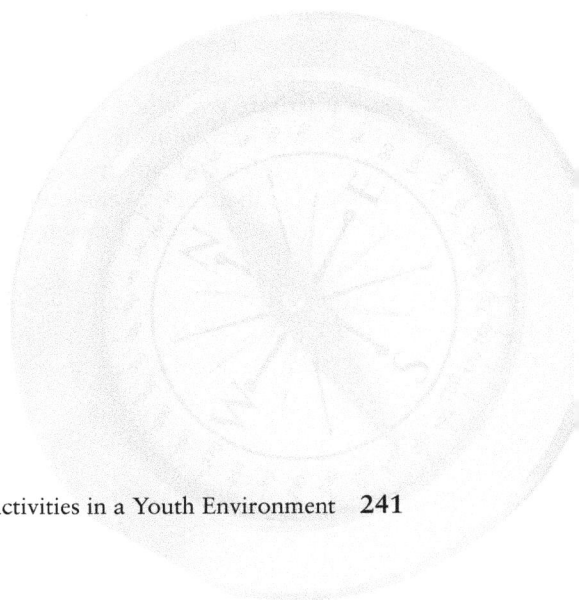

Do You? Does It?

(much like the classic icebreaker Have you ever?)

TYPE

Icebreaker, Perspective

SOURCE

Karl Rohnke, Sam Sikes, & Mary Todd

PROPS NEEDED

sturdy chairs, one for each participant, plus one extra chair for every 10 participants. Could use Carpet Squares or Poly spots as well.

PURPOSE

This activity is all about "triggers." What sets us off? What bothers us and what does not? The more that we learn from our peers as to what their triggers are, the more we can reduce the small "I just don't know what I said" type altercations because we know who responds to what and how.

DIRECTIONS

Sit in a circle (you will need sturdy chairs for this one). Leave a couple of open chairs in the mix. Perhaps three open chairs for every ten folks playing. Begin with one person in the middle asking "Do you or does it?" questions. Questions like: Do you get frustrated waiting in lines? Does it irritate you when you are ignored? Do you "fly off the handle"? If the answer to the question is "Yes" move one to right; if "No" stay seated. As people move around the circle eventually folks will end up on the lap of their neighbors. After a couple of rounds the "caller" can try to grab an empty chair allowing for a new "caller." To keep the new caller from feeling like they are "it," we call this action being "promoted."

VERSION 2

Do you know? You will need a carpet square or a poly spot for each participant, minus one. Scatter the place markers in a random pattern within a defined space. Ask the same sort of questions. If folks have done that thing they must shift to a new spot somewhere within the group. As some point you may shift the questioning to "do you know?" questions that can be used to reinforce concepts and test for understanding. Just like the chair version, the person left without a spot will be promoted and must answer the question that was originally posed to the group. There should be no problem answering the question as you only move if "you have" or if "you know."

DEBRIEFING TOPICS

How did the "stack up" affect the action of the game? Did it change how quickly people responded to the questions? Did it change your interpretation of the questions?

FACILITATOR NOTES

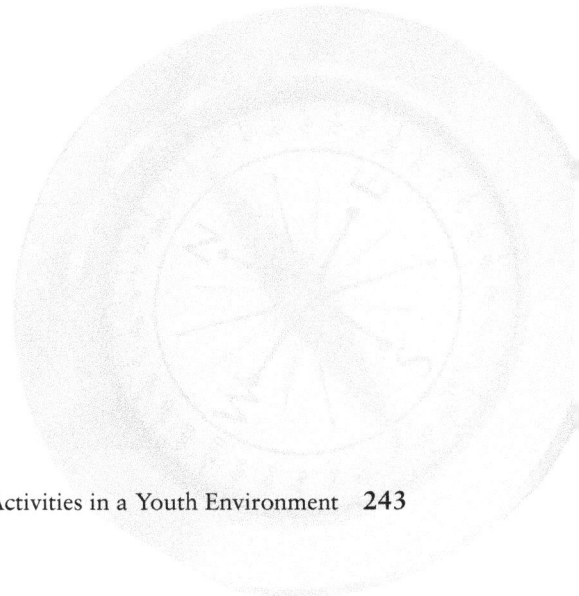

Dots

TYPE OF INITIATIVE

Problem Solving, Diversity

SOURCE

Mosaic Project

PROPS NEEDED

Dot cards, laminated cards, or index cards with colored dots on them. See the directions for the number of cards to use. The colored dot stickers used on file folders also work well.

GROUP SIZE

10–100

PREPARATION/LEAD IN

Choose colored dot cards to give to each of your participants. Be sure to have a wide variety of solid dot cards and mixed dot cards (dots that are half one color and half another color) and 1 unique solid dot color card. Try to have one group that is much larger than the other groups. For example, if you had 30 participants in your group, you could choose 10 yellow dots (majority dot group), 8 blue dots, 5 green dots, 3 dots that are half green and half blue, 2 dots that are half yellow and half blue, 1 dot that is half green and half yellow, and 1 red dot (unique dot card).

DIRECTIONS

Step by Step Procedure

- Invite your participants to make a single file line or circle and close their eyes. Tell them that you will go around and hand them a card that they are to place on their forehead. They must not talk for the rest of the game and must keep their eyes closed even after they have received their cards. As you are passing out the dot cards, make sure you choose the participant that receives the unique color dot sensitively.
- After everyone has a dot card, they may open their eyes. Now tell them you are going to be intentionally vague with the directions, as it is a part of the activity. Instruct them to, "Get into your groups without talking." Make sure you do not tell them to organize themselves according to their dots. Just tell them to get into groups.
- The participants may group themselves however they choose, although they inevitably will do so by the color of their dot cards. They also must not talk during this process. Make sure that you are paying attention to the group dynamics; participants will sometimes push other participants out of the groups. Leaders and followers will arise, and the "Majority dot" group will also lend some interesting dynamics.
- When it seems that almost everyone has found a group and the person with the "unique dot" has some idea that s/he is alone, stop the activity. Participants should look around and then take off their dots to see what color they are.

DEBRIEFING TOPICS

- How did you find your group? How did you help each other out?
- How did it feel to find your group? How did you feel if you didn't find your group?
- Were you happier if your group was bigger or smaller?
- Why did you choose to group yourselves in this way? Remind participants that all you said was "get in your groups."
- Did you try to join any groups but get pushed away? For people with multicolor dots, how did you know which group to join?
- How would this activity relate to real life?
- How do you group yourselves in real life? How do you choose your friends?
- Do people tend to group themselves by the way they look? Think about your friends. Do they look like you? Do they dress the same? Are they the same race?
- Why do you think people group themselves based on how they look?
- Why do you think people hang out with people who are similar to them? Is there any value in seeking out people to be friends with who are different than you? What would be the benefits/advantages? What would make this difficult?
- Did you experience any conflict with other groups? How did you treat those that were not a part of your group?
- What were some behaviors that were demonstrated toward you during the activity?

FACILITATOR NOTES

Dramatic Conflict Resolution

Solving a Conflict with a Friend with Drama

TYPE OF INITIATIVE

Discussion, Story Creation, and Drama

PURPOSE

Children often find themselves in conflicts with their friends and often do not know how to resolve the conflict on their own. By allowing kids to process through different conflict resolution scenarios, it will allow them to practice conflict resolution skills.

PROPS NEEDED

Conflict scenarios, copies of debriefing topics for each small group, flip chart/white board, and markers

GROUP SIZE

1–30, break into small groups of 3–4 people

DIRECTIONS

Break the group into small groups of three to four people and have them read aloud in their small group one of the conflict resolution stories on the following pages:

- Stolen Property
- Sibling Rivalry
- Talking Behind My Back

Each small group should:

1. Read the story aloud.
2. Decide what happens next in the story.
3. Describe ways the conflict could end.
4. Write the ending to the story.

VARIATION

Have the group reenact the story they have read and create new endings that express their ideas on resolving or avoiding the conflict. Allow the other groups to watch the skits.

VARIATION

Have the group write their own conflict story and come up with a positive way to resolve the conflict.

DEBRIEFING TOPICS

- Give the groups enough time to talk through their scenarios with one another.
- Be prepared to offer positive suggestions to help the groups resolve the conflict in their stories.

FACILITATOR NOTES

Stolen Property

The Scenario

Dakota and Tracy were best buddies. They have been best friends since the first grade and played together almost every day. They go to their school's aftercare program every day after school.

One day after school, they were playing their personal Nintendo DS games in aftercare. After playing for 20 minutes, they decided to put their games away and go shoot some hoops. About 15 minutes later, Dakota's mom arrived to pick him up. When Dakota went to get his backpack and coat he realized his Nintendo DS game was missing. Dakota looked around and saw another kid, Josh, playing a Nintendo game that looked like his. Dakota went over and angrily said, "Give me back my Nintendo game!" Surprised, Josh said back, "This isn't your Nintendo game it's mine!" Dakota grabbed the game out of Josh's hand and turned to walk away.

What do you think happens next?

1.

2.

3.

Positive Ways to End this Conflict

Dakota could:

1.

2.

3.

Josh could:

1.

2.

3.

Write the ending to the story here:

Sibling Rivalry

The Scenario

Jarrod and Jake are brothers who are only one year apart in age. At home they share a room and they have two sisters as well. For the most part they get along very well, but lately they have been arguing a lot. They fight about which TV shows to watch, who has to clean their bedroom, and who gets to play with the cool *Star Wars Legos* that they share. Sometimes they get into shoving matches over toys.

For Jarrod's birthday he received several new toys to play with. He was very excited to have received several of his wish list items. A few hours after he opened his presents Jake asked Jarrod if he could play with his new *Pokemon cards*. Jarrod said no and Jake got upset.

What do you think happens next?

1.

2.

3.

Positive Ways to End this Conflict

Jarrod could:

1.

2.

3.

Jake could:

1.

2.

3.

Write the ending to the story here:

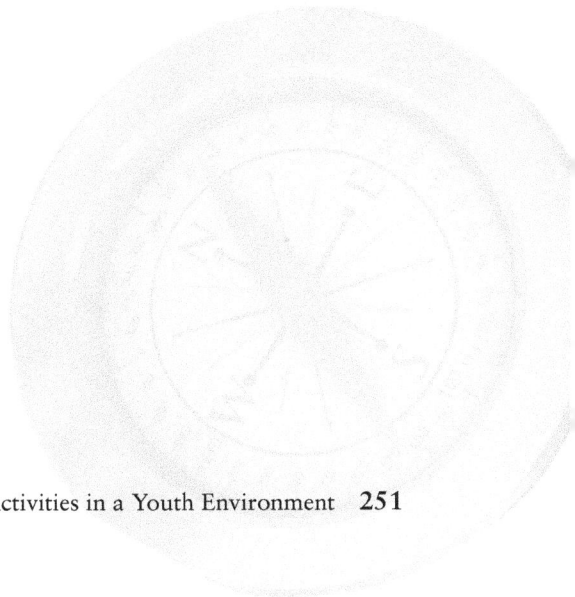

Talking Behind My Back

The Scenario

Kristie and Pam were best friends. They had known each other since the second grade. They were always together and oftentimes spent the night at each other's homes. Pam was sick from school one day so Kristie started hanging out with a girl named Robin, who was very popular in their school. Robin did not like Pam very well and told Kristie unkind things about Pam. A few days later when Pam returned to school she heard some other girls talking about her, spreading gossip and rumors. Pam didn't understand why Kristie was acting weird around her either.

What do you think happens next?

1.

2.

3.

Positive Ways to End this Conflict

Kristie could:

1.

2.

3.

Pam could:

1.

2.

3.

Write the ending to the story here:

Write Your Own Conflict Story

Title:

The Scenario:

What do you think happens next?

1.

2.

3.

Positive Ways to End this Conflict

_____ could:

1.

2.

3.

_____ could:

1.

2.

3.

Write the ending to the story here:

Finger Jousting

(Who Wins the Most?)

TYPE OF INITIATIVE
Problem Solving

SOURCE
Karl Rohnke

GROUP SIZE
2+ people

DIRECTIONS

- Divide the group into pairs. The closer in physical strength people are to each other, the better.
- Ask each person to face their partner and reach out their right hand. Each person joins his/her partner's hand by making a C shape with their fingers and clasp their partner's hand at the thumb. Next, ask them to extend their index finger to create their "sword" (see picture).
- Once everyone is connected with his/her partner, explain "The object of the game is to touch your partner's right shoulder with your index finger. You can only use your 'sword' to gain points and there is no letting go." Then say, "The way to win this game is to get the most touches, so make sure and count each time you touch your partner's shoulder. Ready . . . begin!"
- After one minute, ask each team how many touches they had total and declare the winning team the one with the most touches.
- Most people will think that they are going against their own partner and will be pushing against each other, but really the team with the most total touches wins! The object of this activity is to demonstrate how people tend to work against one other when they should be working together (but don't tell the group this).
- Play another round to see if the pairs continue to work against each other or with one another.

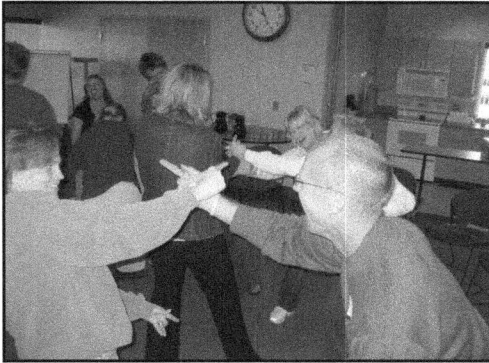

DEBRIEFING TOPICS

- How did you score your points?
- What effect did your methods have on your score?
- How is this activity like trying to solve a conflict between two people?
- When resistance meets resistance, what is the outcome? Describe a real-life example of this.
- When resistance meets submission, what is the outcome? Describe a real-life example of this.

FACILITATOR NOTES

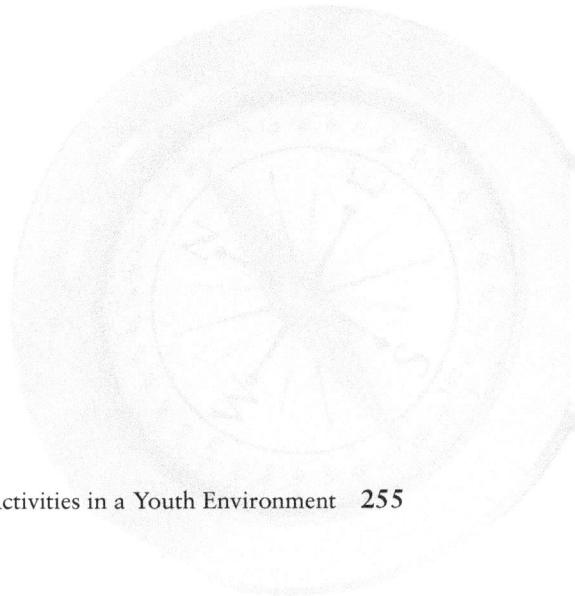

Get Into Your Groups

TYPE OF INITIATIVE
Problem Solving and Diversity

SOURCE
Playing with a Full Deck, Michelle Cummings, pp. 91

PROPS NEEDED
Deck of Playing Cards

GROUP SIZE
12 or more

DIRECTIONS

Invite your participants to get into a circle. Give each person a card and ask them not to look at it. Inform them that it is a non-talking activity, and it should be done in complete silence. Ask each person to put the card to their forehead without looking at their own card. Tell the groups that you are going to be intentionally vague with the directions and then say, "Please get into your groups. Ready, go." There will be some initial confusion as to what 'groups' you are looking for, but people will start milling about and silently helping each other get into groups based on either number, suit, or color.

It is amazing to watch what groups form and whose idea of a 'group' gets followed. Usually a few people will step forward and start placing people together. Sometimes a group will get sorted by number likeness, then get changed by someone else with a different idea of what they think is the right answer—organization by suit or color.

The moral to the story in this activity is that each card would fit into multiple groups. As human beings we often separate ourselves into subgroups or cliques. Conflicts can often take place between people that are 'different' from each other.

To end the activity, ask everyone with a red card to hold their card up. Ask the group, "Couldn't these individuals be considered a group?" Group members reply "yes, but we didn't know what color card we had." Which creates another teachable moment—what things do you have in common with others in this room that you may not have figured out, yet? How can we foster an environment of acceptance and inclusion? A discussion related to inclusion, invitation, and connection is suitable here.

Groups respond very differently to this activity. Some groups are very comfortable with wherever people are placed. Other groups dig deeper into the reality of what is happening. Some individual participants may not let others place them anywhere and choose for themselves what group they want to be in.

This activity should be debriefed well and allow people time to process what happened.

DEBRIEFING TOPICS

- How did you get into your groups?
- Who determined what groups you would be in?
- Did the groups change any during the activity?
- Did you agree with the groups that were formed? If so, why? If not, why?
- Were you uncomfortable in the group that you were placed in?
- How is this activity like everyday society? Do we get to choose the groups we are placed in?
- What is the deeper meaning of this activity?
- How do people respond when they feel excluded from a group based on external appearances?

VARIATION

Like the Blind Shapes activity in this book, you could have one unique card in the deck that does not connect to anyone else in the room (like the 'star' piece in Blind Shapes). This could be a Joker card or a card with a unique color and number. For example, if you had 20 people participating in the activity, you could have the 5 of Hearts be your unique card. The 19 other cards would all be Spades or Clubs (black cards) omitting the 5 of Spades and the 5 of Clubs. The 5 of Hearts should visibly be unable to connect with any other card. When debriefing, the facilitator can ask the "5 of Hearts" participant to talk about their experience of trying to fit into other groups and trying to find their place in the group. What did it feel like to not fit in anywhere? Did other people push you away because you weren't like them? How did that feel?

FACILITATOR NOTES

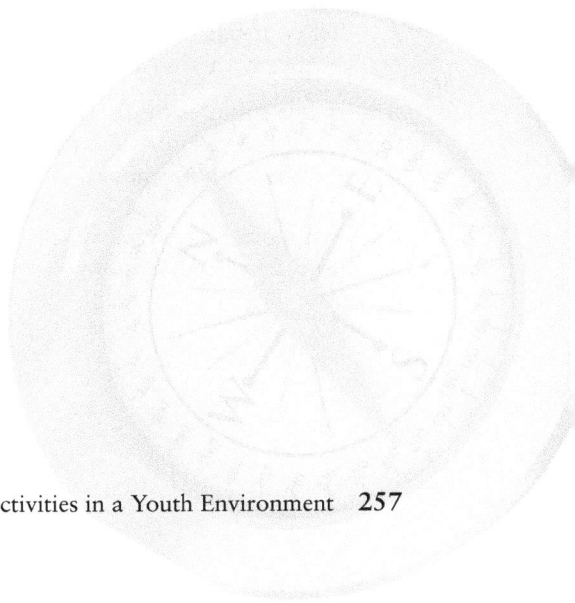

Handshakes and Greetings

This is one of our absolute favorite icebreaker activities. Handshakes are quite simply a great way to mix and greet folks. They are fun, engaging, and get folks talking and laughing. The more your participants interact and get to know each other, the stronger their relationships will be. Many conflicts can be avoided by simply allowing time for personal interaction.

TYPE OF INITIATIVE

Icebreaker, processing and reviewing activity

PROPS NEEDED

GROUP SIZE

10–100

DIRECTIONS

Invite your participants to find a partner. Introduce one of the handshakes that follows and ask a question you would like your participants to share with one another. Questions can vary from lighthearted to more serious.

- Discuss the best meal you have ever had.
- The furthest I have been from this location is . . .
- Three things we have in common are . . .
- Tell your partner about a good book you have read recently.
- Discuss with your partner your typical response to a conflict.

After a few minutes of discussion, tell your participants to remember who their partner is and tell them, "See ya later alligator!" or "Adios Amigos!" and find a NEW partner. Do about four to five different handshakes with different partners.

For each handshake, you will need a new partner. We like to share a story about places we've lived and handshakes we've learned while living in various places. Here are a few of our favorites:

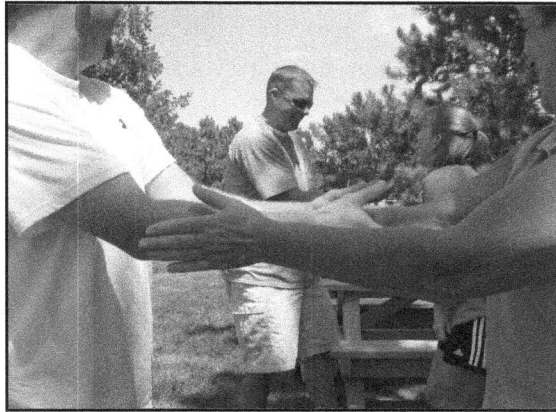

Oregon lumberjack handshake

Begin by giving a thumbs up with your left hand; your partner will grab your thumb and duplicate the sign and so on and so on until all four hands are in use. Now utilizing the same movement as a single jack lumber saw move back and forth saying each others names in a deep, lumberjack voice (Michelle, Mike, Michelle, Mike . . . said in a deep lumberjack voice).

Vermont dairy farmer

With a partner, decide who will be the cow and who will the farmer. Now, for the hand motions, the "cow" will need to lace their fingers together with their thumbs pointing up and as far apart as possible . . . invert your hands so that the thumbs now point down creating the utters of the cow. Now, farmer, you will need to milk the cow and share your name at the same time. Since turn about is fair play, be sure to switch roles and give the cow a chance to be the farmer and vice versa.

South Carolina bass fisherman

Move toward your partner as if you were going to shake hands in a typical fashion, but continue moving your hand until you reach the forearm. Gently slap your hand against your partner's forearm, duplicating the sound of a bass hitting the bottom of a tin boat.

Crush's greeting (from *Finding Nemo*)

Begin with a gentle, backhand high five, followed by a noggin' knock. To safely do the noggin knock, hold your hand backside against your own forehead and gently slap hands together with another person's head while quoting the movie by saying "Dude."

Cappuccino handshake

Hold your coffee in your left hand, high five with your right hand, and then reach down and shake ankles with your right hand . . . all without spilling your coffee!

Crab handshake

Half squat and shake hands through your legs

Texas handshake

Reach across with your right hand, grab hold, and skip around in a circle while exclaiming, "Yee-Haw!"

Sumo handshake

Stomp in a Sumo stance towards your partner and spar with one another!

Come up with your own creative handshake . . . maybe one for your school mascot, state bird, or other fun action that is unique to your group.

VARIATION

At the end of each handshake ask the group to answer a question, share something about themselves, or say good bye in another language.

After you have about four to five different handshake partners do a "Handshake Frenzy." Call out each of the handshakes one at a time and have participants quickly greet their 'bass fisherman' handshake partner. Then after 20 seconds, or long enough that everyone has successfully found their partner and completed their handshake,, call out another handshake. Continue until all handshakes have been called out.

DEBRIEFING TOPICS

Handshakes are great to use as an opener but also as a processing tool. You can keep these same partners throughout the program or length of time the group is together. Use them as partnering tools for discussion questions. Maybe your participants will partner up with folks they usually wouldn't partner with and create a new friend out of their salmon handshake partner.

FACILITATOR NOTES

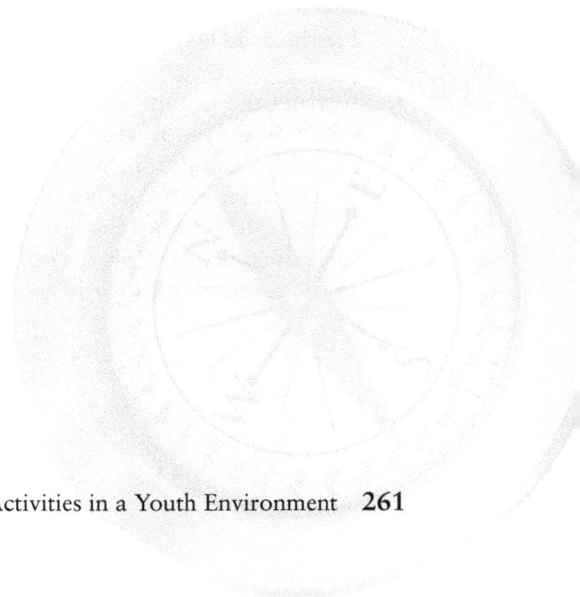

Helium Pole

TYPE OF INITIATIVE
Problem Solving

SOURCE
Karl Rohnke (we think)

PROPS NEEDED
A tent pole or hula hoop, ideally something very light weight

GROUP SIZE
8–20

DIRECTIONS

- Ask the group to divide into two subgroups and stand in two lines facing one another. Ask each participant to stick out their right index finger as if they are pointing at the team across from them. Depending on the overall length of the tent pole, you may be able to accommodate up to 10 people per side. The difficulty level of this activity increases with adding people to each side.
- Explain to the group that you are going to lay the tent pole on their extended index fingers. The only thing that can touch the tent pole is the top of the index finger. They must remain in contact with the pole AT ALL TIMES! The tent pole must continually rest across the top of the right index finger. Encourage the group to keep their fingers straight and pointing at the person across from them. You may want to demonstrate proper form for the pole laying on the TOP of the index finger; otherwise some folks may not do this properly.
- Instruct the group that the object of the activity is to lower the pole to the ground. This sounds easy, but it will challenge them beyond belief. It is a difficult task because it sounds so simple and groups will begin with that assumption.
- It's called Helium Pole because usually the pole will rise above the participants' heads before it will be lowered to the ground. The pole is light enough that any amount of pressure will raise the pole, which is the opposite direction of where they want to go. Groups really have to focus and work together to get the pole to do what they want it to do.

- Facilitate this one carefully, as some groups will get so frustrated that they may want to give up.
- Oftentimes you will see people blaming others for the pole going up and not down, and while they are blaming their fingers are not touching the pole. This is a great example of being worried about what others are doing and not taking care of your own responsibilities.

DEBRIEFING TOPICS

- Why does the pole seem to float higher when the object is for the team to lower it to the floor?
- Why is lowering it so difficult to do while keeping contact with each person's finger?
- After instructions were given, did this seem like an easy task? How did your assumption play into how difficult the task was?
- How important was focus during this activity? Describe behaviors that made it hard to focus. Describe behaviors that made it easier to focus.
- How was the beginning of this activity different from the completion?
- Describe how the group communicated during this activity.
- Did anyone become frustrated with another member of the team? How did you deal with that frustration?
- When you have a conflict with someone, what is your typical response?

DEBRIEFING SCENARIO FOR YOUTH

During the activity we blend into the crowd. We see what other people are doing, which causes us to lose focus. When we lose focus our finger breaks contact from the pole. When we ask 20 people to do a simple task, our sheer determination to accomplish the task can overwhelm the group. With the Helium Pole, our tenacity to keep contact causes us to collectively raise the pole, doing just the opposite of what we want to do. The old saying "there is strength in numbers" is so very true in this instance.

Now imagine being on a schoolyard when a group of rough kids begin to pick on another classmate. The same strength that overwhelms the Helium Pole overwhelms the victim. Think about the conversations that took place among your group when the pole rose higher and higher . . . how did you correct the situation? How will you as an individual correct the conflict or bully situation you are involved in?

FACILITATOR NOTES

How Many Hands

TYPE OF INITIATIVE
Conflict Resolution, Attention Getter, Redirection

SOURCE
This activity was submitted by Edward Caplan, who learned it from a Chicago facilitator named Andy McSchefery

PROPS NEEDED
Your hands

GROUP SIZE
2–10

DIRECTIONS

- Approach a group of two or more people arguing or in conflict. Tell them that you are willing to listen to all sides of the story, but first they must answer a question. Whoever answers the question correctly will get to talk first.
- Place your right hand up in front of the individuals, extend three fingers, and ask, "How many *hands* am I holding up?"
- They will inevitably answer "Three!"
- Inform them that they are not quite right and try again. This time emphasize the word *hands* a little more and say something like, "I'm sorry guys that's not right. Let's try again. How many *Hands* am I holding up?" This time, while holding your right hand up in front of both of them, extend four fingers.
- Usually, if the emotions were high when you first asked, they will be quick to answer incorrectly. Repeat as necessary until someone recognizes that you are only holding up *one hand*.
- Usually, by the third try, a least one of the parties will be slow to answer and start to think about the question instead of reacting. In some situations the person who gets the answer correct first will take the time to explain the answer to the person they were in conflict with.
- This creates a place where two or more people can start admitting to a mistake (not listening to language used or making assumptions) and helping the other person/people to see the situation differently.

A Success Story

Edward Caplan used this approach with two third graders that were in a dispute. Here is his account of what happened:

I approached the two 3rd graders and asked them to breathe. I instantly got the "but he . . ." "then he . . ." I then told them that I would listen to the first person to answer the following question correctly. They both nodded in agreement.

I then placed my right hand up in front of both of them, extended three fingers, and asked, "How many hands *am I holding up?"*

They both responded "Three!" as if their buzzers were broken on a game show.

"I'm sorry guys, that's not right. Let's try again. How many Hands *am I holding up?" I said, holding my right hand up in front of both of them and extending four fingers.*

They again both responded "Four!" as quickly as possible.

"Sorry guys, that's still not right. Let's try one more time." At this point, they are both confused and breathing a little slower.

"How many HANDS *am I holding up?" I said, holding my right hand up in front of both of them extending two fingers.*

This time there was a pause and one boy methodically asked "Two?"

Then immediately the other boy with confidence and with pure "Ah-ha" in his voice said "One!" He then proceeded to explain to his confused counterpart (that he was just wrestling with a minute ago), "Ed said hands, *not fingers." He did this in a non-demeaning way, and the other boy seemed grateful to him for filling him in on the secret.*

Both were now calm and in a better mental and physical state to discuss what had happened.

I have also used this with two high school students that were arguing. I'm not sure exactly why it works, but it appears that by redirecting the negative energy into a concrete brain teaser that they both answer wrong immediately, it creates a point of commonality. This helps them to realize that there may be another way of looking at a situation.

FACILITATOR NOTES

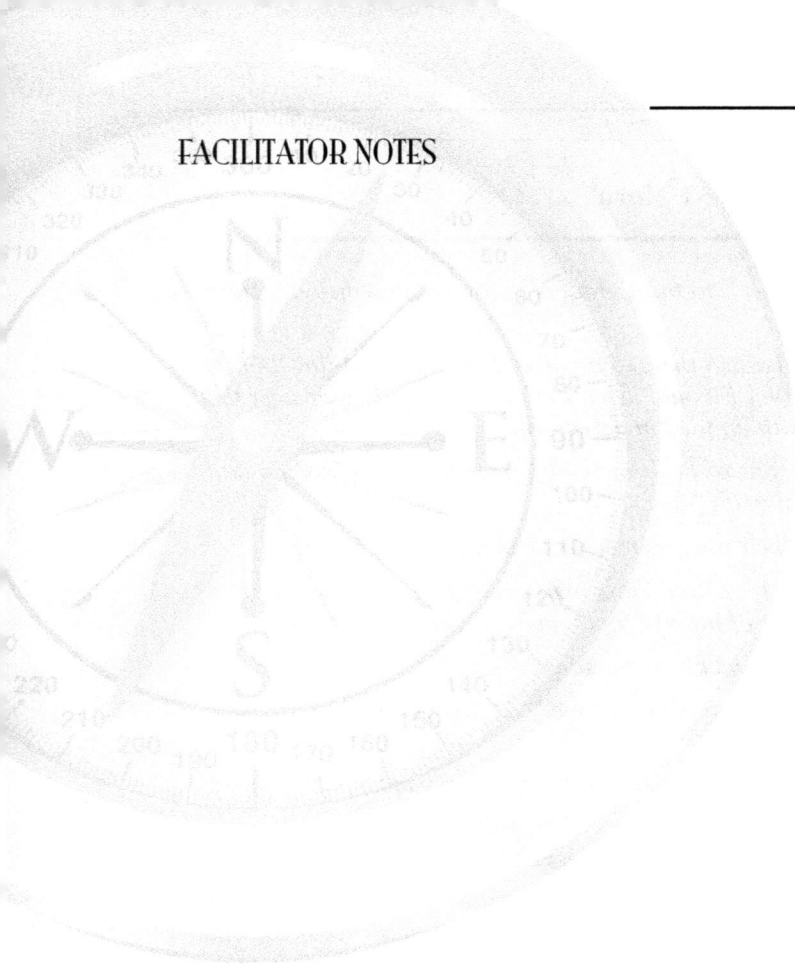

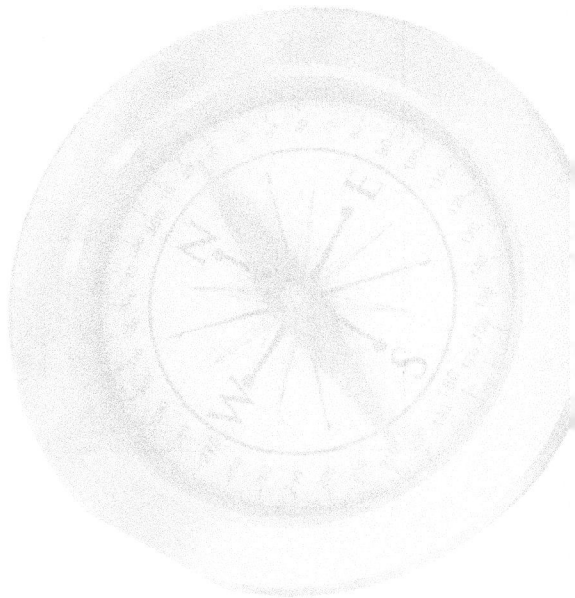

In Group Out Group

TYPE OF INITIATIVE

Diversity Awareness, Conflict Prevention

SOURCE

Originated at The Mosaic Project, further developed by Michelle Cummings

PROPS NEEDED

Flip chart, markers

GROUP SIZE

4–30

DIRECTIONS

Lead In: This activity focuses on differences and stereotypes. Stereotypes are generalizations or assumptions that people make about the characteristics of all members of a group based on an image about what people in that group are like. These images are often wrong. If you assume you know what a person is like, and don't look at each person as an individual, you are likely to make errors in your estimates of a person's character.

In Group   Out Group

STEP-BY-STEP PROCEDURE

Generate a list of all the different types of people in your community. Some possibilities might be "girls, athletes, African Americans, musicians, etc." Aim for 15–20 categories. Divide the room into "in group" and "out group" sections. This could be designated with sheets of paper that say "in group" and "out group." Select one of the categories from your list. Anyone who feels that the description of this category matches them should go to the "in group" side of the room. Those who feel that the description does not match them should go to the "out group" side of the room. Have both sides spend a few minutes creating a list of all the things that they have heard people say about that group. Repeat the process for as many categories as you would like to discuss.

In conflicts, people tend to develop overly negative images of the other side. For example, the opponent is expected to be aggressive, self-serving, and deceitful, while people view themselves in completely positive ways. These stereotypes tend to be self-perpetuating. If one side assumes the other side is deceitful and aggressive, they will tend to respond in a similar way. The opponent will then develop a similar image of the first party, and the negative stereotypes will be confirmed. The stereotypes may grow worse as communication is shut down and escalation heightens emotions and tension.

DEBRIEFING TOPICS

- How different were the lists generated by the "in group" and the "out group" for each topic?
- Why do you think they were similar or different?
- Where do the stereotypes on this list come from?
- How much pressure do such stereotypes place on those people in the "in group"?
- Referring to both the more "positive" and more "negative" stereotypes, what is the benefit of such stereotyping for the "out group"? What are the pitfalls?
- What do you want to remember about this experience?

FACILITATOR NOTES

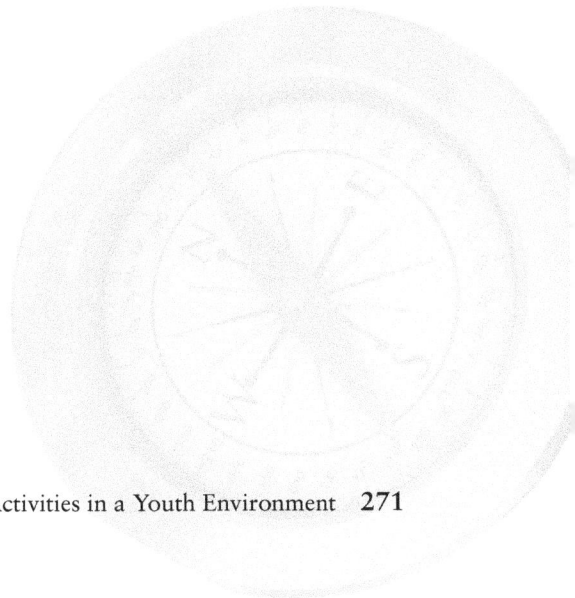

Inside Outside Cards

TYPE OF INITIATIVE

Diversity Awareness, Stereotyping, Processing activity

SOURCE

Michelle Cummings, Training Wheels

PURPOSE

These cards make a great springboard for a discussion of human features and characteristics, both inside and out.

PROPS NEEDED

Inside Outside Cards or paper cutouts shaped like people. Craft materials such as scraps of material, markers, glue, construction paper, scrapbooking paper.

GROUP SIZE

1–30

DIRECTIONS

What is unique about me?

- Invite each participant to pick a card with a skin tone color that best matches them.
- Ask them to decorate the front of the card (the flesh-colored side) with paint, markers, or cut paper. Remind them to pay attention to details like hair, eye color, clothing, accessories (glasses, jewelry), freckles, birthmarks, etc.
- After each participant has finished the outside of their card, ask them to flip to the inside of the card.
- The inside of the card has two sides. Have the participants label one side the 'Public Side' and one side the 'Private Side.'
- Have a discussion on what happens on the inside of us. Talk about the make up of the body with your skeleton, organs, blood, etc. Then move the discussion into other things that happen on the inside, like our feelings. Talk about how some emotions and feelings are easy to show, but other feelings we keep locked up inside and do not share.

- Have the participants draw some feelings they show easily on the 'Public Side.'
- On the 'Private Side,' invite them to draw feelings they keep hidden from others or things they do not share with others. Participants may use dark-colored ink or pencils to write on this side if they do not wish to share these feelings with others. White chalk, crayons, pastels, paint, gel pens, or even white-out can be used to see the writing against the black background.
- When participants have finished, invite them to try to match each project with the participants who created it.
- Allow time for each participant to share their unique creation.
- This is a great opportunity to talk about how outside appearances may differ, but everyone has the same makings on the inside. Our feelings may be different, but our internal structure is all the same.

VARIATION

You could pick any stereotype or group and focus the activity around that. For example, ask participants to pick out a card that looks like a bully to them. Have them decorate their card specific to what a bully looks like on the outside. Then discuss feelings that are easy for a bully to show. For the 'private side' discussion, ask participants to discuss what might be going on inside that a bully may not talk about but may result in negative behaviors.

DEBRIEF TOPICS

- What are some emotions that bullies may have inside?
- What are some emotions that victims of bullying may keep locked up inside?
- What are some reasons why kids bully others?
- What is unique about each of the cards that have been created here today?
- What are some things on the outside of your card that a bully might pick out to bully you about?
- How would you respond if someone picked on you because of the way you looked?
- What feelings do you think would emerge from an incident like that?

Other stereotypes could be

What does a victim of bullying look like?
What does a gang member look like?

WHERE TO FIND IT/HOW TO MAKE IT

Training Wheels sells these unique cards. There are 24 cards per package with eight skin tones represented (three of each).

You could make your own set of cards by folding construction paper in half and cutting out the silhouette of a person.

FACILITATOR NOTES

The Interview

TYPE OF INITIATIVE

Icebreaker

SOURCE

Modified from 4-H Teambuilding Facilitation Manual, 2002 Penn State University

PROPS NEEDED

PURPOSE

You can use this activity to acquaint members of a newly formed group or help an intact group learn more about one another. By learning more about one another, the group becomes familiar with each other, thus establishing trust.

DIRECTIONS

- To begin the interview, ask the group to get into groups of two to three people. This group should be comprised of participants who do not know each other very well. Groups of three participants are encouraged.
- Each person should interview their partner. Make sure that the participants know their answers will be disclosed to the entire group. The interview questions should touch on where they grew up, family, likes, dislikes, feelings toward conflict, and experience either being bullied or being the bully. Allow those groups with three people a few extra minutes to complete their interviews.
- After the interview process, each person will be introduced to the group by his/her partner.

VARIATION

Ask each person to develop two interview questions to ask another member of the group. Have participants conduct the interview as if they were participating in a press conference. The questions can be thought provoking but should not be too personal. Encourage them to be creative in designing their questions.

DEBRIEFING TOPICS

- Did you enjoy being the interviewer or being interviewed better?
- When given time to share in a small group or partnership, how did your conversation change?
- Did you spend more time asking specific questions, or did you have an open-ended discussion?
- Did you share anything that you normally do not share?
- What is one memorable thing you learned about your partner?
- Did any of the questions make you uncomfortable?
- Why is it important to learn more about people we do not know very well?

FACILITATOR NOTES

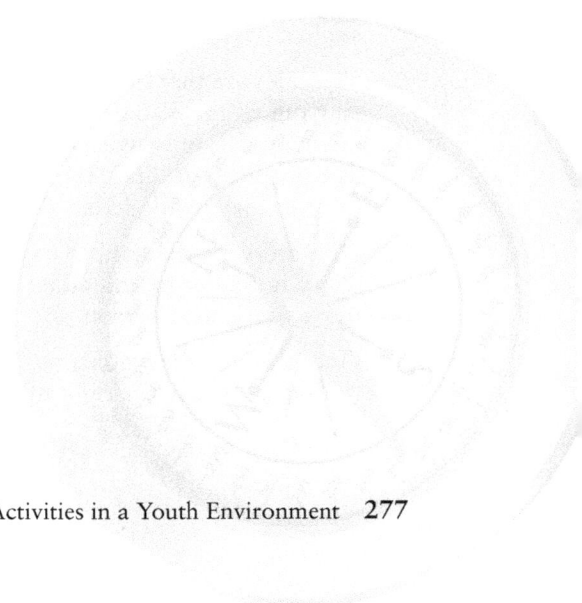

Laughing Matters

TYPE OF INITIATIVE
Being put on the spot, dealing with teasing and conflict

PROPS NEEDED
None

LEVEL
Grades K–5

SOURCES
Journey Towards the Caring Classroom, by Laurie Frank. Adapted from "Mookie," *Adventures in Peacemaking,* p. 123

DIRECTIONS

1. Begin with a discussion about what it feels like to be teased.

2. Introduce a nonsensical word like *fiddlesticks*.

3. Practice saying the word in different ways. How would an opera singer say it, a baby, a goat, a dog, a rapper, a monster, or a ghost?

4. Have the class line up in two lines facing each other.

5. Tell the students that the object is to have someone walk between the two lines without smiling or laughing.

6. The rules are that the walker must keep his or her eyes open. The people in the lines must stay out of the walker's way (give them space to walk) and may not touch the walker in any way. The only word that may be spoken is the nonsensical word that was introduced. The people in the lines, though, may say the word any way they want, and make any kinds of faces they would like.

7. Give everyone the right to pass by starting at one end and asking if that person would like to try it. She or he can either say "yes" and do it or say "pass," at which point you will move to the next person.

8. Once through the whole line, go back to give the people who passed an opportunity to try it. They still have the right to pass.

© 2004 Laurie Frank

DEBRIEFING TOPICS

- Was this hard for you? How? What strategies did you use to try not to smile?
- How did it feel to be the ones saying *fiddlesticks*?
- How did it feel to walk down the line?
- Was it easy or hard for you to decide to take a turn? Are you glad you had the choice?

EXTENSIONS

- Ignoring is one way to deal with teasing. When is it not appropriate to ignore it? Brain storm other ways to deal with teasing.
- Discuss why some people chose to do this while others did not. Go around and ask each person an activity they might choose (or have chosen in the past) not to participate in. What caused them to make that choice?
- Create a chart of activities in school where students have a choice and those where they do not. For example, you might have recess as not being a choice but what they do at recess as a choice. Other times you might have times when students must work in groups, but they have a choice about who they work with.

It is common for adults to tell children to ignore teasing, but youngsters are seldom given concrete strategies to do this very difficult thing. This activity is a way to do that because the strategies used to ignore someone who is trying to make them laugh are similar to the ones used when someone is trying to make them upset. Any strategies they choose to use are acceptable. Common ones include: looking away or focusing on something else, thinking about other things, and getting through it quickly (walking away).

It is imperative that students really feel like they have a choice to do this activity or not. Walking a gauntlet can be intimidating, even if it is about laughing.

ADAPTATIONS FOR STUDENTS WITH DISABILITIES: LAUGHING MATTERS

Cognitive Disabilities	• This activity may not be appropriate for students with cognitive disabilities.
Orthopedic Impairment	• Make sure there is space in and between the lines for a wheelchair.
Hearing Impairment	• Have an interpreter available if necessary.
Visual Impairment	• Have students in the lines use "bumpers up"—hands up in front of them, palms facing out—to help the participant know where the lines are.

FACILITATOR NOTES

Marriage

TYPE OF INITIATIVE

Problem Solving, Diversity

SOURCE

Playing With a Full Deck, by Michelle Cummings

PROPS NEEDED

A deck of playing cards

GROUP SIZE

10 or more

PURPOSE

The object of the Marriage activity is to find the person who has the same color and number card without saying what card you have.

SETTING UP THE CARDS

This activity works best with an odd number of players. You will need one card for each participant. You will need a pair of cards in the same color and denomination (e.g., 3 of hearts and the 3 of diamonds; 5 of spades and the 5 of clubs). You will also need one Joker card.

DIRECTIONS

- Each participant is given a card and asked not to show it to anyone. The goal of the activity is to find the person in the room who has the same color and number of card as they do. For example, if a participant has the 3 of hearts, they will be searching for someone in the room that has the 3 of diamonds.
- **However, participants are not allowed to say the color or number of their card.** As they mingle from person to person they must describe their card without saying the 'taboo' words of *red* or *three*. One might say, "I have an Apple-colored card and my car doesn't work well right now as it is missing a tire."

- When pairs think they have found one another, they link arms and wait until the other participants have finished.
- There is only one Joker in the room. This person will mingle for the duration of the activity and not be able to find a partner. "Pas de marriage," in French means, "no wedding," hence the title of the activity.

VARIATION

Do not allow participants to look at their cards. Ask participants to place the card to their forehead and, without talking, pair each other up according to color and number.

INTERESTING STORY

This activity was played one time using the rules described in the variation. Without talking, participants were pairing people up according to color and number. The participant with the Joker was unaware that they had the Joker card or that there was a Joker card being used. Other participants were trying to be helpful trying to communicate to this participant what their card was. They were gesturing to this participant by pointing and laughing at them. They were trying to communicate that this participant had the Joker card, but what came across to the participant was mean and hurtful communication. This participant believed that since she could not find a partner that others were pointing and laughing at her. There was an amazing debriefing session afterward about nonverbal communication and intention.

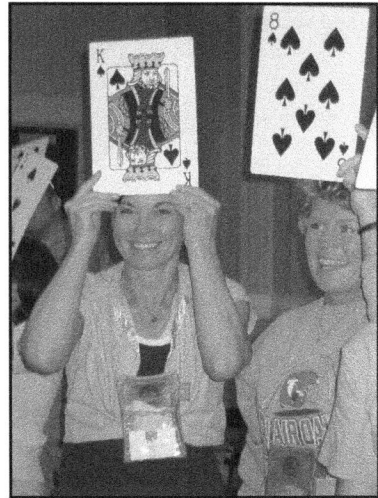

DEBRIEFING TOPICS

- How did you choose to communicate with others in this activity?
- How did it feel to be the Joker? How did others treat you when they realized you did not have the same card they did?
- What did it feel like when you found your partner?
- Did you attempt to help others once you found your partner? Why or why not?
- How is this activity like modern society?
- What were some feelings that came up for you?
- There is one person who could not find a partner. How did this affect the way you played the game?
- What were some feelings you felt toward this person?
- What can we do in our group to avoid situations or feelings like this from happening?

FACILITATOR NOTES

Mix and Match Emotion Stencils

TYPE OF INITIATIVE

Craft, Processing

SOURCE

Michelle Cummings, Training Wheels

PROPS NEEDED

Paper, pencils, markers, emotion stencils

GROUP SIZE

1–30

PURPOSE

Create emotional expressions! Use these stencils to help your participants develop their recognition of emotions and broaden their own range of expressions. They can be used for self-expression to process a conflict or as a group initiative to create a work of art.

DIRECTIONS

Invite participants to gather their choice of paper, paint, yarn, markers, or pencils. Pop out and discard all of the interior pieces from the stencils. Lay out your stencils and ask the participants to create a range of expressions. Tell them they can use just one stencil or mix and match different characteristics of various stencils to create an original face. Use yarn, crayons, and other art supplies to finish off their face.

VARIATIONS

Here are some creative ideas for using your stencils:

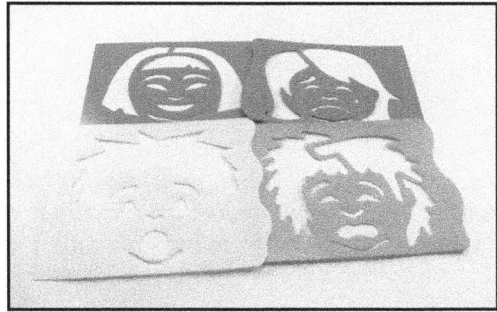

- Make some handsome hand puppets. Trace or paste your face onto a paper bag. Encourage participants to write out a play starring their new puppets. Have them create a conflict situation between a bully and a victim of bullying puppet. Then have them re-create an incident of bullying.
- Emotional discussion. Talk about eight primary emotions: joy, fear, anticipation, sadness, disgust, anger, submission, and acceptance. Discuss other emotions and how they relate to these eight. Ask participants to recreate emotions using different elements of the stencils. Discuss what emotions bullies might feel and what emotions victims of bullying might feel.
- Wall murals and portraits. Create a mural or series of portraits focusing on different emotions for reference when discussing feelings. Use the unique border of the stencils to create a frame for your portraits. Add speech bubbles and label the emotions. When a situation arises, ask participants to indicate on the mural which emotions were expressed.
- Unique cards. Use a variety of expressions to create cards. Draw emotions to illustrate different occasions and greeting cards.
- Use the stencils as a reference when creating or drawing various faces. Combine features to make these emotions silly, sleepy, bored, and excited.
- Have participants create a conflict cartoon. Have them create the different panels using the stencils to draw the characters throughout a conflict situation.

FACILITATOR NOTES

Mood Dudes

There are several ways to use Mood Dudes™. They are helpful for group discussions, counseling sessions, or any program in which you would like people to discuss their feelings. There are five faces depicting sad, happy, disgusted, shocked, and anxious emotions.

SOURCE

Creative Therapy, www.ctherapy.com. The Mood Dudes™ artwork is trademarked by Creative Therapy.

Published in *A Teachable Moment*, pp. 166.

PURPOSE

Having tangible feelings faces for participants to hold onto while talking about their feelings.

PROPS NEEDED

Squeezable Mood Dude™ faces

GROUP SIZE

1–12 per set

DIRECTIONS

Here are a few suggestions on ways to use Mood Dudes™.

- Put them in the center of your sharing circle and let your participants pick and choose which feeling they want to talk about or have experienced.
- Use them with individuals and have them talk about an experience with each expression.

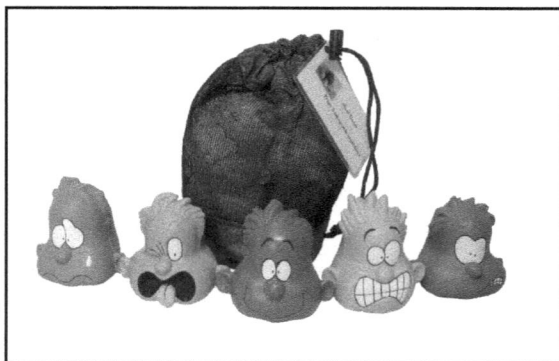

- Use them to talk about the many emotions that come up in conflict situations.
- Use them with character development programs.

Having something tangible for your participants to hold onto while talking eases the experience of talking in front of others. They are made of stress reliever material and are 2 3/4″ × 2 3/4″ in size. Those who are really nervous about talking in front of others may be squeezing the heck out of the faces! You may purchase the faces individually or in a set of five.

WHERE TO FIND IT/HOW TO MAKE IT

Creative Therapy, www.ctherapy.com; Training Wheels, www.training-wheels.com, set of five only.

Other Mood products you can use in conjunction with the Mood Dudes™ are: Mood Postcards, Mood Posters, Mood Cube, and Mood Magnets.

FACILITATION NOTES

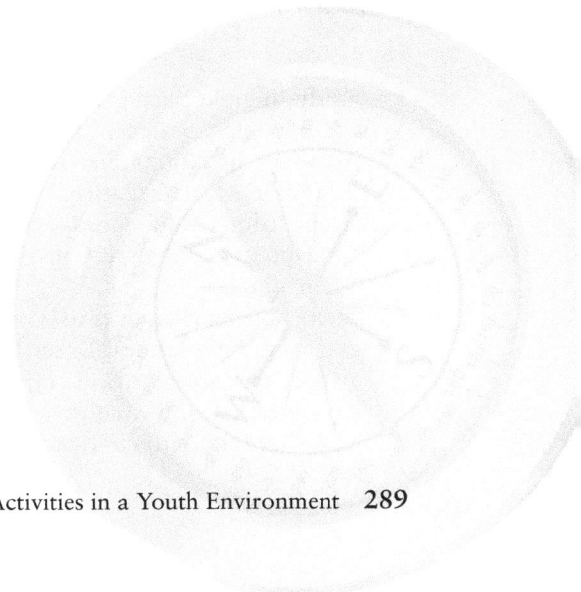

Multicultural Picture Cards

TYPE OF INITIATIVE

Diversity, Processing activity, Reflection tool

SOURCE

Michelle Cummings, Training Wheels

PURPOSE

Illustrated pictures are perfect for learning about relationships, family structures, multiculturalism, people from various generations, and stereotyping.

PROPS NEEDED

My Family Your Family Picture Cards, pictures of people of different ethnicities, genders, and ages. To represent people from various cultures, there are 72 family flash cards composed of 12 individuals from 6 ethnic backgrounds. There are at least three generations represented in each ethnicity.

GROUP SIZE

1–30

DIRECTIONS

Here are a few suggestions on ways to use these cards:

- Study the relationships in your group. Participants can work individually, in pairs, or in small groups. Select a number of character portrait cards, and discuss the relationships between the characters. Are they grandparents and grandchildren? Siblings? Friends? Neighbors? Doctor/Patient? Co-workers? Teacher/Student? Make a list of all of the possible relationships that could exist between groups of people. Participants can write up descriptions of the relationships. Each group can present their discussions to the rest of the group.
- Invite your participants to write a fictional biography. Choose one or two character cards and give them names. Describe where they were born, the school they attended or still attend, their current occupation or what they want to be when they grow up, where they have traveled, and what they are doing now. Discussions can focus around stereotyping and how that relates to conflict.

- Compose a family. Participants can work individually to create a character card family that is similar to or different from their own family. Arrange the individual portrait cards into a family tree. Place the grandparents at the top of the tree, followed by parent and children. You may be able to have four generations represented in your family tree. Describe the relationship between these people—how similar and different are they from your family?

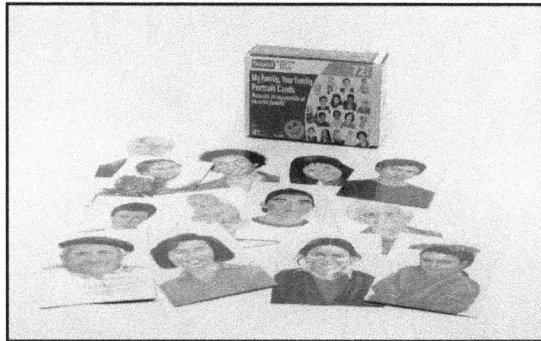

- Fictional bullying story. Invite your participants to choose several cards and create a fictional story about how someone is bullied. One card could be the bully or a group of bullies. One card could represent the victim of the bullying incident. Another card could represent the trusted adult that the victim reports the incident to. Other cards could be the parents of the bully and how they react when they are told about the incident. Invite each participant or group to share their fictional story with the rest of the group.
- Create a conflict situation. Invite your participants to choose cards that match a conflict they have witnessed.
- Choose a bully. Ask your participants to choose one card that looks like a bully to them. Ask them to journal why they chose the card they did and what made that person a bully. You could choose any stereotype for this variation.

WHERE TO FIND IT/HOW TO MAKE IT

Training Wheels sells a set of the My Family Your Family Cards. You could also cut pictures out of magazines representing different ethnicities, generations, and cultures.

FACILITATION NOTES

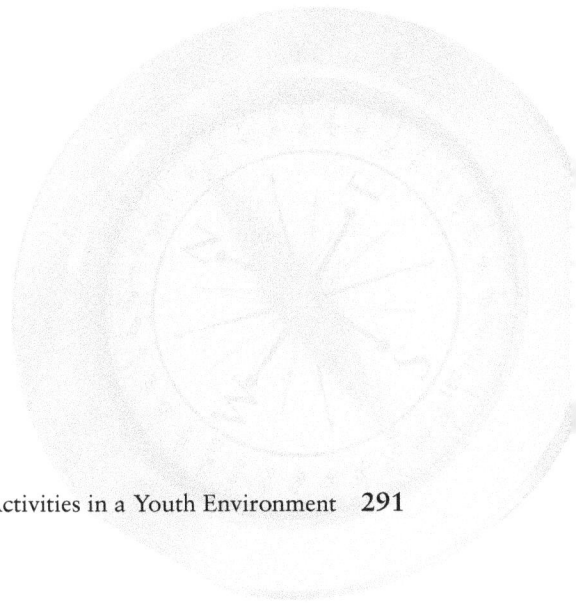

Old Maid or Old Mister

TYPE OF INITIATIVE
Problem Solving and Diversity

SOURCE
Playing With a Full Deck, Michelle Cummings

PROPS NEEDED
A deck of playing cards

GROUP SIZE
17–35 players

PURPOSE
Not to get the Old Maid or Old Mister card

SETTING UP THE CARDS

If you want to play Old Maid, take out all the Queens except the Queen of Spades. If you want to play Old Mister, take out all the Jacks except the Jack of Spades. This is much like the traditional card game Old Maid.

You will need an odd number of people to play the game. Separate the deck into suits. Set aside the Spades and one other suit. You will need pairs of cards and one card per participant. For example, if you have 17 players, you would need the following cards: one Jack of Spades, two 3's, two 4's, two 6's, two 8's, two 9's, two 10's, two Queens, and two Kings.

PLAYING THE GAME

- Divide the group into four teams. Deal each participant a card. They are allowed to show their card to the members of their small group, but not to the other three groups.
- Each group looks for pairs in their small group. If a group has any pairs, those two people may sit down. They are still allowed to participate and strategize with their group, but they may not be selected from other groups.

- Designate which group will start. The first group chooses one person/card from the group to their left. The person selected leaves their original group and joins the group that chose them. This group looks at the new card that has joined their group. If they can make a pair with the new card, the people with the pair may sit down.
- The group who just lost a member is the next group to select a new member from the group to their left. If they can make a pair with the new card, the people with the pair may sit down. If not, the next team chooses their new member.
- Now remember, there is one card out there that no one wants, the Old Mister. It may be hard for groups to mask who has this card. Especially if this card gets chosen by another group. Most groups have a hard time disguising their reactions and feelings when the Old Mister joins their group. Likewise, the group that knows the Old Mister has just left their group also has a hard time masking their reaction to this event. One way to spice up the activity so no one knows who has the Old Mister or the Old Maid is to have the participants hold their cards face down and trade cards with three people in their small groups before the next round begins. This way it is a surprise to everyone as to what card is leaving the group.
- Another thing to consider is the feelings of the person who has the Old Mister card. There will be many topics that come up in this activity for you to debrief the group with after it is over.
- The activity continues until the only person left standing is the Old Maid or the Old Mister.

DEBRIEFING TOPICS

- How did it feel to be the Old Maid or the Old Mister?
- How many different people experienced the Old Maid card?
- How did groups treat you when you entered their group as the Old Mister?
- Give examples of how this is like everyday life?
- How often do we exclude people we do not want in our "group"?
- Have you ever been the only person of your race in a classroom/group?
- How did that make you feel? How can you compare that to this activity?

FACILITATOR NOTES

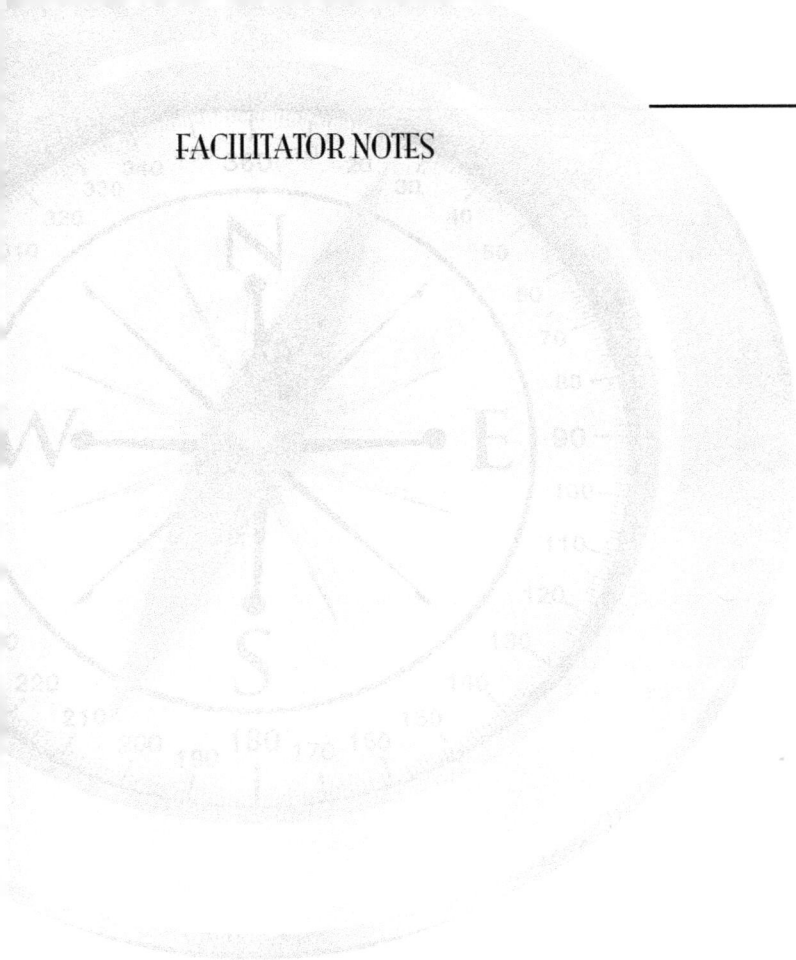

Pocket Processor

TYPE OF INITIATIVE

Processing Tool

SOURCE

Institute for Experiential Education, Buzz
Bocher, Steve Simpson, and Dan Miller
Published in *A Teachable Moment*, pp. 176–177.

PROPS NEEDED

Pocket Processor Cards

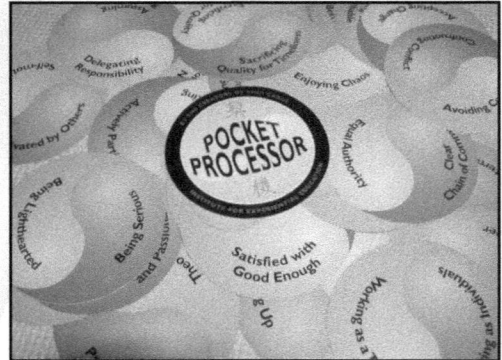

PURPOSE

The Pocket Processor is a processing tool based on the theory of the yin and the yang. This theory describes two ends of a continuum, with each end having the seed of the other. A healthy being does not stay at one point on the continuum but flows continuously between the two extremes. The Pocket Processor helps participants examine the flow along the continuum.

DIRECTIONS

There are several ways to use the Pocket Processor.

BASIC USE

The most basic use of the Pocket Processor is to debrief an activity by spreading all cards out and asking each participant to choose the card that best represents some kind of progress made (either individual or group progress). Then allow each person to explain his or her choice (e.g., "I chose the competing/cooperating card because I am naturally very competitive, but I successfully fought off my desire to complete the initiative faster than the other group").

VARIATION 1

Rather than allowing each person to pick a card, the facilitator may ask the group to come to consensus on the one card (or two or three cards) that best exemplifies progress made by the group. The narrowing down of the cards then may become the topic of discussion, and the participants will start processing all of the issues to narrow it down to the top one. For a direct line to bullying, ask the group specific questions to come to consensus on/around bullying.

Come to consensus on the biggest challenge a victim of bullying would have to deal with. Come to consensus on the card that might best represent why someone would be a bully.

Discuss the cards shown and put the cards in order from the least significant to the most significant card in relation to how a bully might feel. Complete it a second time on how the victim might feel.

VARIATION 2

Fifty-four cards can be overwhelming. Facilitators may choose to narrow the options to a smaller number of cards (7–20) before spreading them out.

FRONTLOADING

The Pocket Processor is an excellent frontloading tool. If a group has multiple goals or a poor idea of what its goals are, spread out the cards prior to the day's activities. Then have the group pick out one or two themes that they want to work on that day. After the day's activities are complete, pull out the cards chosen and ask them to assess their progress on the goals that they set for themselves at the beginning of the day. Goals can be individual or as a group. Rather than setting group goals, a facilitator may frontload by allowing each member of the group to choose his or her own card.

HUMAN CONTINUUM

It is important to remind the participants that the two phrases on each card are extremes of a continuum, not dichotomies. One way to convey this information is through a human continuum.

- Have two sides of a room (or an open space) be two extremes of a continuum. You can place a piece of webbing or rope to mark the center.
- Instruct the participants to stand on the line. Explain that the line has a value of 0 and the walls on either side of the line have a value of 5. The space in between the line and the walls represent from 1,2,3,4, and the walls are 5 on both sides.
- Then read the two sides of the card and allow every participant to physically place him or herself anywhere on that continuum. For example, a facilitator can say, "this side of the room is avoiding conflict. The other side of the room is confronting conflict. I want each of you to find the place on the continuum where you most fit today."
- The human continuum then lends itself to discussion (e.g., "If most of you usually avoid conflict, what impact does that have on our group? If a conflict arises in our group today, how will it get handled? What are the pros and cons of this arrangement?")

WHERE TO FIND IT/HOW TO MAKE IT

To make this activity you could use index cards and write down categories on each card and use it the same way as described. To purchase a deck of the Pocket Processor Cards, contact the Institute for Experiential Education, www.chiji.com, Training Wheels www.training-wheels.com, High 5 Adventures, or Project Adventure.

FACILITATOR NOTES

Pokerface

TYPE OF INITIATIVE

Problem Solving, Diversity

SOURCES

Possiblesbag Teambuilding Kit Activity Manual, by Chris Cavert
Playing With a Full Deck, Michelle Cummings

PURPOSE

This activity focuses on inclusion and diversity.

PROPS NEEDED

A deck of playing cards, preferably jumbo playing cards

GROUP SIZE

Plays well with 10 or more

DIRECTIONS

Playing the Game

- Shuffle your deck of cards and give one to each participant. Ask them not to look at the face of the card. As you explain the directions, ask the participants to hold their card so the face is down toward the floor.
- Tell them that in a moment you are going to ask them to place that card to their forehead. They are not to look at their own card, but everyone else can see their card.
- Instruct them that you are going to be intentionally vague with the directions. Figuring out what to do is a part of the game.
- This activity involves the players mingling around the room, holding their card on their forehead, and treating each other based on the face value of the cards that they see. You can play this game silently or you can allow talking—both ways are powerful. Playing the game silently usually has a more powerful impact. If you choose this option, instruct the group that they do not have the resource of their voice.

- Then ask them to place their card to their forehead and say, "Please treat each other based on the face value of the card that you see. Ready, Go."
- The mingling begins and there is some slight confusion at first. Some participants are uncertain how to treat others.
  - Some typical behaviors are:
    - The royalty cards are usually bowed down to, given high fives, and generally treated very well. Most cards want to 'hang out' with the high cards. Usually royalty cards start grouping together.
    - The middle cards are pretty much ignored. They sometimes get a 'so-so' hand motion demonstrated to them or a shrug of the shoulders.
    - The low cards are treated many different ways. Some get a dismissive hand gesture; some get the letter 'L' sign on a forehead depicting 'Loser'. Some low cards will get a pretend kick their way or dirty looks by others. Some will get a thumbs down motion. These behaviors are obvious and can look somewhat severe to onlookers. Often participants with low cards will form smaller subgroups and begin to back out of the middle of the mingling area.
- After some mingling, ask the players to stop talking and stand still—DON'T LOOK AT THE CARDS YET! Ask the group to separate into what group they think they are in, low cards, middle cards, or high cards. Players place themselves based on how they were treated. When everyone is in a group, ask the participants to look around the room at the order of cards on each player's forehead, and then look at their own card.

DEBRIEFING SEQUENCE:

Start with the low cards and ask them these questions:

- What were some behaviors that were done toward you that led you to believe you had a low card?
- How quickly did you realize you had a low card?

Then move to the middle cards and ask them these questions:

- What were some behaviors that were demonstrated toward you that led you to believe you had a middle card?
- How long did it take you to realize what value of card you had?

Then move to the high cards and ask these questions:

- What were some behaviors that were demonstrated toward you that led you to believe you had a high card?
- How quickly did you realize you had a high card?

The next round of questioning starts with the high cards, then moves to the middle cards, and then moves to the low cards. Ask each group this question:

- After you realized what value of card you had, did it influence the way you played the game?
- What were some specific behaviors you did toward others because of the value of card you had?

The responses to this question are pretty profound. Typically the royalty cards report that they treated others poorly because they had the power. It's interesting to watch the royalty cards get bowed to and the "2" cards get pushed away and treated poorly. During the activity the participants with the low cards will usually back out of the middle of the mingling area. This can lead to a great discussion on one's willingness to fully participate in a group if they are being treated poorly.

This activity also leads to a great discussion on who places value on you. What happens when people feel left out? Isn't the "2" card sometimes the most valuable card when playing blackjack and you have a 19? How would the activity be played differently if there were no royalty cards in the deck? If you were running a race wouldn't you rather be second than tenth? These are great topics of discussion for diversity, cultural norms, and society in general. People of all abilities can play.

NOTE: This game can bring up some interesting emotions that you may have to deal with. These are the teachable moments! Some teachable moments are more powerful than others for different people. Keep a watchful eye over all your players. Make sure they all leave the activity with their self-esteem intact.

DEBRIEFING TOPICS

- How did it feel to be a royalty card?
- How did it feel to be a lower-numbered card?
- What behaviors did you notice going on in the activity?
- How were you treated?
- Did you notice any secluded groups forming?
- How is this activity like everyday society?
- Once you realized what kind of card you had, did it influence the way you participated in the activity?

FACILITATOR NOTES

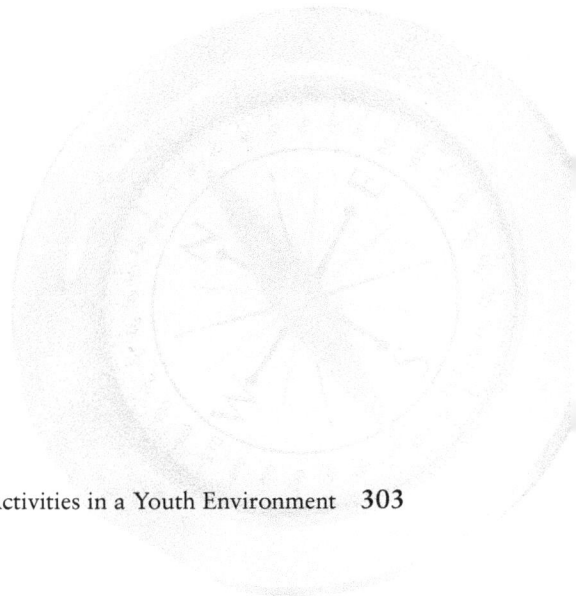

Privilege

PROPS NEEDED

Pieces of candy, fake dollar bills

DIRECTIONS

Come up with a definition for the word *privilege* with the group before starting the activity. After the group has come up with a definition, give them one of the two examples here:

1. A right or immunity granted as a peculiar benefit, advantage, or favor: prerogative: especially: such a right or immunity attached specifically to a position or an office

2. A right enjoyed by a person beyond the common advantages of others. A special right granted to persons in authority, a prerogative.

STEP-BY-STEP PROCEDURE:

Line everyone up, shoulder to shoulder. Then read the following:

- If your family owns more than one car, take a step forward.

- If you have ever been discriminated against based on gender or race, take a step back. If not, take a step forward.

- If you have ever traveled out of the country take a step forward.

- If your parents own their house, take a step forward.

- If you can easily find role models of your own race, take a step forward—if not, take a step back.

- If you are confident in your academic abilities, take a step forward.

- If you are happy with your physical appearance, take a step forward.

- At the end of the last statement, hold up a piece of candy, dollar bill, or some prize and tell the students to race for it. See who is able to grab the prize first.

DEBRIEFING TOPICS

- What might this dollar symbolize?
- Was it fair that certain people were closer to the dollar than others? Why?
- Why might some people have more privilege than others?
- Can you identify privileges that some people have that others may not?
- Where does privilege come from?
- Do you think you have privilege?
- What can we do about privilege?

Make sure you give the students all a piece of candy/fake dollar at the end of the activity.

FACILITATOR NOTES

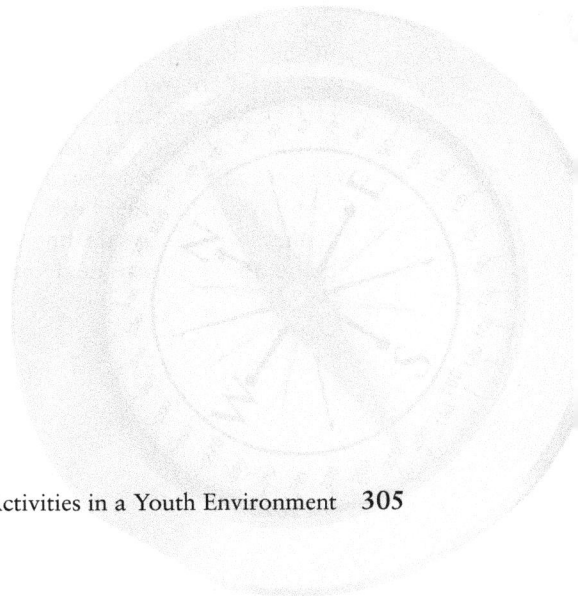

Push Off

TYPE OF INITIATIVE
Opener

PROPS NEEDED
None

DIRECTIONS
Have participants partner with someone relatively their same size. Instruct them to stand about 2 feet apart from one another facing one another. With their feet planted shoulder-width apart, have them place their palms together about shoulder height. The object is to try to push off and release with your hands to make your partner lose their balance and take a step forward or backward. By pushing off and releasing at the right moments you can throw your partner off balance.

This is a quick activity that allows you to talk about resistance met with resistance, aggression met with aggression, and strategies for dealing with someone who is aggressive toward you. This aggression could be verbal or physical. After participants have partnered with someone their same size, have them partner up with someone completely smaller or larger than they are and see how differently the activity plays out.

DEBRIEFING TOPICS
- What were some of your strategies to throw your partner off balance?
- What strategies were consistently the most successful?
- How different was the experience when you partnered with someone who was bigger than you? Smaller than you?
- How could you relate your experience in this activity to dealing with a bully?
- Describe how this activity relates to being in a verbal conflict with a friend.
- What is a good action plan you could take if someone were bullying you?
- Why do bullies use aggression?
- What happened when both parties used resistance as a technique?
- If bullies were always dealing with resistance would they be very successful? What does that tell you about how to deal with a bully?

FACILITATOR NOTES

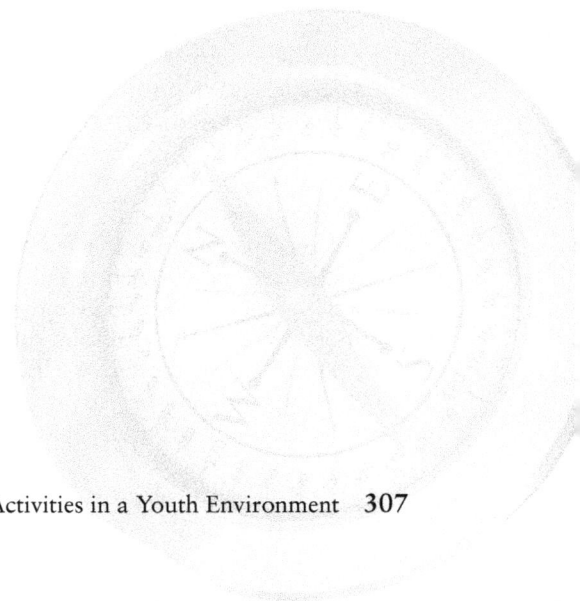

Rejection

TYPE OF INITIATIVE
Diversity, Get to Know You

GROUP SIZE
20 or more

SOURCE
Idea from Rick Bosch

DIRECTIONS
This activity should be played as an initial mixer with a twist. Give each participant a card. Ask them to find a partner with a card that has something in common with their card (this could be the suit, the number, or the color). Depending on the outcomes you have for your program, you could have them discuss one of the following things or come up with your own. Here are a few suggestions:

GET TO KNOW YOU TOPICS
- Find three things you have in common with your partner
- Share a goal you have for the day
- Share why you came to the program/workshop
- Discuss your favorite foods
- Describe the first car you ever owned

Encourage the group to keep mingling and try to connect with at least five to six people. The twist in this activity is in the directions. As you hand out the cards, the participants that receive a red card are given normal instructions for the activity. Participants that are given a black card are given the same instructions with the additional rule they are not allowed to talk to anyone with a red card.

With large groups there are many options for everyone to mill around and find a partner to discuss the chosen topic. At first, those with red cards may be unaware that there are participants in the group that are not allowed to talk to them. After 5 minutes, nonchalantly start exchanging red cards with black cards and give the new instructions to these participants. As the milling about continues there will be visible moments of participants with black cards avoiding the participants with red cards. Stop the activity after this is seen a few times, and ask the group to get into a circle to debrief what happened. Always inform the group of the two sets of rules that were being played so the participants with red cards understand that they were avoided on purpose.

VARIATION

Mike Pollack, Leadership Development International, Tianjian, China, shared this wonderful cross-cultural variation of this activity. Set the Rejection exercise up as indicated and add these instructions:

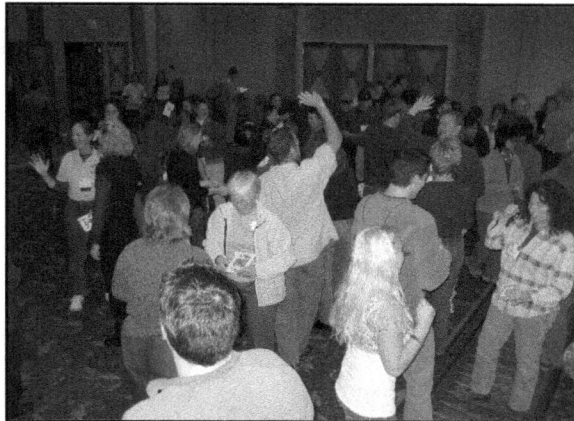

Pairs had to find 3 things in common and had to share a goal for the training day and a goal for the summer trips they were planning.

- Black suits could not talk to red suits was the original rule given only to the black suit cards

However, for added cross-cultural fodder add (taped to the back of the cards):

- Face cards cannot smile
- Odd numbers do not ask or answer direct questions
- Red, even-numbered cards are embarrassed to talk about themselves and will excuse themselves rather than answer

Each person has their own rules, and they are told not to discuss the rules. Each person has to find at least six partners in 10 minutes.

From Mike Pollack: "The results of this variation are great! It definitely stirs up the issues of cross-cultural work with students and staff. It brought up the necessity to defer judgment and to practice patience when we don't know the 'rules' others are playing by, as well as insights about rejection."

DEBRIEFING TOPICS

- How did this activity make you feel?
- How did it feel to have a black card? What were some of your strategies for encountering a participant with a red card?
- If you had a red card, describe an interaction you attempted to have with a black card.
- How is this activity like society?
- Describe how interactions in a conflict situation might mimic the same interactions that were demonstrated or observed here.
- Did anyone experience any anxiety or inner conflict with the rules of the activity?

After a large-group discussion has been completed, invite group members to find a partner and share for a few minutes their experience with the activity. This allows for everyone to verbalize any feelings or thoughts on the experience.

FACILITATOR NOTES

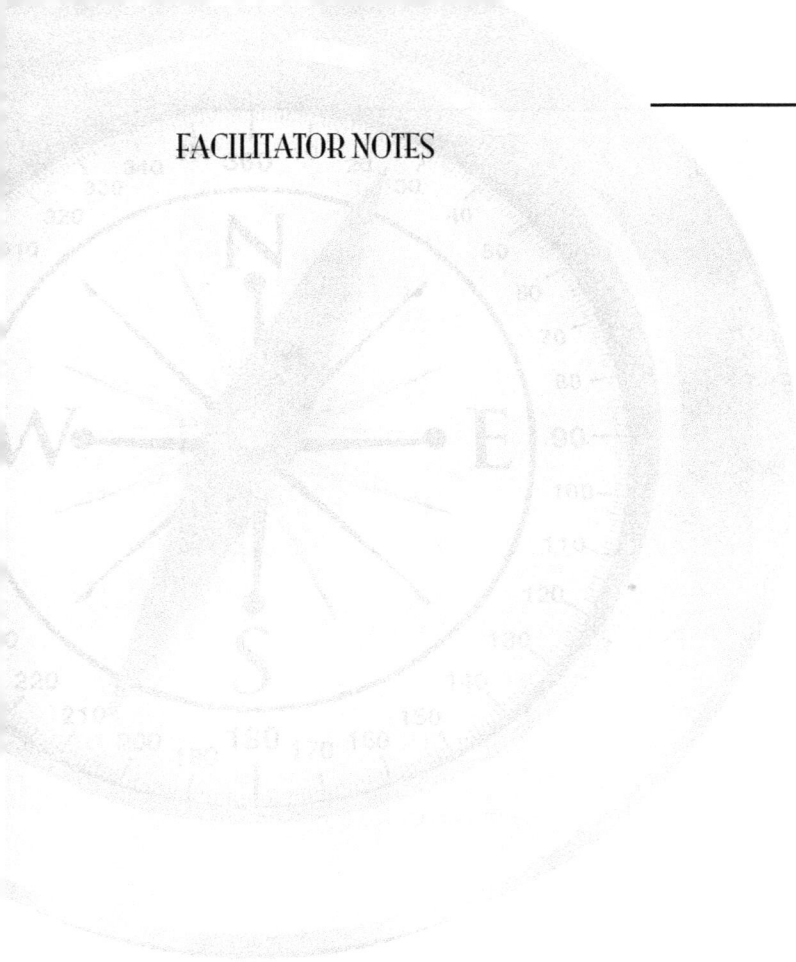

Rope Puzzles

Each of these activities presents a visual puzzle for a team to solve. However, the solution is only part of the puzzle. Working toward consensus within the team is the ultimate goal and the teachable moment for these unique puzzles.

TYPE OF INITIATIVE

Problem Solving, Perspective

SOURCE

Teambuilding Puzzles

PROPS NEEDED

2B or Knot 2B requires five different colors of rope or webbing. Each rope segment should be about 10 feet (3 meters) in length. The Missing Link requires two different colors of rope or webbing. Each rope should be about 10–16 feet (3–5 meters) in length. Not Knots requires just a single piece of soft, flexible rope or webbing. This rope should be about 6 feet (2 meters) in length.

DIRECTIONS

Figure A, 2B or Knot 2B, shows an arrangement of four colorful pieces of rope or webbing that have been joined together by a fifth piece. This puzzle is presented in such a manner that it is not immediately obvious which rope is the one holding the other four together. The challenge for the group is to discover which rope is holding the other ropes together and to achieve consensus on this selection before touching any of the ropes.

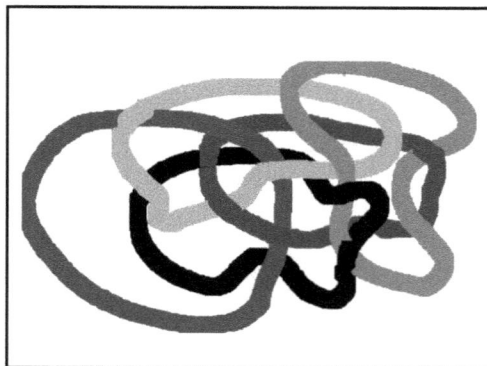

Figure A   2B or Knot to 2B

The goal of **The Missing Link,** shown in Figure B, is for a group to decide if the two segments of rope are linked together (like links of a chain) or unlinked by visually checking them and without touching them.

While the actual solution may be simple or complex, the real value of this activity comes from a team working together to achieve a group consensus, listening to each other, and learning the skills that it takes to get everyone on the same page. We like to begin this activity by a process called 'pairing and sharing,' which involves everyone working with a partner in an attempt to convince one other person before trying to convince the entire group.

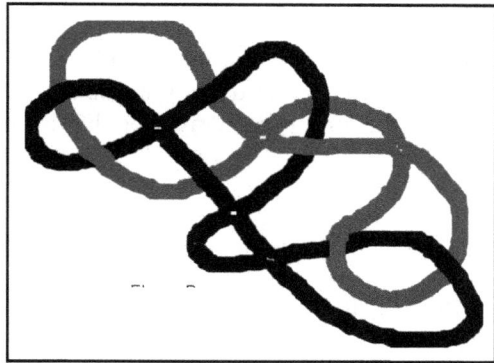

Figure B The Missing Link

A natural consensus-building activity to follow 2B or Knot 2B or The Missing Link is **Not Knots,** shown in Figure C. In this activity, which can be accomplished with only a single piece of rope or webbing, a "doodle" is constructed and the group is given the choice of whether this doodle will create a KNOT or NOT A KNOT (i.e., a straight line), when the ends of the rope are pulled away from each other.

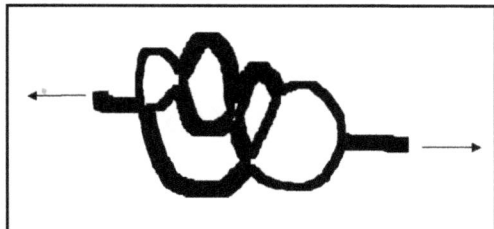

Figure C Not Knots

The object here is to provide the group with some tools to use when they cannot easily form a consensus. Typically, upon analysis, about half of the group thinks the doodle will form a knot, and the other half a straight line. If this is the case, ask participants to partner with another person that has a different viewpoint (i.e., one partner from the KNOT side, and one partner from the NOT A KNOT side). By learning how to listen to a person with a different viewpoint, group members learn how to cooperate. After this discussion, ask participants to choose sides, with the KNOT decision folks on one side of the knot doodle, and the NOT A KNOT folks on the other side. At this point, it is likely that there will still not be a complete consensus within the group. Prior to slowly pulling the ends of the knot doodle, let the members of the group know that you will pull the knot doodle slowly, and they can change sides at any time during the unraveling of the knot doodle (this illustrates the ability to make an initial decision but still be flexible as more information becomes available).

HINTS AND CLUES

For 2B or Knot 2B, consider not only which rope appears to be the correct rope, but also which ropes can be eliminated from the choice because they are obviously not the correct rope. Also, look for the 'hint rope'. Any rope that is only attached to one other rope indicates which rope is the correct one.

For The Missing Link, counting the number of times each rope passes over or under another rope may provide some insight.

DEBRIEFING TOPICS

- How did this activity allow you to see the perspective of another group member?
- Were you persuaded to change your mind after you had more information?
- What are the similarities to this activity and solving a conflict between two individuals?
- Why is it important to hear another point of view or perspective?
- How does personal accountability factor into the answer in these activities? Was there a consequence for being wrong?
- How can we use this information in our group?

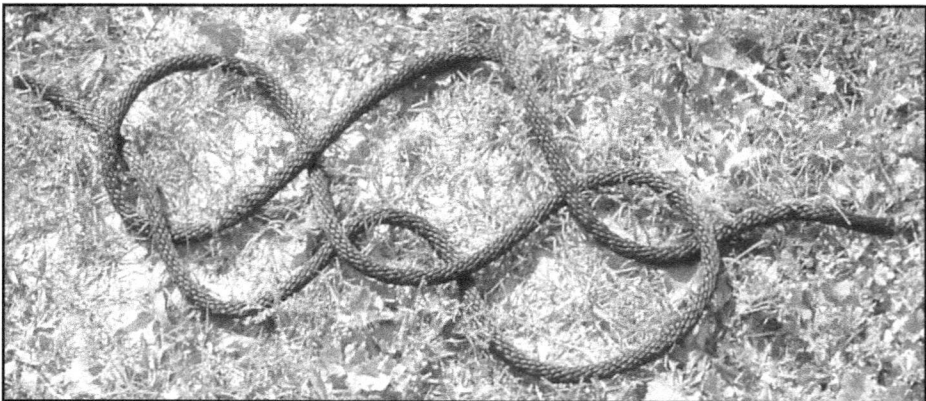

FACILITATOR NOTES

Sharing Connections

TYPE OF INITIATIVE

Icebreaker

SOURCE

Modified from the book, *Teambuilding Puzzles*

PROPS NEEDED

You will need a ball of twine, yarn, or string at least 10 feet (3 meters) in length for every person in the group. 10 people = 100 feet (30 meters). For groups larger than 20, you should increase the length of yarn to 25 feet (8 meters) per person.

DIRECTIONS

- With the group seated in a circle, one person (who happens to be holding a ball of yarn) begins by mentioning various things they enjoy. For example, they might offer, "I like to ride my mountain bike. I enjoy cooking. I like to read."
- When one of these statements rings true for another participant in the group, they hold up both hands, and the person holding the ball of yarn rolls this ball over to them while keeping hold of the very end of the yarn.
- The second person (now holding the ball of yarn) begins sharing some of the activities they enjoy until another participant holds up their hands.
- And so the ball is passed around the group with each participant becoming connected to the other members of their group by the things they have in common. In most cases, group members only catch and roll the ball once. Each person catching the ball holds onto the string as the ball continues along its path to every other member of the group.
- After everyone has caught the ball, the final person must keep sharing information until the starting participant can agree with one of their comments.

VARIATION

Sharing Frustrations

You can reverse the process (essentially rewinding the ball of string by repeating the activity) by discussing things that frustrate and irritate us. Ask the group to think about those little things in life that "set them off." We call them triggers. A trigger is that small, sensitive piece of invisible equipment that each of us has within. Learning what "triggers" others have is an extremely valuable way to reduce the potential for conflict within a group or team. While listening to things that frustrate others, just as before, when a listed situation is shared by

Image © 2010 JupiterImages Corporation.

another member of the group the ball is passed along the string connecting them. Each person, when they receive the ball, carefully winds the yarn back into place before passing the ball on to the next person in the connection line.

DEBRIEFING TOPICS

• Why is doing an activity like this important?
• Name some of the new connections you made or learned in the activity.
• After sharing some frustrations, what are some behaviors we should avoid to prevent a conflict with another team member?
• Based on the web of yarn we created here, describe how one frustration can affect more than one person at a time.

FACILITATOR NOTES

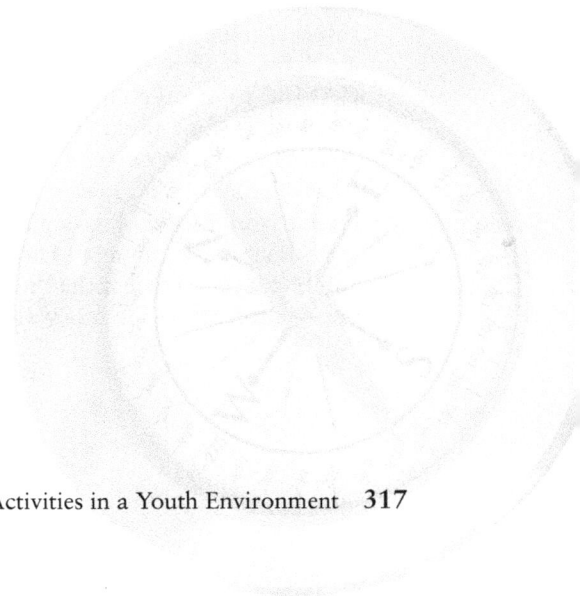

Stop 'N Go Poly Spots

We like to use these spots during the popular game, Have You Ever, from the book Quicksilver, by Karl Rohnke.

PURPOSE

The Stop 'N Go Poly Spots is a frontloading activity using the colors of a traffic light: red, yellow, and green. These colorful spots help guide targeted questions in an icebreaker activity. Incorporating deeper issues into a lighthearted, active game can open the door for deeper conversations after the activity.

PROPS NEEDED

You will need plastic squares or spot markers that are multicolored (one for each participant), plus the three Stop 'N Go Poly Spots. You could also use red-, yellow-, or green-colored construction paper or plastic squares—anything that makes the colors visual and can be stepped on.

DIRECTIONS

- Have enough spot markers for every participant in the circle, and have them stand on the spots. Include the Stop 'N Go Poly Spots in the spot markers.
- Designate one spot as 'the hot spot' (not the Stop 'N Go Poly Spots). This spot will designate who will ask the question for each round. The person on the hot spot must come up with a phrase that completes the fragment, "Have You Ever. . . ." This statement must be true for the person speaking. For instance, if I am on the hot spot and I state, "Have You Ever been to Mount Rushmore?" This statement needs to be true for me.
- After the statement has been made, whoever in the group that also done what was called out should move off of their square and try to find another square to stand on. Moving rules: You may not move to the square immediately to your left or right. You have to make a valiant effort to move to a square across the circle. Stress that it is a 'FAST WALKING GAME!' to avoid collision injuries. Also stress that if there are two people attempting to occupy the same square there should be no body checking others out of the way.
- Whoever ends up on the hot spot is the next person to state, "Have You Ever . . ."
- Example: Have You Ever gone mountain biking? Those people who have gone mountain biking would leave their square and occupy another square. The person that ends up on the hot spot asks the next Have You Ever question.
- **Safety concerns:** Stress the "no body checking" rule when there are two people going for one square. Stress the fast walking rule to keep participants safe.

- After a few rounds have been played, stop the game and add a new rule.
- New rule: Before the new Have You Ever question is asked, the three people that are occupying the Stop 'N Go Poly Spots have to answer a specific question related to the spot they are standing on.
  - RED Spot: What is something I can do to STOP bullying from happening in our group? or What behaviors would prevent me from having a conflict with my parents?
  - YELLOW Spot: What is something I need to be careful of to prevent myself from participating in bullying or being a victim of bullying? or What behaviors do I need to be careful of to prevent a conflict with my parents?
  - GREEN Spot: What is something I do really well to avoid being a bully or a victim of bullying? or How do I handle conflict well?

These questions add targeted conversation into a fun game.

Here are some suggestions for Have You Ever statements:

- Have you ever been to Florida?
- Have you ever gone canoeing?
- Have you ever broken your arm?
- Have you ever gone to the movies?
- Have you ever cooked a meal for more than 10 people?
- Have you ever read a good book?
- Have you ever skipped school when you weren't sick?
- Have you ever worn two different pairs of shoes on accident?
- Have you ever opened a door for a stranger?

You can also ask your participants to directly apply their Have You Ever statements to a specific topic. Here are some suggestions for Have You Ever statements that relate to bullying.

- Have you ever been bullied?
- Have you ever bullied someone else?
- Have you ever witnessed someone getting bullied?
- Have you ever told an adult about a time when you witnessed bullying?
- Have you ever stopped a bully in action?
- Have you ever told a bully to quit picking on someone else?

Here are some suggestions for Have You Ever statements that relate to conflict.

- Have you ever handled a conflict poorly?
- Have you ever felt good about the way you handled a conflict?
- Have you ever started an argument on purpose?
- Have you ever yelled at a friend during an argument?
- Have you ever been a mediator between two friends that were having a conflict?

VARIATON

Begin with one person in the hot spot asking questions that begin with "Do you or does it?" questions. Questions like: Do you get frustrated waiting in lines? Does it irritate you when you are ignored? Do you fly off the handle? If the answer to the question is "Yes" participants would move off of their spot, if "No" participants would stay put. This variation is all about triggers—what sets us off . . . what bothers us and what does not. The more that we know about our peers' triggers the more we can reduce altercations.

There is a keychain activity called the *Stop n Go* created by Brian Brolin that is also designed for conversations for the Red, Yellow, and Green lights and the behaviors that go with them.

WHERE TO FIND

Training Wheels sells a set of Stop N Go Poly Spots at www.training-wheels.com.

FACILITATOR NOTES

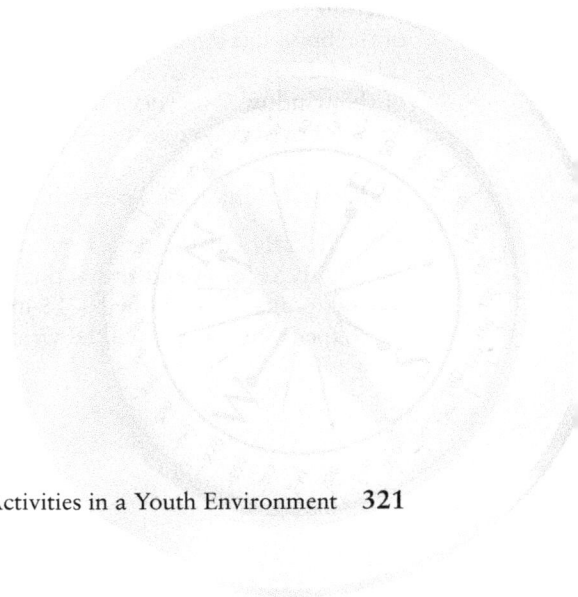

The Other Side

A creative look at perspective

TYPE OF INITIATIVE

Problem Solving, Perspective Awareness

PURPOSE

This activity is designed to stimulate conversation about how there are always two sides to every story.

PROPS NEEDED

One copy of the book *The Other Side* by Isvan Banyai

GROUP SIZE

1–40

DIRECTIONS

The Other Side by Istvan Banyai is a visually dynamic and exciting book. There are few words in this book, but colorful graphic designs on each page offer intimate perspectives on the same scene. Each illustration in the book has another side. As you turn each page over, you will be surprised by the unique perspective on "the other side." The illustrations are amusing, thought-provoking, and surprising. The book is like a kaleidoscope—each page a reflection of the whole, yet showing a different angle and aspect.

The Other Side will have participants wanting to look, and think, twice. For example, one page of the book has a picture of several paper airplanes flying out of an apartment window and the other side of the page shows a boy inside an apartment releasing a flurry of origami planes out of the window. The very next page shows a jet flying over a city, and 'the other side' shows its seated, bored passengers.

To make this book into a conflict resolution activity:

- Carefully cut the pages out of the book and laminate them or use sheet protectors. We highly recommend protecting the pages or it will be a one-time use activity. The activity takes anywhere from 10–15 minutes to complete. By the time someone handles a piece of paper that long, it will be wrinkled, folded, rolled, or torn if it is unprotected.

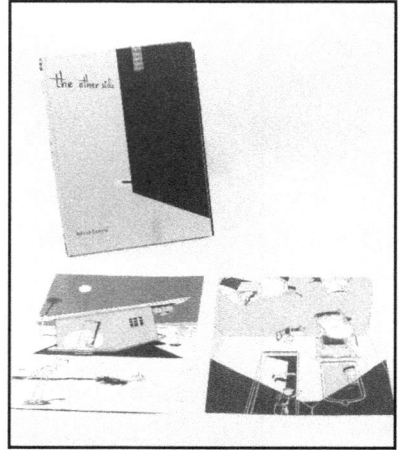

PROCESS

- Invite your participants to find a partner.
- Slide one page of the book in between each pair. Try to distribute the pages to each pair so that each person in the pair only sees one side of the page.
- Have players closely examine their side of the picture for all of the details. Let them know that they are NOT to show their picture to their partner.
- Instruct players to discuss what is happening on their side of the page and then to listen to their partner's perspective from their page.
- Have each pair try to determine what event or story is taking place.
- After several minutes of discussion, allow participants to reveal their pictures to their partner and discuss the differences in the perspective of 'the other side.'

DEBRIEFING TOPICS

It is helpful for participants to debrief with their partner before debriefing with the large group. Ask the pairs to discuss the following questions:

- How was your perspective different from your partner's?
- Were you open to hearing the perspective of your partner's page?
- If you were in a conflict with your partner, how difficult would it be to hear his/her perspective?
- How did you communicate your page to your partner?
- What type of communication did you use to describe your perspective?
- What would happen if you openly listened in a conflict as you did in this activity?
- Why is it important to consider 'the other side' and another perspective?

After participants have debriefed in small groups, invite them to sit or stand in a large circle with their partner and their page of the book. Allow them to briefly describe their page and the different perspective on 'the other side' as well as any learning discovered in their small-group discussion.

WHERE TO FIND IT/HOW TO MAKE IT

This book can be purchased through the Training Wheels website, www.training-wheels.com, or through Amazon.com. It is published by Chronicle Books, www.chroniclebooks.com, **ISBN-10:** 0811846083 **ISBN-13:** 978-0811846080

ABOUT THE AUTHOR OF *THE OTHER SIDE*

Istvan Banyai, the acclaimed Hungarian-born creator of Zoom and Re-Zoom and illustrator of several other books for children, is also well known for his editorial illustrations, which have been published in *The New Yorker* and *Rolling Stone,* among other journals. His perspective, always unexpected (sometimes even to him), has made him one of the most original and iconoclastic illustrators today. He lives in New York and Connecticut.

FACILITATOR NOTES

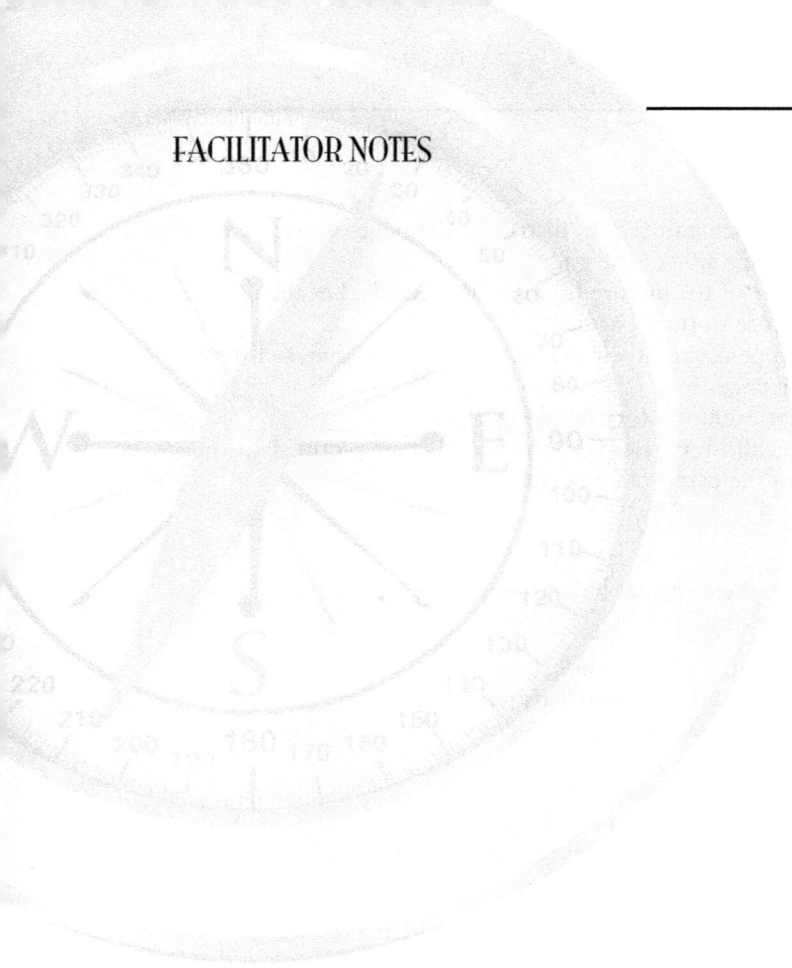

The Sneetches

TYPE OF INITIATIVE

Relationship Building, Discussion tool for prejudice or diversity

PROPS NEEDED

The book, *The Sneetches,* by Dr. Seuss

Dr. Seuss ignites a child's imagination with his mischievous characters and zany verses. Although best loved for children's literature, it is often noted that Dr. Seuss wrote about social issues. This story is one of his best, but least cited, examples of this. This story has significant social meaning. *The Sneetches* is a story of a society of haves and have-nots, in which access to the good things of life are determined by whether you have a star on your belly or not. Although it is a simple children's book, it is certainly a commentary on racial, gender, or any number of other social categories. The story's strength is that it shows just how arbitrary and constructed these categories are. Features—such as a star, but also skin color, gender attributes, etc.—can be used to define people as dominant and powerful or repressed and marginalized. What is at issue is not which characteristics are used to delineate the people into specific social categories or identities, but how people marginalize others by playing up those definitions.

THE STORYLINE

The Sneetches is about a society that is very segregated. There are two types of sneetches: star-bellied and plain-bellied. The star-bellied sneetches are very exclusive and only invite other star-bellied sneetches to their parties and picnics and frankfurter roasts. This makes the plain-bellied sneetches really sad.

"Now, the Star-Belly Sneetches/Had bellies with stars./The Plain-Belly Sneetches/Had none upon thars."

Everything changes, though, when Sylvester McMonkey McBean shows up. He has a machine that can put a star on plain-bellied sneetches, so of course, they all get stars. But when the original star-bellied sneetches find out about this, they're really mad. They get their stars taken off by Sylvester. Soon, a horrible mess is made. Everyone is getting their stars taken off and then put back on until they realize that it does not matter whether they have stars or not.

The Sneetches is a great book. It teaches that looks do not matter; instead, we should accept people just the way they are. In some school districts there is a lot of talk about social and emotional literacy. This book demonstrates to students that differences and individuality are what make everyone unique and exciting. This book has been used with students as old as 14 years old (seventh grade). The older students loved the fact that someone was reading to them. For many students it had been a long time since an adult had read them a storybook. Please know your audience. This book will not be well received by all age groups or populations. This book is geared toward younger kids, but with the right group it could be used with older kids as well.

DIRECTIONS

1. Read the book, *The Sneetches,* by Dr. Seuss out loud as a group.

2. Discuss the following questions:

- How did the star-bellied sneetches treat the plain-bellied sneetches?
- Were the star-bellied sneetches any better than the plain-bellied sneetches?
- Why did the plain-bellied sneetches want to be like the star-bellied sneetches?
- Does it matter what people look like on the outside?

After a brief discussion on the storyline, also discuss with the group some points about prejudice.

Each of us is unique with our own talents, skills, and experiences to offer. There are many ways that people can be different from you:

- moral or spiritual beliefs
- cultural background
- intellectual strengths and weaknesses (e.g., being better at languages or math)
- social skills and preferences (e.g., being shy instead of outgoing)
- tastes, interests, and hobbies (e.g., liking sports or music)
- physical features (e.g., sex, size, skin color, body shape)
- sexual and/or gender orientation or preferences

While we all benefit by being surrounded by people with different beliefs, skills, and experiences, these differences can sometimes cause people to be targets of hatred and prejudice.

To understand what prejudice is, it's important to be able to define words like *stereotypes* and *discrimination*. Prejudice can have some serious effects, but there are many things you can do to recognize and reduce prejudice in your own life.

After the discussion, ask students to find a partner and ask them to find three things they have in common with one another.

FACILITATOR NOTES

Traffic Debrief

TYPE OF INITIATIVE

Processing tool

PROPS NEEDED

Items shaped like or resembling a stoplight, hard hat, school bus, traffic cone, police car, tire, or fire extinguisher.

GROUP SIZE

1–15

DIRECTIONS

One of our favorite processing tools to debrief conflict is the Traffic Debrief. Set these parts out in front of your group to set the stage for targeted metaphoric processing. Each part can be used independently or as a complete set. Following are examples of processing questions and information that relate to each traffic metaphor.

Stoplight

This is one of our favorite metaphors to use to debrief a conflict.

A traffic light is used to help direct motorists while driving to keep them from crashing. The lights signify things a driver should do to keep things flowing smoothly. The three colors on the stoplight can be used as metaphors for behaviors: What are you doing well? (green light) What do you need to be careful of? (yellow light) What do you need to stop doing? (red light)

When a group has started to show negative behavior patterns, or if a conflict arises, use the metaphor of the stoplight to debrief the situation. Frontload your discussion with examples for each color. You could also have the group give suggestions for each color.

- RED: What are things happening in the group that need to STOP in order for us to be more successful? The usual answers are to stop teasing, horseplay, put-downs, blaming, etc.
- YELLOW: What are things we need to be CAREFUL of as we continue? Suggestions have included keeping everyone safe, listening to all ideas, being aware of personal choices and boundaries, etc.

- GREEN: What are things we want to GO for? This could be group goals, as well as behavior suggestions. Ideas have included being respectful, encouraging more, setting time limits, etc.

If it wouldn't be a distraction, the stoplight can be handed out to a specific individual who will monitor those ideas for the group. This person can be asked to report on what they observed at the end of the activity or session. For example, the person designated to carry the stoplight is asked to let the group know any time he sees an infraction of behavior norms. He could call a group discussion, point to the yellow light and say, "We had stated we wanted to be careful of listening to everyone's ideas before we started. Are we listening to everyone?"

Hard Hat

A hard hat is a type of helmet predominantly used in workplace environments, such as construction sites, to protect the head from injury by falling objects, debris, bad weather, and electric shock. Inside the helmet is a suspension that spreads the helmet's weight over the top of the head. It also provides a space of approximately 1 1/2 inch between the helmet's shell and the wearer's head so that if an object strikes the shell, the impact is less likely to be transmitted directly to the skull.

Here are some specific debriefing questions for the hard hat:

- What areas are you being hard headed in?
- What do you need to protect yourself from?
- Often, hard hats are worn in construction/dangerous areas. When do you put on your construction hat each day?
- Describe an area of your life where you metaphorically put on a hard hat before you enter. What types of feelings do you experience as you go there?
- How would a hard hat be helpful/hurtful when dealing with conflict?

School Bus

A school bus is a bus used to transport children and teenagers to and from school and school events. In some cases public bus services may run field trips and high school athletic events. In North America, however, the school bus is a specific type of government-regulated vehicle that is very distinct from other buses. Canada and the United States have specially built and equipped school buses, which by law are finished in school bus yellow and equipped with various forms of warning and safety devices. Every morning across the country yellow school buses make their rounds. For many students, the bright splash of color reflects their eagerness to board the bus and see friends. But there are others for whom the yellow means caution: bullies on board. In the United States, about 160,000 children miss school every day for fear of being bullied, according to the National Association of School Psychologists. Some of these children endure rides on buses where bullies have the run.

Here are some specific debriefing questions for the school bus:

- School is generally where we learn new things. What did you learn today?
- What does the school bus represent to you? For some, it is transportation that takes us to sporting events where we can shine at our natural talents. For others, it is an unsupervised cage where kids are mean to each other, or it takes kids to a place where bullying and conflict happen on a daily basis. What does the school bus mean to you?
- Have you ever witnessed a situation where there was little adult supervision and a crowd of kids encouraging negative behavior?

Traffic Cone

Traffic cones are usually cone-shaped markers that are placed on roads or footpaths to temporarily redirect traffic in a safe manner. They are often used to create merge lanes during road construction projects or automobile accidents, though heavier, more permanent markers or signs are used if the diversion is to stay in place for a long period of time.

Here are some specific debriefing questions for the traffic cone:

- What problems do we need to avoid?
- What do we need to be careful of?
- What behaviors should you avoid when confronting a friend?

Police Car

A police car is the description for a vehicle used by police to assist with their duties in patrolling and responding to incidents. Typical uses of a police car include transportation for officers to reach the scene of an incident quickly, transportation of criminal suspects, or patrolling an area while providing a high visibility deterrent to crime. For some people, the symbol of a police car is something positive. For others, it has a negative connotation and would be the last place they would go for help.

Here are some specific debriefing questions for the police car:

- Who do we go to if we need help?
- Who protects us?
- Do we follow the rules all of the time or just when the "rule enforcer" is nearby?
- What emotions do you feel when you see a police car?

Tire

Tires are ring-shaped parts that fit around wheels to protect them and enhance their function. They are used on many types of vehicles, such as bicycles, motorcycles, cars, trucks, and aircraft. Tires enable better vehicle performance by providing traction, braking, steering, and load support. They form a flexible cushion between the vehicle and the road, which smoothes out shock and makes for a comfortable ride. We all know what happens when we get a flat tire and the obstacles this event presents us.

Here are some specific debriefing questions for the tire:

- What do we need to keep the wheels turning?
- How do we continue forward motion?
- How does our group respond if a conflict happens and we have to stop and 'fix the flat,' meaning, resolve the conflict?

Fire Extinguisher

A fire extinguisher is an active fire protection device used to extinguish or control small fires, often in emergency situations. It is not intended for use on an out-of-control fire, such as one that has reached the ceiling, endangers the user (i.e., no escape route, smoke, explosion hazard, etc.), or otherwise requires the expertise of a fire department. Typically, a fire extinguisher consists of a hand-held cylindrical pressure vessel containing an agent that can be discharged to extinguish a fire.

Here are some specific debriefing questions for the fire extinguisher:

- Where's the fire? What started it?
- What do we need to do to put out the fire?
- How do we prevent the fire from getting bigger?
- Is the fire/conflict one we can handle on our own, or do we need to call in the fire department/parents/counselor?

WHERE TO FIND IT/HOW TO MAKE IT

Training Wheels sells a set of these—7 parts packaged in a 5 × 8-inch, snazzy stuff sack. The stress relievers are all made of polyurethane. Latex free. You could also use Matchbox cars, pictures of these items, or the actual items themselves. www.training-wheels.com

FACILITATOR NOTES

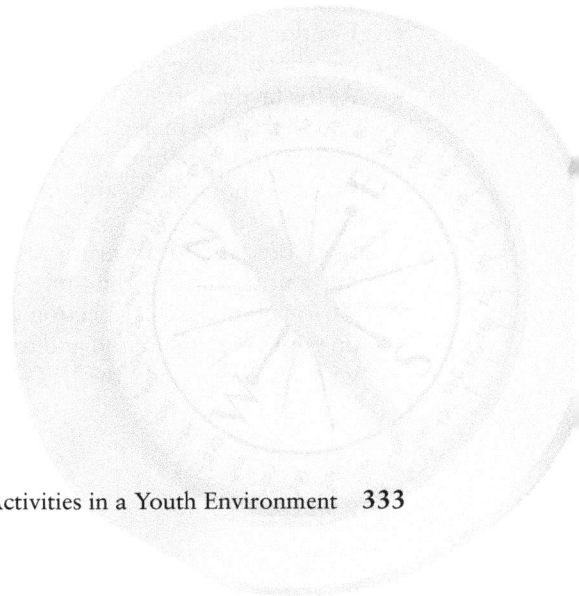

UFO Ball—The Value of Connection

TYPE OF INITIATIVE
Debriefing tool, Attention Getter

PROPS NEEDED
UFO ball

GROUP SIZE
1–225

PURPOSE
This UFO ball may look like a simple ping-pong ball with two pieces of metal, but when both pieces of metal are touched simultaneously, the ball lights up and makes noise.

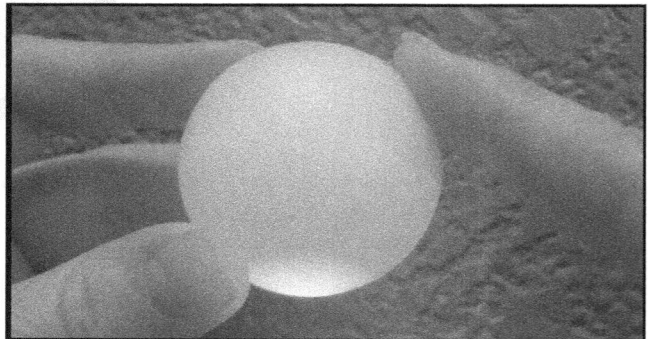

DIRECTIONS
- Invite your group to stand or sit in a circle.
- Conduct a brief discussion on the value of connection. Why is it important? What are the benefits of being connected to a group or an individual?
- As the facilitator, hold the UFO ball in your left hand and touch one of the metal plates with your left index finger. Ask 'Bob', the person on your left, if he will demonstrate the activity with you. Invite him to touch the other metal plate on the UFO ball with his right index finger without physically touching you (meaning, no skin-to-skin contact between the two of you).
- Now describe to the group that you may not know very much about 'Bob,' your partner, but you both go to the same school (which is represented by the UFO ball). Explain that when you make a connection with 'Bob' exciting things can happen. At this moment reach up with your right hand and touch Bob's left hand. The moment you make physical contact with Bob's left hand the UFO ball will light up and make noise.

- Notice the "Ooooh's" and "Ahhhh's" that erupt from the group.
- This is a wonderful tool used to teach the value of connection in your team.
- Next, disconnect hands with Bob and invite the entire group to hold hands with the person standing next to them in the circle.
- Once everyone is connected hand to hand, reconnect hands with Bob. The ball will immediately light up and start making noise again. If one person disconnects from the team the ball will stop making noise. This is a powerful metaphor to debrief the effects on a team when someone is not giving 100%.
- The largest group we have experimented with was 225 people. It took about 45 seconds for the current to travel through the participants before the ball lit up.

VARIATION

For school teachers and educational programs, it can be used to teach the science of closed circuits with amusement. If you use several UFO balls in one circle, you can teach polarities. Invite a group of participants to try and figure out how they can make all of the connections light up with four UFO balls in the circle. This initiative of determining the polarity sequence within the circle can take up to 15–20 minutes to complete.

VARIATION

Use the UFO ball in a one-on-one debriefing session. You can have a connection with yourself. If you are connected to yourself, your treatment plan, your exercise goals, your relationships, your (insert topic here); then we can have more meaningful relationships with others. After all, how can we expect to connect with others when we do not have a connection to ourselves? Plus, the attitudes and energy we bring to our external connections have an effect on those around us. If someone is committed to being connected to their treatment plan, they can have a more positive impact on their family or their team. The UFO ball can help make this point.

DEBRIEFING TOPICS

- In what ways are we connected to each other?
- How can we cultivate the connections on our team?
- When someone disconnects from the team, how does it affect the others?
- Describe a time when you felt disconnected.
- How can we keep a healthy level of energy in our team?

WHERE TO FIND IT/HOW TO MAKE IT

Training Wheels carries the UFO ball. It is often carried in science stores and other novelty shops. www.training-wheels.com

FACILITATOR NOTES

Unfair Game

TYPE OF INITIATIVE
Diversity Awareness

PROPS NEEDED
You will need a variety of art supplies that vary in quality and quantity. Some suggestions are: tag board, markers, glue, tape, construction paper, crayons, tissue paper, a snack, notebook paper, etc.

LEAD IN
As a group, discuss the different communities around them. Let them know that this activity gives them the chance to make a community just the way they would like it. Brainstorm the essential elements of communities before you divide them into smaller groups. Decide on 3–5 elements that each group must include in their communities.

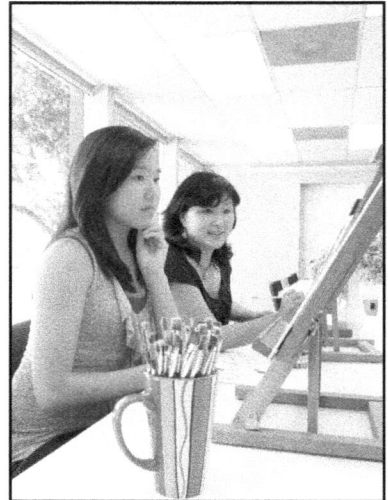

STEP-BY-STEP PROCEDURE
- Have the group count off by 4 and then divide them into 3 groups. For example, have groups 1 & 2 join to form a large group, and make a point to move a few from group 4 into group 3. Now you should have a large group, medium group, and a small group.
- Groups should be spaced apart from one another, giving the smaller group the most comfortable and desired space to work. The medium group should receive the second most desired work space, and the large group should be given a small, undesired work space.
- Then give each group their art supplies.
  - Start with the smallest group. They receive the highest-quality supplies and in the largest quantities. This group should also receive a snack to eat while they are completing their task.
  - The medium group receives their supplies next. The supplies are not as plentiful or as high quality as the small group.
  - The large group receives their supplies last. They receive the lowest quality and quantity of supplies.
  - Allow participants to see the other areas where groups will be working.

- Once the groups have been separated, have students take some time to plan their community. Ask participants to think with their group about how their communities will look—remembering the essential elements to each community. Have them create their communities on their tag boards to present to the other groups. Allow 30–40 minutes to complete the task.
- Bring the groups back together, and have them present their communities to one another. After each group has finished tell them these are neighboring communities.

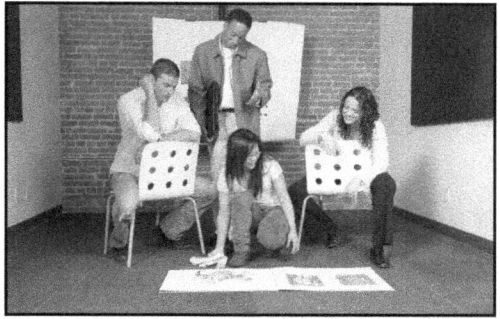

DEBRIEFING TOPICS

- Is the distribution of supplies fair?
- How did it make you feel to see the differences in the work spaces and art supplies?
- What did each group find most difficult?
- How did groups deal with difficulties?
- How did the size of your group play into the success of your project?
- Did any groups make special arrangements? Were they successful?
- What was the effect of differences in supplies?
- How does this activity tie into our communities?
- How can we use this activity to look at the larger global community?
- What types of conflicts could arise between the different communities?
- Give some examples of community conflicts you have heard about.

FACILITATOR NOTES

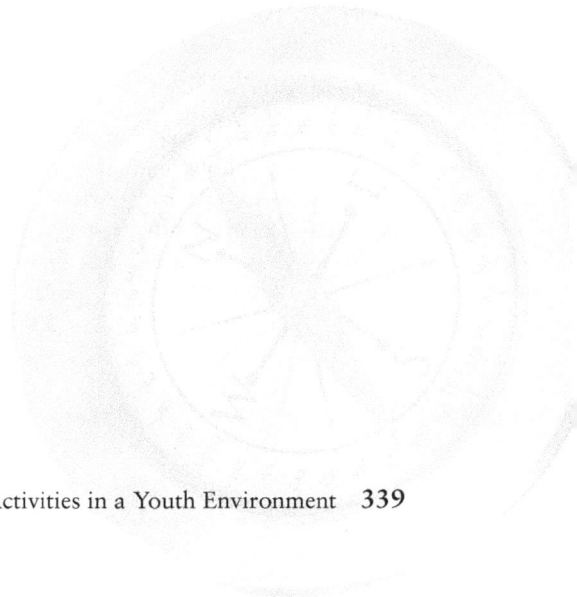

We're All Different

TYPE OF INITIATIVE
Processing

PROPS NEEDED
Index cards and writing utensils for each participant.

GROUP SIZE
2–30

DIRECTIONS
Different people bring different feelings and experiences to every activity or group. To demonstrate this point, give each participant a writing utensil and a large index card. Ask each participant to think of one word that describes how he or she is feeling at that moment. Then, ask the participants to write that one word on the index card in large letters. Go around the room, asking participants to hold up their cards and look at each others' responses. Follow up with these questions to start discussion:

1. How do our different feelings and experiences change how we might act in a group?

2. How can these feelings and experiences contribute to conflict?

3. How can we use our different experiences and feelings to make our group's conflicts positive?

VARIATION

Musical interests

Create a play list of various styles, types, and genres of music. You only need about 30 seconds of each song. Play a segment of each song and ask everyone to write a single word on an index card that describes how they feel about that particular song. When the clip is done, ask everyone to raise their cards and cluster in like groups. Give them a few seconds to discuss why they like or dislike that song. Play another selection.

A sample play list might include segments of songs from the following list of artists:

Jack Johnson
INXS
Faith Hill
Chemical Brothers
Metallica
Eminem
Nelly
P.Diddy
Garth Brooks
Marlyn Manson

Keith Urban
Paverotti
Bach
Cole Porter
Benny Goodman
Jimmy Buffett
The Allman Brothers
Frank Sinatra
Ella Fitzgerald
Black Light Burns

DEBRIEFING TOPICS

- How does recognizing our differences contribute to preventing a conflict?
- Why is it important to learn about the likes and dislikes of others in our group?
- How does doing an activity like this help us prevent conflict?
- Did anyone learn anything new about another teammate? Did you find you had something in common with someone you do not hang out with on a regular basis?

FACILITATOR NOTES

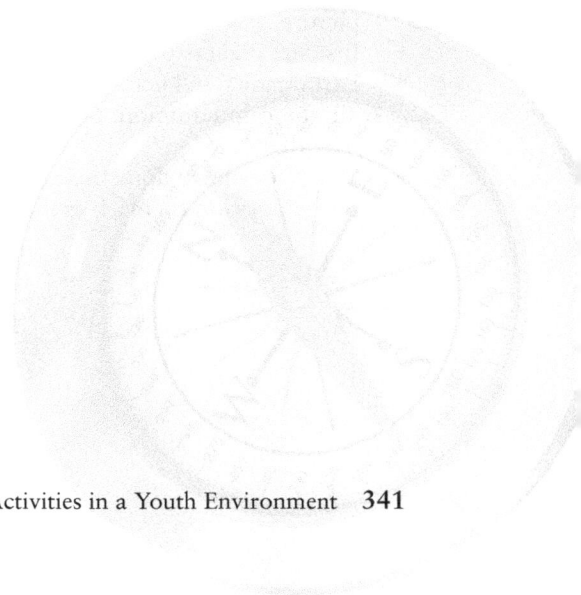

Zoom or Re-Zoom

TYPE OF ACTIVITY

Problem Solving, Communication activity, Discussions on Perspective

PROPS NEEDED

One *Zoom* book, with pages cut out and laminated. Typically, one page per participant (also see Variations). There are 30 pages in *Zoom* and 33 pages in *Re-Zoom*. The activity is based on the intriguing, wordless, picture books *Zoom* and *Re-Zoom* by Istvan Banyai, which consist of 30 sequential "pictures within pictures." The *Zoom* narrative moves from a rooster to a ship to a city street to a desert island and outer space. The *Re-Zoom* narrative moves from an Egyptian hieroglyphic to a film set to an elephant ride to a billboard to a train.

There are many variations of this activity. From a sequencing point of view, this is a good activity to do after your initial icebreakers and energizers.

DIRECTIONS

The challenge is for participants to get themselves lined up sequentially, so that their pictures tell a "story." And, they must do this without looking at each other's pictures. If you are using a portion of the book, make sure a continuous sequence is used.

PROCESS

- Distribute one page to each participant.
- Have players closely examine their picture for all the details. Let them know that they are NOT to show their picture to anyone else and are NOT allowed to look at anyone else's picture.
- Instruct players to line up in the correct sequence according to the picture they received.
- Participants will generally mill around talking to others to see whether their pictures have anything in common. Sometimes leadership efforts will emerge to try to understand the overall story.
- When they have done their best, allow them to reveal their pictures to the rest of the group and reposition themselves if they made any errors.

DEBRIEFING TOPICS

- How did the group first start solving the problem?
- Why was it hard to get the story together? (everyone had a piece, but no-one had the big picture)
- How many people stayed within their sub-group once they found someone who had similarities on their page? How is this like the real world? Do we tend to gravitate toward those who are similar to us?
- What type of communication was used?
- Imagine if, at the outset, the group had taken the time to let each person describe his/her picture to the rest of the group. What would have happened then? Would the solution have been found faster? What prevented such strategies from being considered?
- What kind of leadership was used? Who were the leaders? Why?
- What style of leadership might have worked best?
- How does one's perspective play into the success of this activity?
- What can we learn from this activity that will be helpful to the team?
- What real-life activities are similar to this activity?

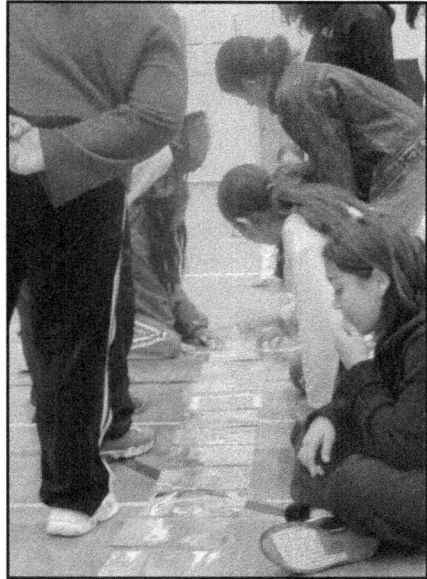

DISCUSSIONS ON PERSPECTIVE

Perspective is one's "point of view"—the choice of a context for opinions or beliefs and experiences. Your perspective can be very different based on where you stand. In the Zoom activity, a page at the beginning of the storyline had a very different perspective than a page at the end of the storyline. Both pages were crucial to the success of the activity. In teams, people with different responsibilities have very different perspectives. Both are valuable and important to the team's success. They are both part of the big picture. How these perspectives are valued and communicated can impact the relationships of the team members.

The outcomes of this activity change dramatically with a few variations.

VARIATIONS

- For groups ranging from 25–32 people: Give each person one page of the book and tell them that this page is 'super glued' to their hand. They must always keep this picture in their possession. Any remaining pages may be passed around the group.
- For groups larger than 32: If you have a group of 35–40, you can double up a few people on one page.

- For groups larger than 50: If you have a group larger than 50 people, you could consider doing *Zoom* and *Re-Zoom* at the same time. Split your group into two subgroups and have them complete the activity separately. *Re-Zoom* is a more difficult storyline, so be prepared for the *Re-Zoom* group to take longer than the *Zoom* group.
- For smaller groups, take the first several pages of the book and set them aside. Then hand participants random pages of the book and lay some pages face down on the ground. The pages on the ground could be looked at 3 times for 20 seconds each.
- With 10–14 people you can take the first 10 pages of the book and set them aside. Hand the 14 participants random pages of the book and lay 8 pages face down on the ground. The pages on the ground can be looked at 3 times for 20 seconds. The task is to get themselves and the pages on the ground in order from the beginning of the book to the end of the book.
- Another variation is to use it for conference presentations dealing with community development. As people enter the room, greet them, introduce yourself, and hand them a page from *Zoom*. Ask them to find their place in the group based on their *Zoom* page. This typically leads to many great conversations about assumptions, connections in community, etc.
- Use as an icebreaker by handing each participant a picture on arrival. When everyone has arrived, explain that each person is holding part of a story, and the group task is to find out what the story is by putting their pictures in sequence.
- Use a time limit to increase difficulty and enhance focus on teamwork.
- Team performance can be measured (e.g., for a competition) by counting how many pictures are out of sequence.
- You can also take a few pages from *Re-Zoom* and put them into *Zoom*. Ask the group to determine which pages do not belong.
- For youth groups or groups that are not able to make the connections between the pages, you could allow a "5-second frenzy" where they can show their page for 5 seconds to anyone they want. After time is up, the page is turned back around.
- For younger groups you can facilitate a no-talking version, but they can show their page to everyone.

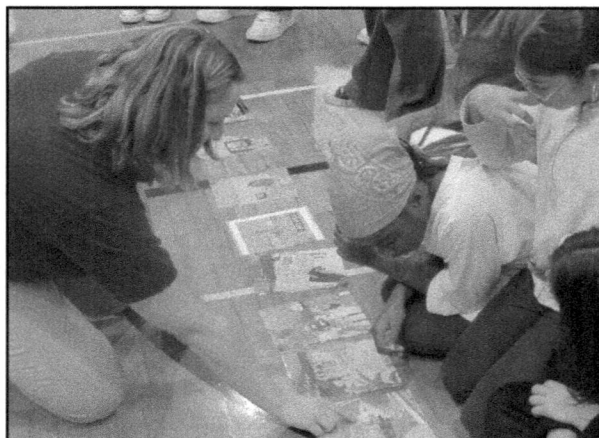

RECOMMENDATIONS

Carefully cut the pages out of the book and laminate them or use sheet protectors. We highly recommend protecting the pages, or it will be a one-time use activity. The activity takes anywhere from 30–45 minutes to complete. By the time someone handles a piece of paper that long it will be wrinkled, folded, rolled, or torn if it is unprotected.

WHERE TO FIND IT/HOW TO MAKE IT

Training Wheels, www.training-wheels.com or www.Amazon.com.

FACILITATOR NOTES

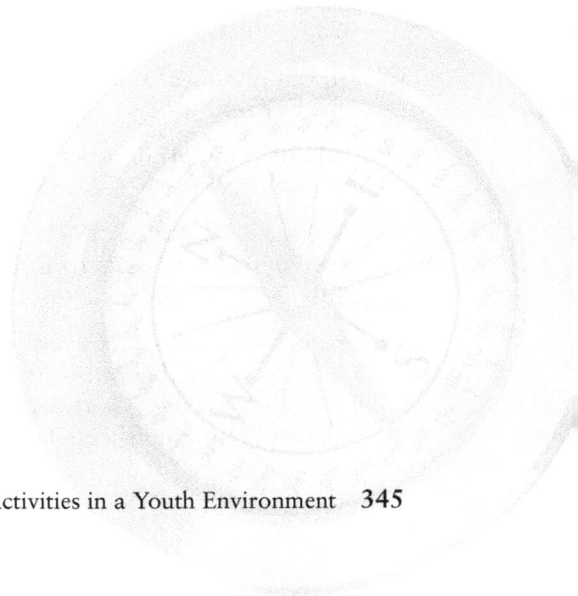

References and Suggested Readings

A key part of our philosophy for writing this book is our desire to effect change that is significant and that can last a lifetime. Change of this magnitude doesn't come about simply by attending one training session or by participating in one activity. Change of this magnitude requires ongoing support and an attitude that learning is a journey.

To support you in your journey of learning, we've put various resources together in this section so information on subjects like negotiation, conflict management, bullying prevention, and relationship building is available beyond the pages of this book. If you know of other great references to add to this list, we would love to know about them. Please e-mail them to either Michelle or Mike, and we will post them on our website for this book, www. settingtheconflictcompass.com.

Experiential Activity Titles

Sikes, S. (1998). *Executive Marbles and Other Teambuilding Activities*. Tulsa, OK: Learning Unlimited Publishers. ISBN 0-9646541-2-1

Sikes, S. (2003). *Raptor and other Team Building Activities*. Tulsa, OK: Learning Unlimited Publishers. ISBN 0-964654172

Cummings, M. (2007). *Playing with a Full Deck*. Dubuque, IA: Kendall Hunt Publishers. ISBN 07575-4094-5

Cavert, C. (2000). *Affordable Portables*. Bethany, OK: Wood N Barnes Publishing. ISBN 978-1-885473-40-0

Frank, Laurie. (2004). Journey Towards the Caring Classroom, Bethany, OK: Wood N Barnes Publishing, ISBN 978-1-885473-60-8

Rohnke, K., & S. Butler. (1995). *Quicksilver—Adventure Games, Initiative Problems, Trust Activities and a Guide to Effective Leadership*. Dubuque, IA: Kendall Hunt Publishers. ISBN 0-7872-2103-1

Anderson, M., J. Cain, C. Cavert, & T. Heck. (2005). *Teambuilding Puzzles—100 Puzzles for Creating Teachable Moments in Creative Problem Solving, Consensus Building, Group Decision Making, Goal Setting, Communication and Teamwork*. AZ: Dubuque, IA: Kendall Hunt Publishers. ISBN 0757570402

Cain, J., & B. Jolliff. (1998). *Teamwork & Teamplay*. Dubuque, IA: Kendall Hunt Publishers. ISBN 0-7872-4532-1

Rohnke, K. (1993). *The Bottomless Bag—Again*! Dubuque, IA: Kendall Hunt Publishers. ISBN 0-8403-8757-1

Cain, J., & T. Smith. (2002). *The Book on Raccoon Circles*. Tulsa, OK: Learning Unlimited Publishers. ISBN 0-9646541-6-4

Peer Mediation Articles

Type: Reference

Source: Eric Digest

Johnson, D.W., R.T. Johnson, & B. Dudley. "Effects of Peer Mediation Training on Elementary School Students." *Mediation Quarterly* 10 (Fall 1992): 89.

Johnson, D.W., & R.T. Johnson. "Students as Peacemakers: Peer Mediation Training." *The Fourth R* 3 (February/March 1992): 7, 11.

Lam, J.A. (1988). *The Impact of Conflict Resolution Programs on Schools: A Review and Synthesis of the Evidence*. Amherst, MA: National Association for Mediation in Education.

Lane, P.S., & J.J. McWhirter. "A Peer Mediation Model: Conflict Resolution for Elementary and Middle School Children." *Elementary School and Guidance Counseling* 27 (October 1992): 15–24.

Meek, M. "The Peacekeepers." *Teaching Tolerance* 1 (Fall 1992): 46–52.

Newton, A. (1993). *Students as Mediators, Project Seed* Auburn, ME: Maine Center for Educational Services.

Robertson, G. (1991). *School-based Peer Mediation Programs: A Natural Extension of Developmental Guidance Programs*. Gorham, ME: University of Southern Maine.

Satchel, B.B. (1992). *Increasing Prosocial Behavior of Elementary Students in Grades K-6 Through a Conflict Resolution Management Program*. Lakeland, FL: Nova University.

Sorenson, D.L. *Conflice Resolution and Mediation for Peer Helpers*. Minneapolis, MN: Educational Media Corporation, 1992.

Wolowiec, J., (Ed.). (1994). *Everybody Wins: Mediation in the Schools*. Chicago: American Bar Association.

Johnson, M. "Perception and Imagination." *Journal of Experimental Psychology* 117: 390–394.

Lerman, L. "Towards a Process for Critical Response." *Alternate ROOTS* (fall/winter 1992).

Bodine, R., & D. Crawford. (1997). *Conflict Resolution Education: A Guide to Implementing Programs in Schools, Youth-Serving Organizations, and Community and Juvenile Justice Settings.* Office of Juvenile Justice and Delinquency Prevention.

Bodine, R., D. Crawford, & F. Schrumpf. (1994). *Creating the Peaceable School.* Champaign, IL: Research Press, Inc.

Bodine, R., & D. Crawford. (1999). *Developing Emotional Intelligence.* Champaign: Research Press.

Covey, S.R. (1990). *Principle Centered Leadership.* New York: Fireside, Simon & Schuster, Inc.

Fisher, R., & W. Ury. (1983). *Getting to Yes.* New York: Penguin Books USA.

Fisk, E. (1999). *Champions of Change the Impact of the Arts on Learning.* Committee on the Arts and the Humanities.

Gardner, H. (1983). *Frames of Mind: The Theory of Multiple Intelligence.* New York: Basic Books.

Glasser, W. (1984). *Control Theory.* New York: Harper & Row.

Glasser, W. (2000). *Reality Therapy in Action.* New York: HarperCollins.

Goleman, D. (1995). *Emotional Intelligence.* New York: Bantam Books.

Harrison, M. *For the Fun of It: Selected Cooperative Games for Children and Adults.* Nonviolence and Children, Friends Peace Committee, 1515 Cherry Street, Philadelphia, PA 19102.

Nelsen, J., L. Lott, & H. S. Glenn. (1993). *Positive Discipline in the Classroom.* Rocklin: Prima Publishing.

Schniedwind, N., & E. Davidson. (1983). *Open Minds to Equity: A Sourcebook of Learning Activities to Promote Race, Sex, Class and Age Equity.* Prentice Hall, Inc. 200 Old Tappan Road, Old Tappan, NJ 07675.

Schrumpf, F., D. Crawford, & R. Bodine. (1997). *Peer Mediation: Conflict Resolution in Schools, Revised Edition.* Champaign, IL: Research Press, Inc.

Book Resources

Before Push Comes to Shove: Building Conflict Resolution Skills with Children, by Nancy Carlsson-Paige and Diane E. Levin, Redleaf Press 1998, ESR*, 93 pp.
By using the children's book *Best Day of the Week* as a starting point (see below), *Before Push Comes to Shove* shows how teachers of young children can begin to build conflict-resolution skills with young children in ways that are meaningful to them and embedded in their everyday school experiences. Topics range from the basics of conflict resolution to curriculum development. A helpful list of resources. Gr **K–6**.

Creative Conflict Solving For Kids, for Gr 5, PEF*
Forty pages of activities involve students in brainstorming, decision making, and critical thinking and fit easily into social studies, science, and language arts curriculum. The curriculum actively involves students in discovering creative ways to manage conflict. Includes poster Rules for Fighting Fair. **Gr 5**.

Fighting Fair, by PEF* 1993
How to resolve conflict within the framework of Dr. Martin Luther King's philosophy of non-violence. Students learn to defuse anger, confront fear, and speak out against injustice. A variety of supporting materials available at additional cost. **Gr 8**.

He Hit Me Back First, by Eva Fugitt, Jalmar Press
Activities and approaches to help children use their creative imagination to become responsible, self-directing, and self-correcting individuals. Guide to removing learning blocks, evoking self-esteem, and activating learning potential. Also in French.

Keeping The Peace: Practicing Cooperation and Conflict Resolution with Preschoolers by Suzanne Wichert, CCRC*
Many concrete and practical suggestions and insights for creating an environment that facilitates creative conflict resolution. Good list of children's books; chapter on war play and alternatives. **Ages 2½–6**.

A Volcano in My Tummy: Helping Children to Handle Anger, by Elaine Whitehouse and Warwick Pudney, NSP*, 80 pp.
Designed for use with 6-to 13-year olds, this book helps caregivers distinguish between anger the feeling and violence the behavior. Offers well-organized activities. **Gr 1–8**.

Conflict Resolution in the Middle School: A Curriculum and Teacher's Guide by William J. Kreidler, 1997, ESR* 384 pp.
This highly acclaimed guide features 28 skill-building sections to help students address the conflicts that come with adolescence, teaching active listening, perspective taking, negotiation, and mediation with over 150 classroom-tested activities. Recent additions to the guide include seven implementation models; how to create a classroom for teaching conflict

resolution; an infusion section that includes math and science; and an exploration of gender and race. Students learn about conflict through discussion, role-plays, and journal writing. Student workbook and journal are now available at additional cost. **Gr 6–8.**

Ready-to-Use Conflict Resolution Activities for Elementary Students, by Beth Teolis, The Centre for Applied Research in Education 1998, CRN*
Includes more than 100 lessons and activities for K–6 students. Two other sections cover conflict resolution activities for educators and building the groundwork for conflict resolution.

Diversity in Action: Using Adventure Activities to Explore Issues of Diversity with Middle and High School Age Youth, by S. Chappelle and L. Bigman, with F. Hillyer, Project Adventure 1999, ESR*, 415 pp.
Over 100 Adventure activities adapted toward issues of diversity—ranging from gender to race to class—and facilitation tips. Background information and discussion guidelines for thirteen diversity topics will help you develop a safe atmosphere where all youth will feel respected, valued, and listened to. Teachers, afterschool programs, youth groups, and others will find this book a valuable tool for empowering young people. **Gr 5–8.**

Bully Busters: A Teachers' Manual for Helping Bullies, Victims and Bystanders, by Dawn A. Newman, Arthur M. Horne, and Christi L. Bartolomucci, Research Press 2000, CRN*
For middle-school children. Seven modules increase awareness of bullying, how to recognize the bully and the victim, how to intervene, how to help the victim, the role of prevention, and coping and relaxation skills for teachers and students. **Gr 6–8.**

The Bully Free Classroom: Over 100 Tips and Strategies for Teachers K–8, by Allan L. Beane, Free Spirit Publishing 1999, CRN*
A clear, easy-to-follow guide with practical, student-friendly activities and strategies for teachers on how to prevent and intervene in bullying situations. Includes "Top Ten Facts About Bullying," a bibliography, and sample letter to parents. Gr **K–8.**

Making the Peace: A 15-Session Violence Prevention Curriculum for Young People, by Paul Kival and Allan Creighton with the Oakland Men's Project, Hunter House Inc. 1997, ESR*
Written to help young people break away from violence, develop self-esteem, and regain a sense of community. A variety of activities cover issues such as dating violence, gangs, interracial tensions, sexual harassment, etc. The program has three parts: The roots of violence; race, class and gender; and making the peace now. **Gr 9–12.**

Playing with Fire: Creative Conflict Resolution for Young Adults, by Fiona Macbeth and Nic Fine, $24.95. NSP*, 192 pp.
A practical ready-to-use guide for teachers, counselors, and group leaders working with young adults. It provides a training program that helps young adults explore conflict and interpersonal violence while learning skills and strategies to turn conflict into dialog.

Partners in Learning: from Conflict to Collaboration in Secondary Classrooms, by Carol Miller Lieber, Educators for Social Responsibility 2002, ESR*, 384 pp.
Provides ten essential core classroom practices that enable teachers and students to become partners in creating a respectful, responsible, and productive community of learners. Classroom-tested methods that make a positive difference in students' motivation to learn and succeed. Includes classroom discipline and management and day-by-day plan for the first month of school. **Gr 9–12.**

Anger Management for Youth: Stemming Aggression and Violence, by Leona Eggert, National Education Service 1994, CRN*
This step-by step training guide teaches participants to identify their anger 'triggers'; how to express anger constructively and how to use appropriate controls. **Gr 7–12.**

Ready-to-Use Conflict Resolution Activities for Secondary Students, by Ruth Perlstein and Gloria Thrall, The Centre for Applied Research in Education 1996, CRN*
Part one addresses basic conflict resolution concepts, Part two explores the application of these concepts in different settings, and Part three provides a framework for establishing a peer mediation program. This is a practical resource filled with activities, scenarios, role-plays, and handouts. For use with youth in or out of the classroom. **Gr 9–12.**

Challenging Activities for Challenging Kids: Taking Conflict Resolution to the Streets, by Conflict Resolution Network Canada 2001, CRN*
Activities designed especially for at-risk youth include use of drama, warm-up games, trust builders, as well as communication skills and adventure-based approaches to conflict resolution. **Gr 9–12.**

About the Author

TRAINING wheels

Michelle Cummings M.S.

Owner/Trainer/Big Wheel
7095 South Garrison Street
Littleton, CO 80128
888-553-0147 phone
303-979-1708 phone
888-553-0146 fax
michelle@training-wheels.com
www.training-wheels.com

Michelle Cummings M.S. is the Big Wheel and founder of Training Wheels, a known leader in the Team Development industry. She is an accomplished author and sought-after speaker and consultant on leadership, teambuilding, and experiential learning. Michelle has created a wide variety of facilitation, debriefing, and teambuilding activities that have collectively changed the way trainers and educators work.

Michelle has delivered innovative leadership programs for hundreds of non-profit and for-profit organizations. Michelle works with professional associations, corporations, universities, and non-profit organizations throughout the world. She is currently working with Stephen M.R. Covey and his associates at CoveyLink on developing experiential activities for Stephen's most recent book, *The Speed of Trust*.

Michelle received her bachelor's degree in psychology from Kansas State University and her master's degree in experiential education from Minnesota State University at Mankato.

Michelle speaks at more than twenty-five local, national, and international conferences each year and authors a monthly teambuilding newsletter called *The Spokesperson* that has over 12,000 subscribers in sixty-five countries. Michelle Cummings has authored four books: (1.) *A Teachable Moment: A Facilitator's Guide to Activities for Processing, Debriefing, Reviewing, and Reflection*; (2.) *Bouldering Games for Kids, an Educational Guide for Traverse Walls;* (3.) *Playing With a Full Deck, 52 Team Activities Using a Deck of Cards;* and (4.) *Setting the Conflict Compass: Activities for Conflict Resolution and Prevention.*

Michelle currently lives in Littleton, CO, with her husband, Paul, and two sons.

About the Author

Who is this Mike Anderson guy anyway?

Mike Anderson, M.Ed

Chief Recreation Officer
The Petra Cliffs Group
Burlington, VT
(914) 393-9140
www.petracliffs.com
mike@petracliffs.com

Mike Anderson is a tattoo-collecting father of three who first discovered adventure play in 1991 as a recreation leader for the City of Atascadero, in California, where he grew up. Since then he has worked as a summer camp leader, program director, rock climbing guide, ropes course builder, trainer, conference center manager, middle school teacher, and the owner of two businesses. Since 2005, Mike has been the owner, chief recreation office and training czar of The Petra Cliffs Group, which includes an indoor climbing center, a full-time guiding service, a very well respected team-development program, an extremely successful summer day camp, as well as an international consultancy that has assisted numerous programs develop their own adventure-based learning programs.

All of this experience has allowed him to hone his skills and develop his own style and areas of interest among adventure professionals. Mike holds a bachelor's degree in recreation administration and a master's degree in education. Mike has authored *The INTERACT Curriculum* and co-authored *Teambuilding Puzzles*, with Jim Cain, Chris Cavert, and Tom Heck. Mike is also a contributor to numerous other texts on adventure play, including the *Book on Raccoon Circles I and II*, *The More the Merrier*, *A Teachable Moment* as well as two science-based texts.

Some of Mike's specialty areas include insight building, games and initiatives training, and conflict resolution programming. Mike has presented in-service trainings and conference workshops on these topics and many others all across the United States and internationally. Additionally, he has delivered pre-conference and session workshops at many of the adventure and challenge industry's largest conferences. A typical year has Mike delivering, on average, 100–150 program days a year all over the world. Mike has delivered programs on four continents, in six countries, and thirty-eight states.

Mike is the creator of many teambuilding exercises, including the Table Web, Adventure Puzzle, Image Chips, the raccoon activities Believe it or Knot and Cutting the Cake, Decomposition Line, the Go-No-Go Hand, as well as Phobia and the Web We Weave. Mike is also responsible for the adaptation of Cup Stacking to a teambuilding activity.

Mike now lives in Vermont with his wife, Megan, twin daughters, Rory and Emma, and son, Harper.